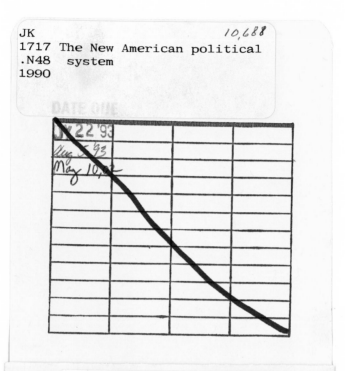

The New American Political System

The New American Political System

Second Version

**Anthony King,
editor**

THE AEI PRESS
Publisher for the American Enterprise Institute
Washington, D.C.

Distributed by arrangement with

University Press of America
4720 Boston Way   3 Henrietta Street
Lanham, MD 20706   London WC2E 8LU England

AEI Studies 501

Library of Congress Cataloging in Publication Data

The New American political system / Anthony King, editor. — 2nd
   version.
    p. cm.
    ISBN 0-8447-3709-7 (alk. paper).—ISBN 0-8447-3710-0
(pbk. : alk. paper)
    1. United States—Politics and government—1977- I. King,
   Anthony Stephen.
   JK1717.N48   1990
   320.973—dc20   89-18458
                                                          CIP

THE AEI PRESS
Publisher for the American Enterprise Institute
1150 17th St., N.W., Washington, D.C. 20036

Printed in the United States of America

Contents

Preface

The American Enterprise Institute published in 1978 a book entitled *The New American Political System.* That book became AEI's best seller, perhaps because of the puzzlement felt by many American political scientists—and by many ordinary American citizens—when they contemplated the workings of the nation's political system in the late 1970s. The old landmarks were still there. The Supreme Court and Congress still met, the White House still stood, the national nominating conventions still selected two presidential candidates every four years. Yet the old landmarks were features of a landscape that had changed in all sorts of ways, some dramatic, some more subtle. To take just a single example, the nominating conventions, although they still met, were no longer actually choosing presidential candidates. They were engaged in little more than a process of ratifying choices that had been made elsewhere, by other people, acting under different rules, and motivated by different considerations. The book published in 1978 sought to describe the major changes that had taken place, to explain them, and to assess their significance.

This book is also called *The New American Political System.* It covers many of the same subjects as its predecessor volume and elaborates on many of the same themes. Like the 1978 volume, it is concerned with describing, explaining, and assessing some of the most important changes that have taken place in the American system in recent decades. This is, however, as the title page indicates, a genuinely new version of the previous book rather than merely a new edition of it. Apart from the editor, only two of those who contributed to the first version, Austin Ranney and Martin Shapiro, have also contributed to this one, and one of them, Ranney, now writes on a different subject. The 1978 version of the book still stands as a statement of what its authors then had to say about the political changes that were taking place around them. This 1990 version is intended to make a new statement about a political system that continues to surprise all who study it by its seemingly endless capacity for rearranging old elements and absorbing new ones.

ANTHONY KING

Contributors

Anthony King, editor
Professor of Government
University of Essex

James W. Ceaser
Professor of Government and Foreign Affairs
University of Virginia

Charles O. Jones
Hawkins Professor of Political Science
University of Wisconsin, Madison

Richard P. Nathan
Provost, Nelson A. Rockefeller College of Public Affairs
and Policy
State University of New York, Albany

Nelson W. Polsby
Professor of Political Science
Director, Institute of Governmental Studies
University of California, Berkeley

Austin Ranney
Professor of Political Science
Chairman, Department of Political Science
University of California, Berkeley

Robert H. Salisbury
Professor of Political Science
Washington University

Martin Shapiro
The James W. and Isabel Coffroth Professor of Law
School of Law
University of California, Berkeley

Martin P. Wattenberg
Associate Professor of Political Science
University of California, Irvine

Aaron Wildavsky
Professor of Political Science and Public Policy
University of California, Berkeley

1
The Separated Presidency—
Making It Work
in Contemporary Politics

Charles O. Jones

In his classic work *Presidential Power*, Richard E. Neustadt observed that "the constitutional convention of 1787 is supposed to have created a government of 'separated powers.' It did nothing of the sort. Rather, it created a government of separated institutions *sharing* power."[1] This formulation encourages Neustadt to define presidential power as the power of persuasion.

> When one man shares authority with another, but does not gain or lose his job upon the other's whim, his willingness to act upon the urging of the other turns on whether he conceives the action right for him. The essence of a President's persuasive task is to convince such men that what the White House wants of them is what they ought to do for their sake and on their authority.[2]

Presidents have advantages in persuading their fellow shareholders in authority to support their attempts to apply power to social, economic, and political issues. But so do their shareholders—a fact that both creates the bargaining situation and sets its conditions.

This essay benefits from the research I am doing on post–World War II cycles of presidential power, supported by the Brookings Institution and the Glenn B. and Cleone Orr Hawkins Chair in Political Science, University of Wisconsin, Madison. I am grateful to Anthony King for reading the manuscript and providing needed improvements.

In looking ahead to the 1960s, Neustadt expressed doubt that Congress would consistently support the president—any president. In fact, he predicted, "If ballot-splitting should continue through the Sixties it will soon be 'un-American' for President and Congress to belong to the same party."[3] He foresaw a "fighting time." "Bargaining 'within the family' has a rather different quality than bargaining with members of the rival clan."[4]

As it happened, ballot splitting did continue to character-ize voting in the 1960s, but the Democrats were successful in controlling both branches for the first eight years of the decade. For two of the eight years (1964–1965) the presiden-tial and congressional Democratic parties seemed as one. That situation was not to last, however. The election that was to terminate the Republican party (1964) failed to do so. President Lyndon B. Johnson ran afoul of Congress on his Vietnam War policies, and he chose not to seek reelection in 1968. Since that time Republicans have won the White House five times, losing only in 1976. They have captured 77 percent of the total electoral vote in those six elections, ranging from 98 percent in 1984 to 45 percent in 1976. Democratic candi-dates have garnered an average of 43 percent of the popular vote in the past six presidential elections, exceeding 50 per-cent only once (50.1 percent in 1976). The "Democratic South" has delivered only for a southerner and then just once. Excluding the 1976 election, Democratic candidates have received a total of fifty-six electoral votes from the South since Johnson left office (6.7 percent of the total). Twice they have been shut out entirely in that region. Even with 1976 included, when Jimmy Carter won thirteen of the fifteen southern and border states, Democratic candidates have won just 20 percent of the electoral vote in the region since 1964.

Meanwhile, congressional Democrats continue to do well. They have won 60 percent of the House seats since 1968 and have been in the majority in each of the eleven congresses (twice by a two-thirds margin). Although their fortunes in the Senate have not been as impressive, they have won 55 percent of the seats in this period. On three occasions, however, they were in the minority (1981–1987).

Given these unusual circumstances, it is a fair restatement of Neustadt's sage observation to say that we have a government of separated institutions competing for shared power. The separation of power interpreted as institutions sharing authority finds a president performing legislative-like functions (Neustadt cites the veto) and Congress performing administrative-like functions (Neustadt cites the dispensing of authority and funds). The separation of powers interpreted as a competition for authority in addition finds each institution protecting and promoting itself through a broad interpretation of its constitutional and political status, even usurping the other's power when the opportunity presents itself. Impoundments, budgeting one-upmanship, the legislative veto, congressional foreign policy making, all come to mind, along with covert intelligence operations, as evidence for worrisome mistrust between the branches.

Presidential power as persuasion is altered somewhat under the circumstances of political separation, as are a president's advantages. He may prefer more indirect methods of getting congressional support—for example, persuading the public through use of the media or impressing foreign leaders through foreign policy initiatives. He may not wish to persuade Congress at all on certain domestic issues, preferring that it not act or concluding that there is a strategic advantage in its taking the initiative. One thinks of congressional Democrats declaring Ronald Reagan's several budgets "dead on (or before) arrival." Given the problems of producing a satisfactory budget in a period of staggering deficits, one can only imagine the president sighing in relief as his political opponents accepted a responsibility they could not fulfill. What is best politically may not be at all the same for a separated president as for a sharing president.

The founders may not have created a government of separated powers, as Neustadt contends, but they set conditions under which competitive power centers could emerge. They separated the elections, thereby making it possible to have eight combinations of party control—White House, House of Representatives, and Senate—once the two-party system developed (table 1–1). Presumably James Madison would be satisfied—perhaps he even knew it would turn out this way.

TABLE 1-1
COMBINATIONS OF PARTY CONTROL

Combination	Republicans' Control	Democrats' Control
1	All three	None
2	Presidency	House, Senate
3	Presidency, House	Senate
4	Presidency, Senate	House
5	House	Presidency, Senate
6	Senate	Presidency, House
7	House, Senate	Presidency
8	None	All three

We have experienced five of the eight combinations (1, 2, 4, 7, 8) since World War II. Occasional split party control—as occurred before World War II—is unlikely to reshape national politics since it is exceptional. A prolonged period of partisan division, however, commands our attention. Beginning in 1968 we observe a separation of politics in which the Republicans have successfully laid claim to the White House, the Democrats to Capitol Hill. Most observers consider this condition bad. "It's a poor way for democracy to do business," is how the eminent columnist David S. Broder puts it. Split government encourages each branch "to usurp the other's power."[5] Broder was commenting on an article by James L. Sundquist in which he argued that this new condition of split party control is "an accident of the electoral system." The result is a disjuncture between theory and practice—between the unity of party government and the practice of what Sundquist calls "coalition government" (the split party condition).[6]

Sundquist quite rightly asks for some attention to this development, first to acknowledge its existence, possibly to correct it with constitutional reforms, or perhaps to offer "an alternative theory that tells us how that kind of government can be made to work."[7] I join Sundquist in his call. I proceed, however, from the assumption that the condition is not accidental. Rather, it is an option that is and has been available to voters in our political system—one exercised frequently in recent decades. Large numbers of voters appear to make a conscious decision to separate the president from the rest of the system. We need to explore the nature of that separation to consider the usefulness of the standard expectations of presidential performance during the contemporary period of separated institutions competing for power. We need to understand how presidents accommodate to their separation if we are to respond to Sundquist's challenge for an alternative theory. Actually we may find that theory incorporated in the original thinking that inspired our system.

The Presidency as Separated

What has been separated from what in this truncated system of ours? Seemingly it is the presidency that has been detached by the voters from Democratic party preeminence elsewhere in American politics. When asked, more Americans continue to identify themselves with the Democratic party than with the Republican party. Few facts of American politics have been more consistent in recent decades. Those voters professing independence of the two parties have at times matched the number identifying with the Democratic party, making both parties minorities among the voters. But the Republicans remain the smaller of the minorities.

Democratic party preeminence also shows up within the states. George Bush's impressive victory in the 1988 presidential race had no perceptible effect on state legislatures, where the Democrats held majorities in both houses in twenty-eight states and the Republicans in just eight, with split control of the two houses in thirteen states (Nebraska's single-house legislature is nonpartisan). Majorities in the state legislatures mean control of the crucial redistricting process following the 1990 census and reapportionment. The national Republican party has worked hard to increase the number of state legislators and made some progress during the early Reagan years. But it will once again have to live with Democratic dominance of congressional districting in the majority of states after the 1990 census.

Democrats do less well in dominating gubernatorial races. It seems that the Republicans can find attractive candidates and garner crossover votes from Democrats. Even so, there have been many more Democratic than Republican governors during the past twenty years. After the 1988 election there were twenty-eight Democratic and twenty-two Republican governors. Governors have been an important source of presidential candidates for Democrats.[8]

What have the voters done? The Democrats seem to have been successful in state and local elections in holding their own party identifiers and attracting independent voters. Yet in presidential elections many Democratic party identifiers and huge numbers of independents vote Republican. Here is the record of Republican candidates' advantage among party defectors and independents in the past four elections (proportions of total voters in parentheses):

- 1976: 20 percent Democratic defectors (37 percent); 11 percent Republican defectors (22 percent); 52 percent of independents voted Republican (41 percent).
- 1980: 27 percent Democratic defectors to Reagan, 6 percent to Anderson (43 percent); 11 percent Republican defectors to Carter, 4 percent to Anderson (28 percent); 56 percent of independents voted Republican (23 percent).
- 1984: 26 percent Democratic defectors (38 percent); 7 percent Republican defectors (35 percent); 64 percent of independents voted Republican (26 percent).
- 1988: 17 percent Democratic defectors (37 percent); 8 percent Republican defectors (35 percent); 57 percent of independents voted Republican (26 percent).[9]

Note that even in the 1976 election, the Democrats' only victory since 1964, the Republican candidate, Gerald Ford, attracted a significant number of Democrats and a majority of independents. And the bonus for Republicans is greater than the difference between the percentages of defectors since the proportion of Democratic voters was larger in each of the elections.

Sizable numbers of voters are splitting toward Republican presidential candidates, away from their partisan preferences or, in the case of independents, their other voting preferences. Two conclusions seem reasonable: (1) that the presidency has been separated from the rest of American politics; and (2) that this separation is a result of the preferences of American voters (a combination of stalwart Republicans, a majority of independents, and a significant number of Democratic defectors). Meanwhile the turnout of eligible voters continues to decline (with the exception of a slight uptick in 1984), thereby calling into question the legitimacy of presidential and, even more, congressional winners.

What does it all mean? How is the separated presidency to be managed? What are the effects of a separated presidency on the political system? These are the questions to be treated in this chapter.

Reading the Returns—What the Elections Have Meant

According to the party responsibility model of separated institutions sharing power, the last "pure" election was that of 1964. Incumbent President Johnson won overwhelmingly in both the popular and the electoral vote count, and congressional Democrats won huge margins—295 House seats (68 percent of the total, the largest margin since 1936) and sixty-eight Senate seats (the largest margin since 1938). The post-election interpreters (as distinct from the longer-term survey analysts) were able to spot a definite mandate, and the Eighty-ninth Congress produced a policy record second only to that of the early congresses of Franklin D. Roosevelt.

What seemed like the beginning of another Roosevelt era for the Democrats ended in less than four years. Johnson could do no wrong in 1965; seemingly he could do nothing right soon thereafter. He declined to seek reelection, arguing that he could serve better by removing himself from politics, an unusual position for a Texas Democrat. The 1968 Democratic convention was one of the most contentious in history—both inside and outside the hall. The Democrats became a party in name only—unable to collect themselves as a unit for nominating a winning ticket. Southern Democrats in 1968 were even given the opportunity to vote for a third-party candidate, George C. Wallace (who won five Deep South states). A review of each presidential election from 1968 through 1988 reveals the mixed messages conveyed by the voters and therefore encourages an analysis of governing strategies by presidents.

The 1968 Election. Richard Nixon won by the narrowest of margins (43.4 percent of the popular vote, 26.4 percent of the voting-age population), and a Democratic Congress was returned. The turnout was 60.9 percent. The return rates were, for the House, 91 percent of all members, 96.8 percent of those seeking reelection; for the Senate, 86 percent of all members, 71.4 percent of those seeking reelection.

The message in 1968 was that the Republicans could eke out a victory when the majority party was seriously divided. But a Republican president had to be cautious in his dealings with Democratic majorities in Congress. Although 1968 was a harbinger, it did not confuse the analysts at the time. Nor did it mislead the president. Nixon won because the Democrats were divided. Even then, Hubert Humphrey nearly won in the closing days of the election. There was no strong message from the voters to separate the presidency from the rest of the system. The instructions to Nixon were reasonably clear—govern within the limits of mixed electoral results.

The 1972 Election. Nixon won by a huge margin (60.7 percent of the popular vote, 33.5 percent of the voting-age population), but again a Democratic Congress was returned. The turnout was 55.2 percent. The return rates were, for the House, 83.9 percent of all members, 93.6 percent of those seeking reelection; for the Senate, 87 percent of all members, 74.1 percent of those seeking reelection.

Between 1968 and 1972 the Democrats reformed their nominating process in a manner that accentuated and amplified the party's diversity on issues and provided outside avenues to its nomination. As a result, their platform slipped out of the mainstream, and their ticket of George McGovern and Sargent Shriver lacked credibility among the voters. The candidate of the majority party in the nation won seventeen electoral votes and 37.5 percent of the popular vote. Congressional Democrats, however, retained majorities in both houses, with a net loss of just twelve House seats and a net gain of two Senate seats. Nixon's victory was by the greatest popular vote margin in history and the second greatest electoral vote total. But the Democrats organized Congress. Separation had begun in earnest. Nixon could be excused for believing he had won a strong mandate to govern. He acted on his interpretation, seeking to establish an independent presidency. Yet his actions in foreign, domestic, and budgetary policy invited talk of impeachment even before the revelations of the Watergate hearings. My interest here is in the problem he faced, not the solution he contrived. After his victory Nixon, like his successors, had to calculate how to govern in the politics of a new era. In Sundquist's terms he sought to develop his theory to meet the political practices of a seriously split government.

We will never know how Nixon's approach would have worked through a full term. The Watergate scandal destroyed his presidency, presumably providing the majority party with an opportunity to regain control of the whole government. Congressional Democrats were the first to profit from the voters' negative reactions to the scandal, realizing a net gain of forty-three House seats and three Senate seats in the 1974 midterm elections. Once again they had comfortable margins in each chamber (67 percent in the House, 61 percent in the Senate).

The 1976 Election. Carter won by a very narrow margin (50.1 percent of the popular vote, 26.8 percent of the voting-age population). The turnout was 53.5 percent. The return rates were, for the House, 84.6 percent of all members, 95.8 percent of those seeking reelection; for the Senate, 83 percent of all members, 64 percent of those seeking reelection.

In 1976 two factors contributed to the likelihood of the Democrats' nominating an outsider: (1) further democratizing (or so it was believed) changes in their nominating process and (2) the post-Watergate anti-Washington mood among voters. Going too far out of town risked the selection of a candidate unfamiliar with Congress and the national Democratic party. Selecting from among old Washington hands (such as Henry Jackson, Edward Kennedy, or Walter Mondale) risked losing the advantage of the post-Watergate public mood; but, as it happened, any calculation of risk taking by party leaders was irrelevant. Carter, of Plains, Georgia, well understood the situation and worked the nominating system to his advantage. He did it in part by separating himself from his party, including those like Jackson and Kennedy who would return as majority party leaders in Congress.

The results in 1976 were hardly a triumphal return to the White House for the Democrats. Carter won with narrow margins of both the popular and the electoral vote counts against an opponent who was the first appointed vice president and who trailed Carter by thirty points in the polls after the Democratic convention. Meanwhile congressional Democrats did not appear to suffer from the political distance imposed on them by their presidential candidate. They retained the huge margins they had gained in 1974. Further, Carter's separated campaign left them nearly as independent as though a Republican had won. Carter ran ahead of just twenty-two successful House Democrats and one successful Senate Democrat.

Thus 1976 offers a variation of the separation hypothesis: a Democrat in the White House convinced that he has a mission separate from that of his party and sizable Democratic majorities in Congress confident of public support for their legislative approach. Meanwhile there is evidence in the election for voters' support of separation: (1) the probability of a Republican victory if Watergate had not occurred, (2) Ford's near victory (a switch of fewer than 10,000 votes in Hawaii and Ohio would have given him a majority of electoral votes), and (3) the independence of Carter (as well as his closeness to Ford on many domestic issues).

Accepting the separation-of-politics hypothesis should lead one to predict serious problems when the separation is expressed within one party—that is, with the president interpreting his election as an instruction to maintain a distance from his party in Congress. Among other effects, a member of the president's own party may be encouraged to challenge the president's renomination on the basis of an argument for party responsibility. That is precisely what occurred in 1979, when Senator Kennedy of Massachusetts announced his intention to seek the Democratic presidential nomination. Carter won renomination, but at great political cost. Kennedy's challenge was important in itself owing to his national prominence, but it also amplified the problems the president faced internationally and in the domestic economy. And it confirmed the separation of the Carter years.

The 1980 Election. Reagan won by a decisive margin (50.7 percent of the popular vote, 26.7 percent of the voting-age population), and the Republicans made significant gains in Congress. The turnout was 52.6 percent. The return rates were, for the House, 83 percent of all members, 90.7 percent of those seeking reelection; for the Senate, 82 percent of all members, 55.2 percent of those seeking reelection.

With Watergate all but forgotten and the Democratic party once again displaying serious divisions, Reagan won a massive victory in 1980. A sitting majority-party president won just six states and the District of Columbia (9 percent of the electoral vote). In 1976 Carter won thirteen of fifteen southern and border states; in 1980 he won two. But something more happened in 1980. The rejection of Carter was strong enough to harm the congressional Democrats too. Although many sought to separate themselves from Carter in the campaign, the Republicans had a net gain of twelve Senate seats (returning a majority for the first time since 1952) and a net gain of thirty-three House seats (the greatest increase for Republicans in a presidential election since 1920).

These results are as close to the party responsibility model of separated institutions sharing power as are ever likely to occur for a minority party (1952 being another recent case). Unless such a sizable victory by the minority party's candidate is followed by realignment (and elections analysts did speculate about that possibility), interinstitutional unity is unlikely to last very long. In this case the congressional elections of 1982 restored a strong majority to the House Democrats, nearly wiping out the losses suffered in 1980. But substantial policy achievements had been realized. Indeed, the agenda was significantly altered as a result of tax cuts, increases in defense spending, and cuts in the rate of growth of many domestic programs and in the so-called social welfare safety net. This combination produced huge deficits, thereby depriving the Democrats of their traditional ability to

TABLE 1–2
APPROVAL ELECTIONS, 1956–1988

	1956	1972	1984	1988
President				
Electoral vote (%)	86	97	98	79
Popular vote (%)	57	61	59	54
House				
Incumbents returned (%)	95	94	95	99
Net gains/losses[a]	−2	+12	+14	−3
Senate				
Incumbents returned (%)	86	74	90	85
Net gains/losses[a]	0	−2	−2	−1

a. For the president's party.

support an increased government role in resolving social and economic problems. In fact, as Aaron Wildavsky observed:

> At one stroke the Democratic party denied its traditional . . . recourse to create employment; it also obligated itself to keep the revenues it can raise from new taxes to reduce the deficit. . . . Even if he had lost the [1984] election, Ronald Reagan would have won the battle over future domestic policy.[10]

But, of course, he did not lose the 1984 election.

The 1984 Election. Reagan won by an overwhelming margin (58.8 percent of the popular vote, 31.2 percent of the voting-age population), but essentially the same Congress was returned. The turnout was 53.1 percent. The return rates were, for the House, 90.1 percent of all members, 95.4 percent of those seeking reelection; for the Senate, 93 percent of all members, 89.6 percent of those seeking reelection.

The 1984 election was a classic "approval" election—much like those of 1956 and 1972. In each case, the voters returned the whole government to an extraordinary degree, as shown in table 1–2. The three Republican presidents won overwhelmingly in the electoral college and in the popular vote; yet the Democrats did relatively well in both houses of Congress, gaining slightly in the House once (1956) and in the Senate twice (1972 and 1984). These second-term victories for Republicans (the Democrats have had none since 1944 when Roosevelt won his second second term) were essentially personal triumphs and therefore not interpretable as providing a mandate. Separation was confirmed by the voters in each case, and Republican presidents were in the position of having to calculate how to govern under the circumstances. Reagan did not attempt the Nixon formula. He settled for protecting the domestic agenda advantage he had gained in the first two years of his first term and concentrating on foreign policy issues.

The 1988 Election. Bush won by a decent margin (53.4 percent of the popular vote, 26.8 percent of the voting-age population) but again with the same Congress. The turnout was 50.1 percent (the lowest in sixty-four years). The return rates were, for the House, 92.4 percent of all members, 98.5 percent of those seeking reelection; for the Senate, 90 percent of all members, 85.2 percent of those seeking reelection.

The previous approval elections (1956 and 1972) were followed by razor-thin Democratic victories. In fact, the Kennedy and Carter victories are astonishingly alike in regional support (a combination of southern, northeastern, and industrial midwestern states) and the separateness of the presidential and congressional returns (Kennedy ran ahead of just twenty-two successful House Democrats, like Carter, and ahead of none of the successful Senate Democrats; Carter ran ahead of one). Both Kennedy and Carter could be expected to have difficulty leading their party in Congress.

Still, better one of "ours" than one of "theirs," and Democrats had historical reasons for optimism about recapturing the White House in 1988, probably, if it were to happen, by the same narrow margin. They even offered a regionally balanced ticket that would presumably repeat the 1960 and 1976 victories (a presidential candidate from the Northeast and a vice-presidential candidate from the Southwest). But there was no domestic policy advantage like the recession of the late Dwight Eisenhower years or political or institutional advantage like the Watergate scandal of the Nixon administration. In fact, there were few obvious reasons

13

for changing the government at all. Therefore, 1988 looked very much like other approval elections, as table 1–2 shows. Without a significant intervening event, voters were satisfied once more to confirm their support for the separated presidency. They were possibly even apprehensive about a change.

Bush, therefore, like his predecessors Eisenhower, Nixon, and Reagan, had to determine what it all meant for governing. But there was a difference. He was not being reelected. His was the first election since Herbert Hoover's in 1928 in which the party succeeded itself when an incumbent left office, and he was the first sitting vice president to be elected since Martin Van Buren in 1836. Here was a new condition in contemporary American politics, a vice president from a successful administration faced with having to distinguish himself from his predecessor while seeking at the same time to manage the political and institutional separation enforced by the voters. Moreover, it was said that his forty-state victory lacked a policy mandate. Yet presumably he was expected to take control of the government.

Mixed and ambiguous messages abound in any recounting of how we have elected our government in recent times. Presidents win with the support of one-fourth to one-third of the voting-age population. Voting turnout declines steadily, with the exception of one small uptick in 1984. Meanwhile, by constitutional design in the Senate (only one-third up for reelection each time) and by electoral preference in the House, over 80 percent of the Congress is typically returned (counting both those retiring and those defeated as members not returning). In the House the return rates of incumbents seeking reelection varied little during this period—90.7 to 98.5 percent. In the Senate the return rates among incumbents seeking reelection varied more widely from one election to the next, ranging from 55.2 to 89.6 percent. Note that on four occasions during this period (1968, 1976, 1980, and 1988) the House returned a higher percentage of its full membership than the Senate even though two-thirds of the senators were not up for reelection.

There is another way, albeit somewhat contrived, of looking at the mixed electoral messages that complicate how separated presidents approach the problem of governing.

TABLE 1-3
PRESIDENT'S ELECTORAL VOTE COMPARED WITH
CONGRESSIONAL PARTY SPLIT, 1968–1988
(percent)

Election	Presidential Electoral Vote[a]	Congressional Party Split[b]
1968	56.2 R	56.2 D
1972	97.2 R	55.7 D
1976	55.0 D	66.0 D
1980	91.4 R	54.0 D
1984	98.1 R	56.1 D
1988	79.6 R	58.9 D

a. Excludes the three electoral votes for the District of Columbia.
b. The combined totals of House and Senate Democrats.

Since the total electoral vote is based on the total number of representatives and senators, it is interesting to compare the electoral count for presidents and for Congress (the latter as measured by the combined party split in the two chambers). Table 1-3 shows the results of this comparison from 1968 to 1988. Even with the forty-nine-state sweeps of Nixon and Reagan in 1972 and 1984, the congressional count still remained very much the same, in favor of the Democrats. Separation is even observed for Carter on this basis, since congressional Democrats retained a two-thirds margin although their party's president received the second lowest electoral vote percentage for any winning candidate in this century. Note also that Bush faces a higher counter vote in Congress than any of his immediate Republican predecessors, indeed higher than any minority party president in this century (that is, at the time of his election).

In summary, recent American politics as conditioned by election results encourages an analysis on the basis of revised models—those that stress separation and competition. Though not exactly meeting Sundquist's challenge, such an analysis clearly draws from similar observations about political and institutional developments. Superficially this new politics appears to demand variable accommodative or independent behavior by presidents. More about the variation later. For now it is enough to acknowledge the changes and accept that they call for revised thought about how national politics and policy making are and should be working. Toward that end it is worthwhile to review the effects of congressional reform and the collateral changes that have taken place in the president's control of the governmental agenda. Both reveal alterations in the political and policy landscape that help sharpen our understanding of the challenges facing the separated president.

Congressional Adjustment—
Presuming to Govern from Capitol Hill

If Republican presidents have the problem of judging what it means to win without their party, so do congressional Democrats have to calculate what role to play when they are reconfirmed without the advantages of winning the White House. It is no coincidence that Congress began seriously to reform itself during the 1970s. The quintessential Republican was elected in 1968 and reelected overwhelmingly in 1972. Nixon was no national hero like Eisenhower or man of the Hill like Ford. He had served as a campaign "hit man" for Republicans. He was unloved—though variably respected—on Capitol Hill, among the press, and within the bureaucracy. He was said to be paranoid. Perhaps so. But even paranoids have enemies.

Thus Nixon's elections were politically foreboding for Democrats. Given their continuing strength on Capitol Hill, it seems in retrospect that reform was predictable, since a Nixon presidency confirmed fears of institutional imperialism within the White House. Those fears naturally encouraged careful review of congressional organization and practices so as to strengthen the legislature as a political and policy base. That is not to say that Nixon in the White House was the only cause of reform, but he was an important contextual stimulus.

There were at least ten reform commissions in Congress during the period 1965–1979, both partisan and bipartisan. Reforms were aimed at the committees, staff resources, presidential power, the budget process, party leadership, administrative capacities, ethics, campaign finance, and the rules. These reforms and other political developments in the decade of the 1970s contributed to the following important changes:

• In congressional attitude—members were more assertive in policy making, expanding individual interests in policy and assuming more institutional initiatives, notably in foreign policy.

• In personnel—committee chairmen were removed, subcommittee chairmanships were distributed more widely among members, and new party leaders were elected.

• In policy capabilities—members of Congress provided themselves with significantly more staff and created special units to provide independent policy analysis (the Congressional Budget Office, the Office of Technology Assessment, and an expanded Congressional Research Service).

• In lawmaking—a new budget process that called for new kinds of law was created, and committee and conference deliberations were opened to the public.

It is unquestionably true, as Samuel C. Patterson has written, that "if Henry Clay were alive today, and he were to serve again in the House and Senate . . . he would find much that was very familiar."[11] Legislatures do have a common look. It is less certain that Clay would understand either the complex policy issues facing Congress or what his role was to be in a legislature in which sophisticated policy analysis was widely available to the members to back up political judgments.

Even more to the point, perhaps, is the likelihood that prereform modern presidents like Johnson, Kennedy, Eisenhower, Truman, and Roosevelt would wonder what on earth was happening. It is not that past congresses simply rolled over in the face of presidential initiatives. Rather it is that Congress has prepared itself to participate broadly in the national policy process, often offering alternatives or intervening in other ways at all stages of that process (from problem definition and agenda setting through program evaluation). In other words, Congress has moved in the direction of functioning as an entire government, alongside, or in competition with, the executive. And it all happened rather suddenly. Here is what Senator Mondale (Democrat, Minnesota) had to say in 1972 about the policy independence of Congress on important issues:

> I have been in many debates, for example, on the Education Committee, that dealt with complicated formulas and distributions. And I have found that whenever I am on the side of the Administration, I am surfeited with computer print-outs and data that comes within seconds, whenever I need it to prove how right I am. But if I am opposed to the Administration, computer print-outs always come late, prove the opposite point or [are] always on some other topic. So I think one of the rules is that he who controls the computers controls the Congress, and I believe that there is utterly no reason why the Congress does not develop its own computer capability, its own technicians, its own pool of information. I would hope that we do so.[12]

At that same time I argued that Congress had the computer capability, roughly, of the First National Bank of Kadoka, South Dakota. That is no longer true. Senator Mondale's hope was realized. Within the decade Congress was able to provide itself with independent computer-based policy analysis to challenge that from downtown.

How is the president to respond to these developments? That is the central question. "The executive Power shall be vested in a President of the United States of America" (Article II, section 1 of the Constitution). Although Article II is rather spare in specifying the details of authority, many of its provisions strongly imply policy and administrative leadership.

> The President shall be Commander in Chief. . . .
>
> He shall have Power, by and with the Advice and Consent of the Senate, to make Treaties, provided two thirds of the Senators present concur; and by and with the Advice and Consent of the Senate, shall appoint Ambassadors, other public Ministers and consuls, judges of the supreme Court, and all other Officers of the United States (sec. 2).

> He shall from time to time give to the Congress Information on the State of the Union, and recommend to their Consideration such Measures as he shall judge necessary and expedient; he may, under extraordinary Occasions, convene both Houses, or either of them . . . ; he shall take Care that the Laws be faithfully executed (sec. 3).

A president who wins office by any margin has a right to assume the constitutional prerogatives commanding the military, creating a government, setting an agenda, convening the legislature, and executing the laws. What, then, is he to think of a Congress that prepares itself politically and structurally to encroach on the executive's authority? He will naturally react strategically, devising techniques for retaining his prerogatives. Given no guidance by the Constitution for dealing with their special situation, separated presidents, too, will try to govern by making the most of their position. We may expect their responses to vary, depending on their personal style, the issues at hand, and their political support.

Agenda Control and the Separated President

Scholars have maintained that the president determines the agenda of government. This common assertion follows from the many constitutional prerogatives just cited and seems suited to the policy and political conditions of a government that is growing. At least from Woodrow Wilson forward, we seem to have measured successful presidents by whether they aggressively pursued an expansive agenda. The failures were those presidents who were too passive. Government simply did not work right if the president did not provide a large agenda. Note, for example, the early assessments of Bush. The postelection judgments were that he lacked a mandate despite having won forty states. Yet the hundred-day review of his presidency criticized him for failing to provide an agenda. Presidents are supposed to drive the system, even when electoral analysis questions their right to do so. They are expected to overcome the weaknesses of their separation.

Upon reflection such declarations as those regarding

19

Bush's first months in office are based on two conditions that have changed dramatically: (1) a government with a limited, if expanding, domestic agenda and (2) a president serving with a Congress in which his party has a majority. When our national government finally caught up to the rest of the world in the scope of its domestic programs and when voters came to support split party control, the old agenda-setting generalizations became less apt. Here is some of what happened.

• Government expanded dramatically during the 1930s and the 1960s. Not even consolidative presidents like Eisenhower could roll back the New Deal, and the Great Society led to a federal budget with a life of its own. Much of the agenda came to be self-generating, deriving from programs already on the books. The budget did not reach $100 billion until 1962. Then it took just nine years to reach $200 billion, four to reach $300 billion, three to reach $400 billion, two to reach $500 billion, and another eight to reach $1 trillion. Ironically, during much of this period of escalation, the country was served by presidents devoted to budget cutting. Nixon, Ford, Carter, and Reagan served during the period when budget outlays grew from just under $200 billion to over $1 trillion. At the very least these numbers suggest that a sizable agenda is already and permanently in place. Therefore, reason dictates that the president's role is properly understood in the context of continuing commitments, which constrain the number and kinds of new policy initiatives that he can take.

• The mixed electoral signals discussed earlier likewise have significant implications for agenda setting. Of the elections since 1968, only that in 1980 could be said to bear a strong agenda-setting message, and even that message was more garbled that we initially thought (that is, we were told later that many voters were rejecting Carter, not endorsing Reagan's program). The other elections separated the two ends of the avenue in policy terms, providing little support for dependence of one branch on the other. Presidents were able to initiate legislation, to be sure. But increasingly their proposals were competitive with those from Capitol Hill—

and responses from both were constrained by an agenda already in place.

• Many of the reforms cited earlier ensured a more aggressive role for Congress in agenda setting. House committee staff nearly tripled and Senate committee staff nearly doubled during the 1970s. Personal staffs increased by 50 percent in each chamber during the same period. Party committee and congressional support agency staff also underwent major increases. Some 25,000 to 30,000 people now go to work on Capitol Hill and in state and district offices around the nation. They are, for the most part, bright, able, and ambitious people seeking credentials for advancement in the U.S. government's company town. They are unlikely to sit around waiting for a president to tell them what to do. Rather they constitute an inchoate policy-making machine. It is true enough that staff or individual members can seldom go all the way in the policy process without presidential support. But on many issues in recent years congressional initiative has been crucial—for example, trade, taxes, environmental issues, drugs—and presidents have had to respond.

Is the president then a captive of these developments? Can he never break out to effect significant change? Under most circumstances separated presidents are indeed captives. Our understanding of their role is enhanced if we acknowledge that fact. But aside from severe crises, recent experience suggests that a president can break free under special conditions. First, the president must have a landslide victory so that there can be no doubt that he has public support (at least as compared with his opponent). Second, some issues must appear to have been decided in the campaign so that victory has policy significance (the 1988 election suggests that this may not always be so). Third, the winner must offer a clear policy message, one that signals definite change if he wins. Fourth, the president's party needs to do well in congressional elections, thus providing at least superficial evidence that winning the White House is not just a personal victory for the candidate. Finally, the election results should exceed expectations in some way—a greater margin for the presidential candidate or more gains in Congress than had been predicted.

When these demanding tests are met, the result is agenda congruity—that is, general agreement at both ends of the avenue (and in the media) on the policy message of an election and a willingness to accept presidential leadership. There are spectacular cases in history when these conditions were met—most notably following the 1932 and 1964 elections. No one doubted that Roosevelt and Johnson had the right to govern as each saw fit, even if surveys might cast doubt on the authenticity of a mandate in policy terms.

One does not expect these conditions to be met during the period of the separated presidency. Yet in 1980 we witnessed a landslide victory for Reagan, definite issues being debated during the campaign, unquestioned policy direction on the part of the Republican candidate, spectacular gains for the congressional Republicans, and surprises both in the size of Reagan's victory and in Republican control of the Senate for the first time since 1955. A Reagan mandate was declared and largely made effective, with congressional cooperation, in 1981.

Even when these extraordinary conditions are met, we cannot expect them to be sustained. An administration is fortunate to be able to carry them through the first two years. The 1982 elections wiped out most of the 1980 gains for House Republicans. In the Senate Republicans held on to majority status until 1986, but much of the president's agenda-initiating capacity had been exhausted. He, like Congress, came to pass the time struggling to manage a deficit-driven agenda for which they were both responsible but over which they had only the most limited control.

Agenda congruity can result in spectacular policy breakthroughs. The Roosevelt, Johnson, and Reagan administrations will forever be marked as having had profound effects on the agenda. Each administration transformed the work of government, with the subsequent effect of creating new issues. The expansive agendas of Roosevelt and Johnson led to a consolidative agenda. That is, quantum increases in government programs were followed by efforts to make them work. A contractive agenda was created by Reagan's sizable tax cuts in 1981. Virtually for the first time in modern history, Washington policy makers sought to keep government from growing or actually to reduce it. Still failing substantially to reduce deficits, they were then faced with a fiscal agenda that concentrated on increasing revenues without paying the political price for such actions. This led to all manner of policy contortions—"revenue enhancement" being one of the more honest forms—but failure at this writing to reduce the deficit ensures that elected policy makers will continue to be managed by the existing agenda.

This brief review points to the weakness of the separated president for performing a vital function in the national policy process—that of agenda setting. Extraordinary political conditions are required to permit him to perform his expected functions of problem definition and priority setting. Congress has become his competitor—albeit a clumsy one—in these agenda-related activities. Yet the public and media expectations are that the president is still in charge. Even when elections produce agenda congruity—a seemingly unifying act for the separated president—the advantage is bound to be fleeting, though not without effect. Once more we are led to ask: How is a president to perform under these circumstances? Having been separated from the rest of government, how is he to meet his responsibilities? The answers differ according to the presidents and the political conditions under which they hold office.

Making It Work

If role playing is about estimating and meeting expectations, playing the president is among the more demanding roles ever conceived. In a recent book on President Carter's relations with the press, Mark Rozell points out that journalists relied on at least two sets of expectations in evaluating the president's performance:

- *General expectations of presidential leadership.* These expectations included the proper ingredients for successful leadership and the leadership approaches presidents should presumably adopt.

- *Expectations of Carter.* These expectations pertained to what journalists thought Carter would and should do as president.[13]

For the first, Rozell reports that journalists often have in mind models of forceful, active presidents like Roosevelt and Johnson. For the second, assumptions about how Carter should perform were based on the journalists' knowledge of the man (or at least what they thought they knew) and the fact that he was a Democrat.

The trick for presidents is to make these expectations work for, not against, them. Reagan was masterly in this regard. Journalists' expectations of the office remained high, but their expectations of the man were consistently low. Thus even ordinary performance was rewarded with praise—without raising expectations of Reagan's performance next time around. The so-called teflon characteristic of Reagan is explained by the low standard that was being employed. Who expects a president taking his nap to be responsible for all that is happening?

In his treatment of the "home style" of members of the House of Representatives, Richard F. Fenno, Jr., employs Erving Goffman's concept "presentation of self." As Fenno describes it, "Politicians, like actors, speak to and act before audiences from whom they must draw both support and legitimacy. Without support and legitimacy, there can be no political relationship."[14] Both verbal and nonverbal elements are involved, and the nonverbal may often be the most important in the judgments that are made. Presidents too "speak to and act before audiences." I maintain that a separated president has a special problem in presenting himself to and between audiences, and that problem derives precisely from the need for support and legitimacy, the more so if, as is frequent, they are not conveyed by the election. Verbal and nonverbal elements are surely involved in the presentation. To understand the importance of the nonverbal, we need only to be reminded of Carter's toothy smile after the reporting of bad news and Reagan's embrace of the astronauts' families after the shuttle disaster.

We observe varying strategies by which separated presidents attempt to gain support and legitimacy. Acknowledging his weakness with Congress in domestic matters, Nixon presented himself as a leader in foreign and defense policy. He was then and remains a credible leader on such issues. In maintaining public support for his initiatives, Nixon sought to govern alongside, or without, the Congress. He appeared to accept the terms of the separation, accommodating it by employing a style of independence. He naturally gravitated to those issues that allowed for greater separation and, therefore, independent action. Ford entered office not having been elected by the American public. As an appointed vice president, he had only congressional confirmation, as required by the Twenty-fifth Amendment, to legitimize his assuming office. His position was only slightly better than that of a cabinet officer (both houses of Congress must approve an appointed vice president, but only Senate approval is required for cabinet appointments). Ford's strategy in serving as Nixon's lame duck was to prevent the huge Democratic majorities of the 1974 election from taking charge of the government. His style was defensive, relying on the veto and his considerable experience on Capitol Hill to thwart nearly total congressional government.

Carter employed a trusteeship style in seeking to gain and maintain support and legitimacy. Like Nixon, but for different reasons, Carter invited the separation that was interpretable from the 1976 election results. As the first president elected after Watergate, he was comfortable in presenting himself as having been entrusted to make the right policy choices for the nation. That style dissuaded the president from uniting with members of his own party in Congress since any such joining would detract from the strength of his adopted position.

Presentation of self is the stock in trade for an actor. Reagan proved himself sensitive to the larger audience, believing correctly that they would not support change proposed in a threatening manner. Thus he consistently gift-wrapped radical change in traditional values and offered it with a disarming twinkle and smile. He appeared to understand what it was that most Americans wanted in a president. In meeting those expectations rather than those current in

Washington, he was able to capitalize on whatever political advantage was offered. Reagan consistently played to the audience that mattered—the American people—and therefore built the kind of trust that Fenno speaks of for representatives. This trust and support provided the leeway for risk taking, even for damage control when, as in the Iran-contra matter, risk resulted in failure. In the end, it seems, others learned to govern with him.

It is too soon to know how Bush will manage his separation. There is, however, evidence about how he will try. In early presentations he has favored directed bipartisanship. Having many more direct policy interests than Reagan, he will tackle specific issues and seek broad support. He prefers to get congressional Democrats committed early to a policy approach, thus defusing the issue and preventing it from making the headlines as a case of presidential-congressional conflict. Bush believes that government can help solve problems—a quite different kind of optimism from that of his predecessor. But he appears to understand that the larger audience is watching and waiting to judge whether his style is presidential and his program effective.

Conclusion

Separated presidents face the challenge of governing under the contrary political conditions set by the American voters, the competitive institutional conditions created by a reformed Congress, and the policy conditions resulting from the huge post–Great Society self-generating agenda. At the very least these changes should encourage us to question previous tests of presidential performance. Thus, for example, it seems inappropriate to judge a separated presidency by the amount of legislation enacted or by policy breakthroughs. Mixed electoral messages force the president to move cautiously or to suffer the consequences of a Nixon or a Carter.

Nor is it appropriate to judge one president's performance by that of the latest occupant of the office, by some earlier "model" president, or by his first year in office. Thus, for example, it is a questionable exercise to evaluate Bush by Reagan's first months in office, Carter's record by Johnson's, or Reagan's last year by his first. More justifiable is an evaluation based on an analysis of the political, institutional, and policy conditions facing a president, combined with consideration of his personal qualities. To what extent did the president maintain support and legitimacy in accommodating those conditions? Judgments about the policy success of separated presidents should be made in this context. That is not bad advice for evaluating any president. But it is particularly appropriate for a president as quarterback of a team over half of which is not on his side of the scrimmage line.

Recent thought about the presidency is consistent with the perspective offered here, even if it is not developed in exactly the same way. Terry Moe concludes that the variations identified here occur "within a long-term historical process whose general path and underlying logic are the fundamental components of institutional development." He finds that politicization and centralization have grown "because of the nature of our institutions and the role and location of presidents within them."[15] Presumably election results are important in determining the role and setting the location for presidents. I propose that the concept of the "separated presidency" captures much of the institutional development to which Moe refers.

Scholars appear to agree with Fred I. Greenstein that dilemmas for presidents are created by "high expectations of performance and the low capacity of Presidents to live up to those expectations" and with Nelson W. Polsby that "Congress and the President are like two gears, each whirling at its own rate of speed."[16] Moe expects that "the gap between expectations and capacity will continue to characterize the presidency."[17] Theodore J. Lowi, describing a pathology of presidential government, believes that "the expectations of the masses have grown faster than the capacity of presidential government to meet them."[18]

These views set an agenda for political scholars—one that encourages analysis of the special challenge facing a president separated from, yet expected to lead, the rest of the political system. Within the broader development that Moe speaks of and that Sundquist and others worry about, the variation in approaches is a worthy subject of study. It

27

begins, however, with the recognition of the changes that have occurred and directs attention to the variability in conditions for each new occupant of the office.

Wildavsky sees all of this as "an antileadership system" in which "Presidents are tempted into action only to discover that whatever they do is not what they were somehow supposed to have done."[19] What that suggests is that presidents must be ever attentive to the constraints as well as the perquisites of power. Defining who you are and where you are is a starting point in the presentation of self. Doing so is an especially sensitive endeavor for the separated president since there is an unusually small margin of error. Presumably presidential attentiveness to position as a source of power would satisfy Madison as one of the "auxiliary precautions" that experience teaches are necessary if government is to control itself.

2

Political Change
and the Character of
the Contemporary Congress

Nelson W. Polsby

The purpose of this chapter is to describe the main characteristics of the contemporary Congress, especially as they have
emerged from slightly less contemporary features of the
political landscape. In a world of change, Americans have
been able to rely upon great stability in their political institutions. They have been deprived of the stimulus of occupying
armies, or the refreshment of an internal revolution, or some
other constitutional upheaval leading to a wholly new and
different political order. Such upheavals have frequently
emerged in the modern world over the past half-century,
transforming the governments under which large chunks of
the world's population exist. Nevertheless I shall argue that
meaningful change has come to the American political system
within living memory, and even to that seemingly rock-solid
fortress of continuity and stasis, the U.S. Congress.

Continuity and Change—An Overview

As we look at the past half-century of Congress as a historical
whole, it is possible to discern an alternating and somewhat
overlapping pattern of activity and retrenchment, of focus
and stalemate in congressional affairs. Three times during
the fifty-year period, Congress has gone through episodes of
high productivity and strong coordination; and through three
somewhat longer episodes, Congress has more or less ridden

at anchor in the political system at large. Neither one mode nor the other is exclusively "natural" to Congress. Although the legitimacy of congressional behavior in either mode is frequently the subject of hot dispute, both roles are historically characteristic of Congress, and both fully express the powers of Congress as contemplated in the overall constitutional design. This design confides to Congress two complementary assignments: to represent the American people in at least some approximation of their variety and diversity and to provide a forum for the taking of significant policy initiatives. When there are great variation and disparity in the opinions of Americans about public policy, this fact is bound to be recognized in pulling and hauling on Capitol Hill; when there are unanimity and resolution, Congress moves its business with dispatch.

I will be brief and schematic in identifying episodes of concentrated congressional activity over the past fifty years. In these historical moments, Congress initiates or ratifies sizable expansions of federal activity, focuses its energies effectively, and undertakes policy innovation. The first of these moments was the enactment of the New Deal (1933–1936) in which the political innovations of Franklin Roosevelt's first 100 days occurred, including the revision of banking laws, the formation of the Securities and Exchange Commission, the establishment of a social security system, and the passage of the Wagner Act, among other events.[1] The second moment was the creation of wartime agencies in Washington (1939–1946), which greatly increased the administrative capacities of central government and broke through congressional resistance to governmental economic forecasting and planning and to an administratively augmented presidency. This episode included, among others, the Budget Act of 1939; the establishment of the Office of War Mobilization and (later) Reconversion; the Employment Act of 1946, which created, among other things, a Council of Economic Advisers; the consolidation of civilian control of the armed services into a Defense Department; and the establishment of the Central Intelligence Agency, the Atomic Energy Commission, and the National Science Foundation.[2] The third moment was the New Frontier–Great Society (1963–1969). This period saw the completion of the New Deal: the enactment of Medicare and civil rights laws and the creation or enhancement of federal bureaucracies (such as the Department of Housing and Urban Development) dedicated to less-advantaged clientele.[3]

Interspersed with these episodes of innovation have been episodes of stalemate and retrenchment. We remember, for example, the thwarting of the later New Deal (1937–1941), in which President Roosevelt attempted, and failed, to pack the Supreme Court after the Court found many early New Deal measures unconstitutional. Roosevelt then attempted, and failed, to defeat conservative Democratic members of Congress in the 1938 election, and Congress no longer produced a cornucopia of new legislation. In time, "Doctor New Deal" gave way to "Doctor Win-the-War." Then, from roughly 1950, when the Truman administration began to be bogged down in loyalty-security issues, and all through the Eisenhower administration, when the threat of a presidential veto prevented all but the most consensual of congressional initiatives, on into most of the Kennedy presidency, in which the dominance of conservative committee chairmen in Congress narrowed the president's agenda (1950–1963), Congress and the presidency existed in a sort of equilibrium described by one liberal commentator as a "deadlock of democracy."[4] Since 1968, there has been a period of consolidation in reaction to the most recent set of policy innovations, and during most of this time Congress has been in Democratic while the presidency has been in Republican hands. During most of these three periods, political innovation has been resisted or at a stalemate, and little or no consensus has existed favoring new departures in governmental policy. Private authority has been preferred to the authority of central government.

That periods of stalemate should last, on average, about twice as long as periods of innovation ought not greatly to surprise even the most casual student of human nature. In important respects, the U.S. population resembles the population that attempted to build the Tower of Babel. The point of that Biblical fable is perfectly straightforward: to undertake great public works, it helps if everyone speaks the same language. Finding that language in the expression of common goals and organizing concerted strategies toward those

31

goals are not trivial tasks when formal power and autonomy are dispersed and it is necessary to mobilize the consent of majorities several times over—first in subcommittees, then in committees, and then on the floor of each of two legislative chambers. The most prevalent alternative form of coordination—dictatorship—is scarcely relevant to the politics of a free and self-governing people. Far more relevant is the simple fact, illustrated in table 2–1, that it takes time to gather up the consensus necessary to move a bicameral representative body that exists independently within a constitutional separation of powers.

Crises of various sorts—notably, a depression, a war, and a presidential assassination—have done a great deal to press Congress toward bouts of innovative activity.[5] In contrast, reforms of congressional procedures have played little or no role in galvanizing forward motion on the policy front. The era's most comprehensive overhaul of procedures, the reform of the committee system in 1946, came at the start of a long period of stalemate.[6] Other important institutional changes included Lyndon Johnson's redesign of the seniority rules for assigning Democratic senators to committees, which occurred during the Eisenhower lull, the 1961 packing of the House Rules Committee, and various reorganizations and reforms of the House in the mid-1970s.[7] All these changes were significant in creating institutionalized settings for a more successful and better coordinated deployment of the resources of the majority party in Congress, but none was sufficient in and of itself to create an avalanche of new and innovative public policies. Avalanches require the cooperation of the president. Even so, the most important facts about

TABLE 2–1

PERIODS OF CONGRESSIONAL INNOVATION AND STALEMATE,
1933–1989

Innovation	Stalemate
New Deal (1933–37)	1937–41
Wartime (1939–46)	1947–63
Great Society (1964–68)	1969–89

SOURCE: Author.

the capacity of Congress to respond—to presidential leadership or to leadership within Congress itself—are encoded in Congress's own organizational structure and in the ways in which the changing composition of Congress makes an impact upon congressional organization.

The Contemporary Senate

The chief changes that have overtaken the U.S. Senate in the past half-century can be compactly described. It has become a more national and outward-looking and a less state-oriented and inward-looking institution.[8] Now, as a matter of course, senators interest themselves in constituencies beyond those mobilized exclusively in their home states and seek to influence national policy on the assumption that it is politically useful to them to achieve national recognition and national resonance in their work. This sea change in the expectations of senators and in the way they do their work, and therefore in the role of the Senate in the political system, I believe has been driven, in large part, by a fundamental change in the career prospects of U.S. senators that occurred in the early 1950s as the result of the arrival on the scene of national television.

We are fortunate in having a superb baseline from which to measure the transformation of the Senate. In 1957 William S. White, congressional correspondent of the *New York Times*, published a book, *Citadel*, which admirably captures the spirit of the place—the prevailing institutional ideology, in effect— as it had been handed down and as he experienced it.[9] What he described was a rather stuffy and comfortable club, complete with leather chairs, snoozing members, obsequious attendants, cigar smoke, and bourbon and run more or less exclusively for the benefit of a small number of elderly and important men. Internal norms of "clubability" were what mattered, White explained. Ideology did not matter, although it seemed to be coincidentally the case that the most significant people in the place, the old bulls who constituted the "inner club," as White called it, just so happened to be themselves conservative, mostly southern, and ill-disposed toward much of the New Deal, though not the part, presumably, that sent resources to southern farmers, or invented tax breaks for the oil industry. And they tended to be against the advance of civil rights, sometimes immoderately so, even though the institution was alleged to prize moderation. White made the claim that the more progressive senators tended to give offense primarily because of their lack of deference to the collegial norms of the place and not because of the substance of their views. One could not do well in the Senate by seeking publicity, he argued, or by running for "other" offices—presumably the presidency.

White argued that in its essence the Senate of those days was fulfilling its historic constitutional purpose of "cooling the legislative tea" by providing a calm, skeptical, and carefully deliberative counterweight to an allegedly more impulsive House of Representatives and a demonstrably more innovative and demanding presidency. What he described, however, was in large measure the very successful pursuit of parochial interest, sometimes clothed in statesmanship, sometimes not. The southerners who ran the place, insofar as they actually did so, attended with great care to the local prejudices of the small and lily-white electorates that sent them to Washington. No doubt they were obliged to do so to stay in the Senate, but nevertheless this was a clear prerequisite that allowed the more able among them to adopt an interest in broader concerns, such as foreign or military affairs or health care.[10]

There were some questions about the descriptive accuracy of White's portrait by the time it reached print. On the whole, it was accepted by a great many of those journalists and biographers who wrote about the Senate during the 1960s and even thereafter. It is common to find in magazine profiles of senators of that era, for example, some attempt to assess whether the subject was "in" or "outside" the "inner club," and one writer once went so far as to publish what he advertised as a guess at a comprehensive listing of the club's members.[11] This suggests that White captured something about the Senate that had high credibility among observers.

By the time *Citadel* was published, however, two forces were transforming the Senate radically. One was television, as I have mentioned, and the other was Lyndon Johnson. Television, it appears, happened very suddenly indeed to the U.S. Senate. In March 1951, a senator who had not much weight in the institution, Estes Kefauver of Tennessee, became an overnight media star as the result of the daytime broadcast of hearings of his committee's investigation of organized crime. Kefauver went on to run in the 1952 presidential primary elections—very successfully—and more or less on the strength of his lucky burst of publicity, he became a factor in the presidential nominating politics of the Democratic party for the rest of his life.[12]

From the 1950s onward, senators in wholesale lots, if they could manage it, began to maneuver themselves toward active roles in presidential nominating politics. Some of them simply used the Senate as a publicity springboard from which they could launch themselves. Kefauver and, more successfully, John Kennedy pursued that strategy. Others, following the early lead of Arthur Vandenberg and Robert A. Taft and, notably, Hubert Humphrey sought to use their position in the Senate to pursue national policy goals in a way that would commend themselves to the party leaders who in those days controlled the presidential nominating process. In short, they began to invent the Senate as an arena within which, and not merely from which, one could launch a presidential bid.

Lyndon Johnson's ambitions led him to the latter strategy. Under the patronage of elders of the old inner club, he became the Democratic leader of the Senate mid-way through his first term as senator. He managed the business of his party in the Senate in part with an eye toward national office—refusing, for example, to join the southerners who put him into the leadership in overtly opposing civil rights initiatives.

Johnson's leadership of the Senate also greatly changed the institution itself. Decisions by consensus of senior members were replaced by the accretion of powers, large and small, in Johnson's own hands. Ralph Huitt, Joseph Clark, and others have left us a picture of a body that was being explicitly managed by an assiduous, indeed a compulsively driven, leader anxious to make a record and advance his career by coordinating as many different things as he could reach within the institution.[13]

By the time Johnson ascended to the vice presidency in 1961, the old citadel had largely disappeared. Senators were

35

in no mood to continue the highly centralized pattern of leadership that Johnson had imposed on the institution. It was a great virtue that Mike Mansfield, Johnson's successor, vastly preferred a lighter touch on the reins.[14] But the Senate did not return to the collegial pattern of the old inner club. In the meantime the goals of senators had shifted perceptibly. A senator was in the White House—the first one originally elected to the presidency since Warren G. Harding. He had beaten a former member of the Senate in the general election as well as several in the prenomination period to get there. And a senator was vice president. At least ten senators— Russell, Kerr, Lodge, Johnson, Kefauver, Kennedy, Taft, Vandenberg, Symington, and Humphrey—had been serious contenders for the presidency over the past couple of nomination cycles.

In the 1930s and 1940s, it was unusual for senators to run for president, to cultivate national constituencies in the pursuit of policy initiatives, or to go out of their way to court publicity. Now all these activities are usual. Indeed, for a senator not to do so nowadays may even occasion comment.[15] These changes in the way individual senators conduct their jobs—facilitated by an enormous increase in staff, space, and equipment—have also wrought changes in the Senate's role as a corporate entity in the political system. As it has become a less collegial and reactive body, it has become more enterprising and innovative with respect to public policy. The Senate is now a place in which public policy ideas are tried out, floated, deliberated, and sometimes parked as they await the proper constellation of forces leading to eventual enactment. The careers of senators, and of the staffs of senators, depend far more on engagement with the new and far less upon the preservation of the old than was true forty or fifty years ago.

The Contemporary House of Representatives

As recently as twenty years ago, an observer might have said that, of all of the institutions of American government, the House of Representatives had been least touched by change since the creation of most of the institutions of modern

America in the early years of the twentieth century. Not since 1919 had an ongoing committee assignment in the House violated the criterion of seniority.[16] New committee assignments were doled out by committees on committees of each party, much influenced by the leaders of key state delegations.[17] Committee chairmen—those most senior in committee service in the House majority party—dominated the policy-making process within their respective domains, sometimes collaborating with ranking minority members, sometimes not. The Republican conference—the assembly of all Republican members—was considerably more influential than its counterpart body, the House Democratic caucus, in expressing a party mainstream ideological position. This was understandable in light of the fact that Republicans in the House were, on the whole, far more ideologically united.[18] For the most part, both the conference and the caucus were moribund, meeting to do serious business only once in every two years, to nominate and elect party leaders and to ratify the work of their respective committees on committees. For the rest of the time, party leaders—the Speaker, majority and minority leaders, and party whips—had custody of all the routines and schedules that are at the heart of the management of a complex legislative body, but they were constrained to exercise their power more or less in the fashion of tugboats urging a gigantic ocean liner along a course it intends to pursue anyway.

In recent years, however, change has finally come to the House of Representatives. Its main outlines are these: committee chairmen, once beyond reach, have been deposed and threatened with removal on several occasions since 1950, mainly for being out of step with maintream sentiment among the Democratic members of the caucus; committees on committees have been reconstituted to give party leaders much more power, including the power unilaterally to appoint members to the key scheduling committee, the Rules Committee; and uniform rules of committee conduct have been written so as to spread power downward and outward to subcommittees and their chairmen. As subcommittees have gained autonomy and party leaders have gained responsibilities, power has slipped away from the chairmen of full

committees, who have been the major losers in the transformations that have taken place.[19]

The main engine of change has been the House Democratic caucus. Because the House has been firmly in the hands
of a Democratic majority since 1954, what has happened to
the Democrats is of paramount concern in following developments in the House. From 1937 until quite recently, the
divisions within the caucus were sufficient to neutralize any
attempts to use the caucus to coordinate the majority party.
Southern Democrats—about 100 strong during most of the
period, and virtually all of them from safe seats—made up
almost half the Democratic members of the House—sometimes a little less, depending on Democratic electoral fortunes
in the rest of the country. And about two-thirds of the
southern Democrats were Dixiecrats, which meant that they
were opposed to Democrats from the rest of the country on
most issues of public policy and were perfectly willing to
make coalitions with House Republicans to stop liberal legislation. So the actual ideological division in the House as a
whole was frequently closely balanced when conservatives
were not slightly in the lead. This made of the House the
graveyard of many liberal proposals during the Truman and
Kennedy presidencies.[20]

From time to time, House members closer to the mainstream of the national party would become restive. A small
uprising of the peasants took place after the 1958 election, for
example, when a flood of newly elected liberal Democrats
descended on the House. As Speaker Rayburn saw all too
clearly, this was bound to have no legislative consequences
over the short run, since liberal initiatives could not in any
event survive an Eisenhower veto. In their impatience a few
young leaders of the party in the House—notably Eugene
McCarthy, Lee Metcalf, and Frank Thompson—organized
what in time became a programmatically oriented substitute
for the caucus, the Democratic Study Group.[21] This group
soon embraced most ideologically mainstream Democratic
members. It took more than a few years for the House
Democratic leadership to become comfortable with the study
group, which at its most effective acted as the sort of communications system and rallying-point that the official Dem-

ocratic whip system could not provide, because of its obligation to serve all Democratic members, whatever their
ideological stripe.

By the 1970s, the caucus had absorbed many of these
functions of the study group and had revived as an instrument of House leadership after a fifty-year period of quies-
cence. What had happened was this: slightly more than a
score of Dixiecrats had disappeared from the House, and
they had been replaced by Republicans. It is not altogether
intuitively obvious that a gain of about twenty-five Republican seats in the House would be a proximate cause of the
liberalization of the House, but this, more or less, is what
happened. It was, to be sure, not the new Republican members themselves, most of whom were ferociously conservative, who were the instruments of change but rather the
drastic change in the make-up of the Democratic caucus that
did the job, enabling the caucus to take initiatives that only a
few years earlier would have torn it apart.

Indirectly, of course, these changes were the product of
the nationalization of the South, of demographic changes
that made the South more like the rest of the country, and of
the party realignments that made it possible for southern
Republicans to run for House seats and win. Promiscuous
and ill-founded claims of party realignment at the national
level have given the whole idea of realignment a bad name
among careful analysts. If there has been a party realignment
anywhere in America these past fifty years, however, it has
occurred in the South, and it has led to liberalization in the
House of Representatives.

Congressional-Presidential Relations
and the Growth of Congressional Staff

The president is the most interested observer of Congress
and its most devoted lobbyist. Congress, despite its full
complement of internal institutional imperatives, must nevertheless somehow coordinate its activities with the president. Hence, significant changes in the presidency over the
past fifty years have had a great impact on Congress. Of
these, two have had the greatest importance. The growth of
a systematic congressional liaison service—a staff of full-time

professionals in the White House that deals exclusively with Congress—is the less significant of the two.[22] More important has been the capture by the presidency of executive agencies—notably the Bureau of the Budget, now the Office of Management and Budget (OMB)—that once provided more or less neutrally competent ad hoc service to the legislative branch.

Starting with the Johnson administration, and accelerating with the Nixon presidency, a great many of the underlying facts and numbers on which legislation depends, and which used to be supplied routinely to Congress by the executive branch, became subject to presidential political influence. Mistrust of the presidency, known in Johnson's day as a "credibility gap," began to develop on Capitol Hill along a broad front, and not only with respect to the Vietnam War. Soon, Congress felt the need for access to its own information and completely changed its pattern of staffing.

The sheer numbers are staggering.[23] Two entirely new congressional agencies were created: the Office of Technology Assessment in 1974 and the Congressional Budget Office (CBO) in 1975. The CBO in particular had an almost immediate impact. Staffed by nearly 200 economists and other professionals, the CBO's budget estimates quickly developed a reputation for realism that overshadowed the increasingly partisan and massaged numbers of the OMB. Very soon it became a commonplace of Washington practice to conduct bipartisan or nonpartisan discussions of live economic issues using Congressional Budget Office, not Office of Management and Budget, numbers.

Between 1960 and 1980, the staff of the Congressional Research Service of the Library of Congress was increased fourfold; and the numbers of employees assigned to the House and the Senate, to individual members and to committees, jumped comparably. By 1985, roughly 25,000 staff members worked for Congress. This includes only the Congressional Research Service component of the Library of Congress, and only the one-third of the General Accounting Office employees who work directly for Congress. In 1957, 2,441 staff were employed by House members and 1,115 by Senate members; by 1985, those numbers had turned into

7,528 and 4,097, respectively. In 1960, 440 staff were employed by House standing committees, and 470 by Senate
standing committees; in 1985, those numbers had become
2,009 and 1,080, respectively. The growth in a couple of short
decades has been remarkable. The growth in another measure is even more remarkable: in the forty years from 1946 to
1986, while the consumer price index rose 450.8 percent,
legislative branch appropriations rose 2,859.3 percent.

An inspection of the year-to-year figures shows double
digits in the growth of congressional appropriations after
Lyndon Johnson's 1964 landslide, continuing right through
the Nixon era. There is no adequate way to quantify the
attitudes of mistrust that appear to have caused these figures
to lift off the planet earth when and as they did, but it is
possible to speculate about the causes of the creation of a
legislative bureaucracy after so many years in which the
legislative branch found it possible to live comfortably with a
comparatively thin roster of professional staff. Loss of comity
with the executive branch, driven by the development of a
greatly augmented presidential branch of government, is by
far the most plausible explanation.[24]

Under the old dispensation, what congressional staff
were professional at was looking after the political needs of
members, mixed in, in exceptional cases like the House
Appropriations Committee, with some attention to oversight
of the executive. On the whole, service on the staff of Congress did not require much interest in or competence at public
policy analysis, much less political innovation. Expertise
came with long years on the job rather than as the result of
professional training. Today, while the numbers of professionals employed by Congress has burgeoned, their average
age has shrunk, and they now come to Capitol Hill with
professional credentials.[25] Many more of them—not just in
absolute numbers, but as a proportion of the whole—focus
on policy and on promoting their employers' interests
through the advocacy or adoption of public policy positions.
This is most noticeable in the Senate, where senators are
stretched so thin by the multiple responsibilities of committee
work that it is largely impossible for them to keep track of
everything personally. Their staff members do it for them,

and in the process not infrequently engage in sophisticated forms of political entrepreneurship on their principal's behalf. Sometimes it is a part of a staff member's duties not only to seize and promote a policy position or to make or adopt an issue in behalf of one's principal, but also to engage the interest and approval of the principal as well.[26]

Staff members with these extraordinary opportunities to affect public policy tend not to devote their lives to congressional service as so many of their predecessors did, but to job hop around the policy subcommunity on which they are making a mark. So not only are congressional staff different today in their sheer numbers, but also they are different in the ways in which they define their jobs, different in their training, and different in their career expectations. Collectively, they resemble their counterparts in the political entourages of the presidential appointees who run the federal agencies of downtown Washington far more than they do preceding generations of staff members on Capitol Hill. They have brought increased capability to Congress to deal substantively with policy, and they have done much to provide a link between Congress and the increasingly specialized and professionalized worlds of policy makers, policy advisers, and lawyers and foundation, university, and think tank personnel who make up the various policy subcommunities of Washington and throughout the United States. There was a time when Congress, and congressional staff, stood aloof from the communications networks maintained by these policy subcommunities.[27] This is no longer true.

Five Stories about Change

We are now in a position to begin to think about the proposition, frequently asserted, that as a piece of eighteenth-century political machinery, Congress is ill-equipped to deal with twentieth-century challenges by virtue of its resistance to and incapacity for change.[28] Fair-minded observers must concede that there may be many reasons to find fault with Congress and with many aspects of public policy as they emerge from Congress. It seems doubtful, however, that a lack of change can be pinpointed as the source of difficulty.

Students of Congress will be familiar with analogous complaints in the 1960s and 1970s about the incompetence and senility of conservative congressional committee chairmen who were, in the mysterious exercise of their diminished and enfeebled powers, completely thwarting the forward march of liberalism as orchestrated by competent and nonsenile presidents, journalists, public interest advocates, and professors. The proper diagnosis should have been: if only these committee chairmen had actually been senile, how much easier it would have been for liberals to get what they wanted.

As an institution that is venerable in years, certainly as governmental institutions go, well bounded, highly legitimate, and resourceful, the Congress of the United States cannot be expected to transform itself into something unrecognizable with the touch of every passing breeze. Yet changes have come to Congress, and many of these changes have proved to be meaningful for the life of the institution and consequential for public policy. Over the long run, at least two sources of change, not yet discussed here, have shaped congressional structures and outcomes. In addition, we might review the three avenues of change that have mattered over shorter time periods during the most recent half-century.

Institutionalization. At an early point in the life of the Constitution, Congress had not developed a large number of the organizational characteristics that are familiar to present-day observers. The development of some of these characteristics has been studied in the case of the House of Representatives under the rubric of "institutionalization."[29] This refers to the growth of organizational features tending to define and harden the external boundaries of the institution, manage and promote internal complexity, and establish universalistic criteria for internal decision making. Many of these features were observed to have developed over the course of the nineteenth century, to have slowed down during the Civil War, and to have achieved very nearly their contemporary form soon after the turn of the twentieth century. These included the modern committee system, modern criteria for the selection of party leaders, as well as the diverse duties adhering to the positions of party leadership themselves,

43

seniority in committee assignments, and judicialized methods for disposing of contested elections.

Critical Elections. At least three times in history, electoral changes affecting the composition of Congress were massive enough to have an immediate and dramatic impact on public policy by more or less permanently changing the majority party in the House, the Senate, and the presidency simultaneously. The Civil War era, the 1890s, and the New Deal era all qualify by stringent criteria as periods when critical elections transformed Congress. The foremost student of these elections, David Brady, has argued that conditions no longer exist at the congressional district level to facilitate massive changes in the composition of Congress such as were made possible by the narrow electoral balances in many congressional districts in earlier times.[30] Nowadays, the vast majority of members of Congress hold seats that are fortified against small or even major swings of national sentiment. Because they can withstand landslides at the presidential level—at least landslides favoring Republican presidential candidates— the likelihood of far-reaching changes of public policy owing to wholesale changes in the party composition of Congress in the near future seem dim. But this in no way invalidates the historical significance of critical elections as an avenue of congressional change.

Technology. Change in the modern Congress has also come in part as a response to changes in various underlying conditions of modern life. A technological innovation, such as television, with its power to focus the attention of millions, could be counted upon to impinge upon the lives of politicians who depend upon millions of people for their votes, though no one could predict precisely how it would do so. The nationalization of the South, with its eventual impact on the rise of southern Republicans and, paradoxically, on the liberalization of the House, rests in turn, at least in some respects, on a technological footing: for example, the mechanization of agriculture that depleted the nation (and especially the most rural part of the nation, the South) of its rural population or air conditioning, which made intolerably hot places habitable and made some of these places targets for retirees seeking better winter climates.

Sociopolitical Movements. Changes in Congress can equally be seen as the product of social and political movements. The demographic movements that brought rural southerners to the cities and northern Republicans, such as well-to-do retirees, to the South have already been mentioned. World War II attracted southerners, both black and white, to the North to work in factories supporting the war effort. This greatly accelerated the movement of black Americans into the voting population and helped to create safe Democratic congressional seats in the urban North.[31]

Political Innovations. Finally, political changes elsewhere in the system have had an impact on Congress. Some, like the changes creating myriads of safe congressional seats, may well have retarded the prospects for other changes, at least those changes that come through the medium of a critical election. Other political events may have facilitated change. As the presidency expanded, for example, Congress found that it too had to expand its capabilities in order successfully to exercise its responsibilities to check and balance and to keep track of what was going on. It is possible to trace the recent growth of congressional staff and its professionalization to the stimulus of institutional innovation in the modern presidency.[32] Changes in the rules and procedures of presidential nominations, not trivially abetted by television, have given Washington politicians added visibility and influence in what has come to be a process dominated by primary elections and hence by publicity. At the same time, the influence of state party leaders has diminished. This combination of technological innovation and political reform may be the best explanation available to account for changes in the career possibilities confronting U.S. senators and therefore changes in the role of the Senate in the political system.

Conclusion

Change happens frequently enough, and in sufficiently unexpected ways, even in the life of an organization as stable as the U.S. Congress, to require the attention of observers as they monitor the performance of contemporary American political institutions. It has not been my purpose here to give an exhaustive census of changes that may have affected Congress, but only to call attention to some of the more important ways in which even Congress has adapted in recent days to the complex and surprising challenges of life in our times.

3

The Supreme Court from Early Burger to Early Rehnquist

Martin Shapiro

The Supreme Court handed down its major abortion decision in 1973 and its major death penalty decision in 1977. It was a Court that took the policy lead on matters of life and death. In the 1980s, commentators found it increasingly difficult to characterize the role of the Court or to discover any central tendencies in its development of new constitutional policies. It was clear that the Court was active rather than self-restrained, but not so clear what it was active at.

There is indeed a new central tendency in the Court's jurisprudence, but one that does not lead to big new constitutional rules of the type that so clearly identified both the scale and policy direction of actions by the Warren Court and early Burger Court. This new central tendency is, in a sense, a return to a position ostensibly and ostentatiously abandoned by the New Deal Court. The newest Supreme Court has reasserted its claim to be the ultimate judge of whether each and every government action is reasonable. Whatever is unreasonable is, in the eyes of the justices, unconstitutional. If nine justices view their job in this way, but do not share a common, well-defined ideology, the result is a great deal of Supreme Court action, but action that results in continuous piecemeal adjustments rather than ringing new rules like one person one vote or abortion on demand.

In the twenty-five years before 1977, the Supreme Court had been a major domestic policy maker in the United States. It had initiated at least five major policies: school desegregation, reapportionment, reform of the criminal justice system, an emasculation of federal and state obscenity laws, and the opening of birth control and abortion services to millions of working-class women and girls. In addition to these major policy breakthroughs, there had been dozens of smaller policy changes that had a substantial impact on American life. For instance, the Court had substantially affected welfare administration by abolishing residency requirements and requiring hearings before benefits were cut off. It had expanded the legal concepts of standing and class action to facilitate a much broader use of litigation as a form of interest group politics. It had given women, government employees, students, convicts, and illegitimates whole sets of new legal rights.[1] In all five major areas and most of the smaller ones, the Court could have readily anticipated more political opposition than support. Few American politicians would care to run on a platform of desegregation, pornography, abortion, and the "coddling" of criminals.

The Court as Enunciator of Diffuse Values

The distinguishing feature of the Supreme Court's interventions has not been their utility in building a support coalition of politically powerful, focused constituencies. Rather, it has been their consonance with some widely held but inchoate values of the American people and with ideas whose "time has come." Few politicians in 1962 could have won an election on the slogan "one man one vote." Those who sought to overturn the Court's reapportionment decisions nevertheless found that one man one vote was too close to the democratic bone to be attacked successfully. Neither the clichés of states rights nor the sophistications of political science voting analysis could stand up against a Court armored in democratic truism. The rules that excluded from trial truthful evidence that would have sent guilty persons to prison were, and remain, a political liability to the Court. But the root holding, that everyone accused of a crime is entitled to a lawyer, could hardly be attacked successfully. Most Americans cannot help believing that everyone accused of a crime is entitled to a fair trial, which obviously means having a lawyer among other things.

As to desegregation, obscenity, and abortion, they were all ideas whose time had come. After World War II, few white Americans outside the South could openly defend government discrimination against blacks. The question in 1954 was not how the Court could announce desegregation. It was how the Court, at that late date, could possibly have held racism to be constitutional. By the 1960s and 1970s, American sexual mores had so changed that the Court's recognition in its obscenity, birth control, and abortion decisions of the prevalence and problems of sexual expression was little more than a legal confirmation of the felt necessities of the times.

It is precisely this phenomenon of Supreme Court expression of diffuse but basic beliefs and values that makes the Court such a political mystery. As a number of other chapters in this book make clear, political science is extremely uncomfortable about the relation between generalized public opinion or basic political values on the one hand and political action on the other. In the light of the striking parallelism between what the Court has done and the general drift of American life and thought, it is difficult to depict the Court as a pure example of a political elite doing whatever it pleases. In the light of its massive policy initiatives, it is also impossible to depict it as a mere ritualistic legitimizer of what those political actors more closely linked to particular political forces choose to do.

The Court as a Member
of the National Governing Coalition

All of this is not to deny that the Court remained a partner in the national governing coalition. Most of its major interventions were primarily against state governments in areas that traditionally had been left to the states (such as education, police, and morals) but have increasingly become the targets of actions by the whole array of national government institutions. Of course, two of the most memorable decisions of the 1954 to 1977 period were ones in which the Court seemed to act not with but against another branch of the national

49

government.[2] Neither *New York Times Co.* v. *United States* nor *United States* v. *Nixon* is nearly as antipresident as the decision looked at the time. Indeed, the former carefully avoided a real constitutional test of the system of secrecy classification of government documents, just as Congress and the president have carefully avoided the kind of full-scale reconsideration of the system that might lead to a real "official secrets" act. The latter decision did quash presidential pretentions to be above the law. It is, however, actually the first decision that acknowledges the constitutional validity of the executive privilege doctrine—that is, the position that the president holds a pool of independent powers drawn directly from the nature of government itself rather than drawn exclusively from grants of power found in specific language of the Constitution.

In the 1980s the Court ruled on separation of powers issues raised by congressional innovations such as the legislative veto and budget-balancing legislation. In these decisions it showed itself to be a member of the Washington coalition whose views could not be ignored by its fellow players, but it certainly did not provoke confrontations with its fellow branches.[3]

The Court as Effective Policy Maker

Thus, although the Court turns out to have been a major policy maker in recent times, its movement seems to have been largely in the same direction as the nationalizing tendency of American politics, the liberalizing trend in American thought and mores, and the general constellation of Washington forces. Yet many of its decisions (such as those on obscenity, the rights of the accused, abortion, school prayer, and desegregation) have been highly controversial. How has a Court, which is not elected and has neither a large budget with which to buy support nor an enforcement arm to compel it, gotten away with these decisions? Five complementary answers may be offered.

Partial Success and Outside Assistance. First, the Court has not gotten away with them completely or unaided.[4] Neither the Court's school desegregation goals nor its ambitions to impose national, uniform standards of police conduct have met with more than very partial success. And frequently what success the Court has had has depended on the efforts of Congress in passing new legislation, or on the federal bureaucracy in wielding the carrot and stick of federal funding to local authorities, or on the willing compliance of local authorities who favored its decisions.[5]

Interest Group Allies. The second answer is a variant of the first. Court decisions may call into being, encourage, or greatly strengthen interest groups that will then aid the Court in achieving its policies. The Court's school desegregation decisions were not only a tremendous boost to the NAACP but also a major catalyst for the growth of political and civil rights organizations among southern blacks signaled by the emergence of leaders such as Martin Luther King. Both the school prayer and abortion decisions accelerated the creation, growth, and vehemence of interest groups. We are more apt to view with alarm those that attacked the Court than to remember that many such groups provided the Court with powerful support against its attackers.

Summating Preferences. A third and closely related approach to the Court's political viability is in terms of its ability to summate constituencies. Along one dimension this summating capacity involves intensities. A relatively weak, very widespread, diffusely held value may receive little expression by the legislative or executive organs of national or state governments, most of which are better designed to respond to intensely held values concentrated in specific, easily identified constituencies. Supreme Court decisions may tap highly diffuse support (for instance, pro freedom of speech sentiment) that rarely becomes sufficiently focused or organized to generate direct pressure on legislative or administrative bodies. Along another dimension the Court may bring together groups. At the time the governor of Arkansas used state troops to resist court-ordered school desegregtion, those who cared about integration were joined in supporting the Court by those who cared about obedience to law.

51

Working Out the New Deal Program. A fourth answer to the question of the Court's success in the twenty-five years before 1977 is to be found by reviewing the events of the past forty. The Warren Court and the early Burger Court confirmed the New Deal stance of the 1930s that constitutional rights were for the members of the New Deal coalition (that is, the poor, minorities, government employees, and intellectuals) and not for the New Deal's enemies (that is, the business community and the propertied). The early New Deal Court had practiced judicial self-restraint. It had stripped the business community of constitutional rights created for it by earlier courts, but it had done little to assert new rights of any sort. The Warren Court announced due process and First Amendment rights that protected government employees and the beneficiaries of government welfare programs. It upheld equality as the central constitutional value and thus the underdog as the principal constitutional beneficiary. The Warren Court received broad support because, a decade or two after the New Deal, it finally moved to incorporate service to the New Deal victors into constitutional law, just as Congress and the presidency earlier had incorporated such service into statutory law. The Supreme Court got away with its activism because it was activism on behalf of the winners not the losers of American politics.[6]

The Court and the Law. The fifth and final factor to be examined in accounting for the success of the Court in policy making is that the Court retains its status as an institution and as guardian of the Constitution. At the level of thought and feeling that can be tapped by survey research, the public's sense of the legitimacy of the Court tends to fluctuate over time along just about the same curves as the felt legitimacy of other American institutions. The Court fairly consistently scores somewhat higher than does Congress and the presidency, but in recent years its level of popular support has run at only about 50 percent. None of these data yields a very clear picture of why the Supreme Court is considered a court or why what it says is considered to be the law. Nevertheless, of key importance to explaining the success of the Court is the fact that it retains its public image as a court.

All else being equal, and particularly when someone else's ox is being gored, a Supreme Court pronouncement is the law. So long as the Court does not gore too many oxen at any given moment, it will continue to tap American respect for the rule of law and the rule of the Constitution as higher and better law. We do not know why Americans still identify the Court with the law of the Constitution rather than with simple policy making. It may be that this illusion is carefully fostered as a political tool by liberal elites.[7] For whatever reasons, the illusion persists.

The Policy-making Process

How does the Supreme Court make policy? What determines the policy choices of the justices? These questions may be approached along a number of different routes. The judicial behavior school tells us that the justices follow certain basic ideological patterns along two dimensions, one involving civil rights and the other economic liberties.[8] In each individual case, a justice's vote for one or the other party is triggered by the correspondence of the issues or parties to his attitudinal set. Thus, a justice who has conservative attitudes in the economic realm will vote for business and against government in regulation cases. A justice who is a liberal in the civil rights and liberties realm will vote for the speaker and against the government in freedom of speech cases.

There has been considerable debate about whether the research techniques of the behaviorists can "prove" that "attitudes" determine votes or even whether the attitudes identified by the behaviorists are truly independent variables that can properly be used to explain anything. What is shown indisputably by their work, however, is that many of the justices vote with very considerable consistency for certain classes of parties over other classes: government over business, unions over management, the accused over the state, and so on. Whatever theory of judicial psychology we wish to construct from these facts, the brute fact of judicial preferences remains.

For some years political science has been concerned with the internal dynamics of small decision-making groups such as congressional committees. Some work on the Supreme Court has also stressed its small-group processes, suggesting that both votes and the wording of the controlling opinion in a case may be influenced by coalition building and bargaining among the justices.[9] The justices circulate draft opinions among themselves for comment. Scholars working on the justices' papers have discovered that a great deal of such comment occurs at times and that at least some tacit bargaining takes place.

In recent years a number of works by scholars and journalists and a number of interviews with and speeches by the justices have exposed to public view what most knowledgeable observers had known about the Court's inner workings all along but had been remarkably unwilling to state in print.[10]

Each year the Court receives several thousand petitions for certiorari and appeal. In theory, appeals are treated differently from certiorari. In fact, they are processed in about the same way. Each justice's clerks work their way through the papers guessing which ones will be of interest to their justice. The clerks are recent law school graduates, typically at the top of their class and with law review experience. They usually come from the most prestigious law schools, although a kind of geographic distribution modifies this somewhat. Some have clerked for other judges before coming to the Court. Most stay two years. Some justices do part of the petition-culling work themselves. Some indicate what kinds of things they want to see. Others barely supervise the work of their clerks. Each justice eventually prepares a list of pending cases he or she wishes the Court to consider. Any case listed by any one justice is likely to receive some personal attention from the others. Eventually any case that four justices wish to take will be accepted by the Court.

Although this work is done rapidly and largely by the clerks, there is little need for a more elaborate process. Certain clues like conflict on the circuits or appeal by the government easily tag many cases as ready for the Court.[11] Everyone around the Court has a general sense of the big issues of the moment and the current trends in litigation. Each term dozens of cases will raise approximately the same issue. It is highly unlikely that any major issue that the justices would want to consider if they knew about it slips by them in the clerk-dominated petition stage. Even if it did so in one term, it would undoubtedly be back the next. Indeed, the principal problem seems to be that the Court takes too many minor cases that do not really require its attention.

Once a case is accepted, both parties file written briefs, and a date is set for oral argument. Today's Supreme Court brief in any major case really consists of two parts, although they may be interwoven. One is a legal argument citing, distinguishing, and otherwise disposing of the cases in point and the legal arguments made by opposing counsel and in treatises and law review articles. It may sometimes influence the outcome of cases, but its principal role, like that of most lobbying, is not to persuade "the guys on the other side" but to provide good arguments for "our guys." The brief will contain, in addition to the law, a public policy analysis of the issue raised and supporting data to show that the resolution recommended by counsel will constitute the best outcome for society at large and the fairest treatment of the two parties. The root of the modern brief is not the legal analysis but the attempt to persuade the Court what the best thing to do would be.

Some of the justices read some of the briefs before some of the oral arguments. No one seems to suggest that all of the justices read all of the briefs before all of the oral arguments. The oral argument itself usually lasts an hour, which is split between the two opposing counsel who address the whole Court in the Supreme Court chamber. The justices interrupt with questions. At weekly or biweekly intervals the justices meet to vote on the cases they have heard argued. Some justices apparently vote in many cases on the basis of what they have heard in oral argument or read in memoranda written by the clerks. Clearly, all the justices have not thoroughly read the briefs in all the cases and evaluated them on the basis of their own independent research before they cast their initial votes.

The chief justice speaks first and then the others in order of seniority on the Court. As each justice speaks, he or she indicates his or her vote. The justices keep informal track of the voting. If the chief justice is among the majority, he assigns the task of writing a draft opinion to one of the majority justices. If he is not, the majority justice who is senior in length of service on the Court assigns.

The justice assigned the opinion prepares a draft and circulates it to the other justices, and those justices who choose to prepare concurrences and dissents also write drafts. It is clear from reading the opinions that there is some reading of one another's drafts. It is also clear that dissenters often do not bother to meet the specific arguments of the majority and vice versa, although a real debate occurs in some instances. Real collaboration or even bargaining takes place rather infrequently among the majority. For the most part the justices and their clerks act as nine separate law firms would act rather than as a collegial body. In many instances a majority justice simply votes silently with the majority in spite of language in the majority opinion he or she does not like. Since the 1950s there has been a rapidly growing tendency to file brief concurrences to indicate differences over language or rationale. Many opinions of the Court are signed by only four justices. In a number of important cases in recent years, the Court has resorted to a brief per curiam opinion signed "by the Court" and then individual opinions by each of the justices. It is now fairly routine for five or six justices to file written opinions in a single case.

Clerks write most of the words in most of the opinions. At one extreme, a justice may tell his or her clerks which party he or she wants to win in a given case and then let them do the whole job; the justice will then read the clerks' finished product and sign it. At the other, a justice may write the entire opinion and ask his or her clerks only for research assistance on particular points. Some of the justices fall near the first extreme in the handling of nearly every case. Others choose to do a good deal of original writing in certain cases. A few justices may actually write a majority of the words they sign as their own each year. The justices are clearly hard working.

Justices' complaints of overwork, however, must be evaluated in the light of their tendency to take many cases that involve no major point of law. The Supreme Court is not a place where nine scholarly men and women think, study, discuss, and carefully ponder their decisions and then write reasoned elaborations of the careful path of legal analysis that they have pursued collegially before coming to a conclusion. Most cases seem to be decided by most justices after a little reading and talking and some more or less structured thinking, and on the basis of their best guess about which resolution of the issues will be fair to the parties and promote the best public policy. Most of the justices are not practicing legal scholars of the first order. Few are policy specialists with a vast fund of expertise in any area of government operations or social or economic affairs. They do the best they can under the circumstances—and the circumstances are that, like most other politicians, they confront too many problems, for most of which neither the state of our social knowledge nor the capacity of our social technology provides clear solutions.

All of this is not to say that the justices act "by guess or by God" or by delegating decision making to the parties or to their clerks. Few of the issues that reach the Court are brand new. Most cases involve only a slight variation on facts and issues that have been before the Court dozens of times. A justice may have made up his or her mind, after a half a dozen vehicular search cases, that the cops ought to be allowed to search cars whenever they have any half-way decent reason for doing so. The justice does not have to spend more than a few minutes on the latest case, which may be novel only in the sense that this car was in a parking lot and the cars in the previous six cases had been in the street. The justice need only look at the facts briefly to make sure the police were not acting in a totally arbitrary way. If they were not, his or her vote is routine.

Moreover, the justice may be quite certain where all the other justices stand and be pretty sure that they will not be convinced to change their views by any facts or arguments at their disposal. Under these circumstances there is little reason for the justice to rethink the basic questions, seek to convince or bargain with fellow justices, or spend time carefully honing an elaborate opinion. Even if the justice is assigned the opinion-writing chores for the majority or feels compelled to file a separate opinion, there is no reason why one of the clerks should not compose it.

In short, like most other government policy makers, the justices are usually confronted with choices that they can treat as incremental variations on choices that they have made in the past. Such incremental tactics free some of their attention for major policy decisions when they choose to make such decisions. In order to understand the policy directions of the current Court, some background on the Court under Earl Warren and Warren Burger is necessary.

The Warren Court

After its first few terms of incremental adjustments,[12] the Warren Court took a fairly clear direction: to serve the value of equality and to incorporate that value more deeply in the Constitution. Although the structure was never completed, the blueprint was clear. The Court moved toward the creation of constitutional guarantees of national basic minimums in education, housing, subsistence, legal services, political influence, birth control services, and other facets of the modern welfare state. This value of equality turned up in the Court's decisions not only on the equal protection clause, but also on due process, privacy, travel, counsel, voting, and all sorts of other cases that purported to be about rights. The Warren Court was attempting to change the Constitution and impose its own will on that of other governmental bodies, particularly the state legislatures. It was pretty clear that by the late 1960s nobody in the Warren-Brennan majority really cared much about anything but the policy outcomes of the cases.

The Early Burger Court

By the time of Chief Justice Warren's retirement in 1969, the Court had gone a long way in the equality direction in the areas of race, rights of accused, voting, and birth control. Although the materials were still scattered and incomplete, the Court seemed on the verge of moving toward declaring constitutional rights to subsistence, housing, and education. The crucial halt to this movement came in 1973 in *San Antonio School District* v. *Rodriguez*, a decision in which the justices refused to create a constitutional right to equal education.[13] In the same year the same bloc of Nixon appointees plus Justice Potter Stewart that had been the majority in *Rodriguez* refused to make sex a suspect classification.[14] With a few minor exceptions, the Burger Court refused to extend the list of suspect classifications or fundamental rights; that is, it refused to extend further the policy areas in which it had announced itself as primary policy maker.

The Burger Court did not retreat from the basic assertions of judicial power or the basic policies made by its predecessor. Yet its policy preferences differed somewhat. As a result, the Burger Court spent its early years largely in marginal readjustments of Warren Court policies.[15]

In the rights-of-accused area, the Burger Court sometimes moved a step beyond the Warren Court. For instance, it extended the right to counsel to misdemeanors as well as felony cases and announced the right of indigents to state-provided psychiatric testimony where an insanity defense is raised. On the key issue of the exclusionary rule, however, it chipped away at the Warren Court position and called for Congress to abolish the rule. Indeed, the Court itself seemed fairly close to abolishing or seriously modifying the rule.

In one area, however, the Burger Court marched on down the path blazed by the Warren Court. The Burger Court's major abortion decisions were not grounded on any explicit constitutional guarantee, but they provided nonetheless a new and very broad right to abortion.[16] The Burger Court went almost as far in the death penalty cases, declaring unconstitutional many state death penalty statutes.[17]

In grappling with the record of the early Burger Court, most commentators have concluded that it was an activist Court but one that tended to use balancing doctrines to reach ad hoc policy judgments in particular cases rather than announcing major new constitutional rights, except in the abortion and death penalty areas. It was indeed typical for the Court to announce that a given case involved a clash of various governmental, social, and individual interests and then resolve the constitutional issue by a purely conclusory statement that, on balance, some of those interests were more weighty than others. At this stage it was difficult to describe the Court's role except in terms of roving policy intervention. The policy product was not clearly liberal or conservative. Justice Harry Blackmun's movement toward the left and the relative centrism of Justices Lewis Powell and John Paul Stevens meant that Burger and Rehnquist could not muster sufficient troops to create a dominant new bloc of Republican appointees even if they had been sure what to do with it. Justice Rehnquist's opinions seemed to introduce new or revived themes of states rights and the autonomy of private individuals and groups from government intervention, but no central value emerged to replace the Warren Court's eroded but far from eliminated commitment to equality.

The replacement on the Court of Burger and Powell by Antonin Scalia and Anthony M. Kennedy gives some promise of creating a new majority, but there is little to suggest that it will be strong enough to move to a new central value position. At least pending another round of appointments, only relatively small changes are likely in the nuances of what the majority finds reasonable. The history of the Bork nomination and the continued balance between a Republican president and a Democratic Senate make it unlikely that even a new round of appointees would take the Court in fundamentally new directions.

The Mature Burger Court and the Early Rehnquist Court

With the benefit of hindsight and new, rather striking decisions, the self-selected role of the mature Burger Court and early Rehnquist Court can now be described more precisely than merely labeling it a roving, ad hoc, balancing-doctrine activism. This new role and central constitutional doctrine have emerged only partially, however. Much of the older ad hoc style remained in at least six major areas of the Court's work: rights of the accused, voting and elections, discrimination, abortion, freedom of speech, and federalism.[18] In the first five of these, the Court's central or core policy was clear enough, but a great deal of uncertainty remains in the application of that policy to marginal situations.

Rights of Accused. The mature Burger Court maintained a

strong allegiance to the right to counsel. It slightly cut back on the requirement that the police act on the basis of search and arrest warrents. Its self-incrimination decisions were mixed.

The key question, of course, was the survival of the exclusionary rule, which requires that confessions or evidence that are the fruit of police misconduct be excluded from trials. The Burger Court came to terms with the exclusionary rule and adopted two basic tactics for confining what it saw as its costs. First, it tended to narrow the standing of defendants to raise exclusionary rule issues in federal courts, particularly when the defendant had an opportunity to raise them in state courts. Second, the Court fastened on the notion that the purpose of the exclusionary rule is the purely pragmatic one of deterring police misconduct. Accordingly, the Court was free to "administer" the rule—that is, to invoke it as such times and in such ways as to actually deter police misconduct and to refuse to "rigidly" or "mechanically" apply it when the police acted in "good faith."[19] The early Rehnquist Court has continued this stance.

Voting and Elections. In the area of voting and elections, the Court is, if anything, firmer than ever on the one-person-one-vote slogan for apportionment in congressional elections. It now appears ready, however, to allow the states fairly large deviations where such deviations are reasonable means of ensuring that voters who live in isolated places or are members of minority races get some representation.[20] The Court's new major area of concern involves race and voting. The Court has made clear that it is unconstitutional either to adopt "at-large" electoral schemes in which a number of legislators are elected from one large district or to draw the boundary lines of single-member districts with the intention of reducing the number of minority legislators elected.[21]

A closely related question is now beginning to come before the Court. Do the Fourteenth and Fifteenth Amendments require states to draw district lines so as to ensure the election of some minority legislators or a proportion of minority legislators approximating the proportion of minority persons in the electorate?

Ever since the Warren Court attacked malapportionment (electoral districts with unequal populations), the justices have been urged to move on to gerrymandering, the practice of purposely drawing district boundaries to give advantage to a particular candidate or party. The Rehnquist Court has indicated it will move against patently partisan gerrymanders, but without any absolute standard like one person one vote by which to judge the shape of districts,the Court will almost certainly pursue some sort of reasonableness standard in this area too.[22]

Discrimination. In the area of racial discrimination and school desegregation, the Burger Court continued its earlier pattern. It left to district and circuit courts nearly all of the work of school desegregation, while it remained firm in its basic holding that dual school systems must be dismantled. It also remained firm, however, that the Fourteenth Amendment forbids only government acts that intentionally discriminate. The Burger Court was deeply divided on how much evidence of discriminatory intent there must be, on what makes an action a government action as opposed to a private action, and on what the scope of the remedies ordered by a court may be once discrimination or segregation is found. It did not challenge district-court-ordered busing as such, but it did forbid throwing districts that historically had not segregated students in with districts that had so as to create large, racially diverse pools of students to be bused.

Disputes about race increasingly arise not in cases that seek to apply the Fourteenth Amendment directly but in those involving the various civil rights acts passed by Congress. After considerable struggle the Court read most of these acts as barring not only intentional discrimination by governmental and private actors but also those actions that have an adverse and disparate impact on minority interests. Also after much struggle and by shaky majorities, the Court upheld governmental and private use of racial classifications to achieve affirmative action under these statutes. The statutes themselves, however, contain certain clauses designed to protect "seniority rights" and other "last-hired-first-hired" practices that tend to perpetuate past discrimination. Where either private or government affirmative action programs came into conflict with such practices or prescribed very severe discrimination against white individuals in favor of minorities, the Court was badly fragmented. In *Regents* v. *Bakke* and *Fullilove* v. *Klutznick,* the Court sought a middle ground that approves some degree of favored treatment for minorities but not an automatic and mechanical shutting out of whites as a class from educational and employment opportunities.[23]

The Court formally refused to elevate gender discrimination to quite the same level of evil as race discrimination. Occasionally it approved a state statute involving a sexual classification. It became divided and uncertain when a sexual classification appeared to be employed to compensate women for past inequalities or in cases brought directly under the Fourteenth Amendment in which government action intended to achieve some legitimate purpose had an incidental adverse impact on women.

One clear problem raised by discrimination cases is, so far, insoluble. If any government or private action, no matter what purposes it is trying to achieve, is unlawful if it results in any degree of adverse and disparate impact on racial minorities or women, then racial and sexual equality are elevated to trump values that displace every other value in American public policy. Let us suppose we seek to improve public school mathematics education by introducing a new requirement that high school math teachers have had some college training in mathematics. Then it turns out that a higher proportion of the current white male math teachers have had some college training in math than have current black or women math teachers so that proportionally more blacks and women will lose their teaching jobs than will men. Must we forgo this attempt to improve mathematics education? Some justices believe that discrimination is so terrible that everything else must give way to its eradication, at least until equality is achieved. Others believe that where an important goal is being pursued some incidental adverse effects on minorities and women are permissible.

About all the justices can do is to distinguish two situations. Where Congress has chosen to bar not only intention but adverse impact, thus making racial and sexual equality trump, or where Congress has chosen affirmative action, the Court will act most favorably toward minorities and women and with greatest disregard of other values. Where the Court is invoking its own interpretation of the Constitution in the absence of a congressional directive, it will be somewhat less harsh toward nonintentional discriminatory impact that occurs as a result of seeking to achieve legitimate public purposes.

A second continuing cause of division is affirmative action. We must correct the continuing evils caused by past discrimination, and one of the few means available is affirmative action. The adverse side of affirmative action is telling some individual that he may not have the job or the education he could otherwise have had simply because he is white and male. Because none of us is comfortable with this insoluble dilemma, it is little wonder that the Court seeks a middle ground. It says that to correct past injustices one may discriminate against white males now, but not too much and not too obviously. It cannot state with any precision just how much and just how obviously.

With the appointments of Justices Scalia and Kennedy, the voting balance on proof of discrimination and affirmative action issues shifted slightly. The result was a series of decisions that somewhat altered the Court's vision of a reasonable balance between seeking racial and gender equality on the one hand and achieving efficiency and fairness to white males on the other. The shift was greeted by the predictable outcry from civil rights groups that the Rehnquist Court was destroying the Constitution and the equally predictable response of journalists in search of a cliché that the Rehnquist Court was now the "conservative" Court. Both responses failed to note sufficiently how divided, uncertain, and ambiguous the Burger Court and public sentiment had been on these issues. The shift of the Rehnquist Court has been of precisely the kind and degree one would expect when a gradually changing set of people is seeking to achieve a delicate balance.

Abortion. The early Burger Court announced and the later

Burger Court held firmly to a nearly absolute right of pregnant women to choose abortion in at least the first three months of pregnancy.

"Pro-life" forces have managed to push through a variety of statutory provisions that limit abortion. The Burger Court was deeply split in responding to these initiatives. It approved some, most notably the withholding of public funds to fund free abortion services, but struck down or severely limited others. Here again the appointments of Justices Scalia and Kennedy have somewhat changed the balance on a divided court and are likely to lead to somewhat more discretion for the states, with the Court retaining for itself the final balancing of privacy versus fetal interests.

Freedom of Speech. In addressing the constitutional problem of freedom of speech, the Court has maintained a rather consistent policy since the mid-1950s. The core of the First Amendment prohibits government from restricting speech on the ground that its content is politically objectionable. Freedom of speech cases typically come to the Court in one of two postures. It is claimed that government is covertly seeking to restrict politically unpalatable speech under the guise of doing something else, or it is claimed that government may be genuinely pursuing some legitimate non-speech-restricting goal (such as making the city more beautiful by removing the blight of outdoor billboards), but at an impermissible cost to freedom of speech. These cases become even more complex as counsel seek to include various kinds of activity, such as the refusal of reporters to name their confidential sources to grand juries under the speech umbrella, while opposing counsel argue that the activity is not really "speech" at all or is only at the periphery of what is normally considered speech.

Besides these problems of restricting covert and incidental speech and drawing the boundaries between speech and nonspeech, the Court has also declared that certain categories of speech, such as libel and obscenity, may be restricted by government because their content is disapproved. In dealing with most of these categories, however, the Court has introduced a number of "ifs," "ands," and "buts" that produce much litigation and many close cases.[24]

The later Burger Court and the early Rehnquist Court maintained as their central doctrine of free speech the same doctrine first established early in the Warren Court. Under this "balancing" doctrine, they embraced a strong preference for freedom of speech but in each case the value of the speech infringed was weighed against the government's interest in infringing. If the government, for example, can show that a "compelling" governmental interest, such as national security, is being served by the infringement upon speech, and that this compelling interest could not be equally well served by means that infringe upon speech less than the one chosen, then the Court may approve the restriction on freedom of speech. Thus, the Court may uphold a statute that punishes the publication of military information in time of war because, although speech is clearly restricted, the restriction is, on balance, justified by the national interest in winning the war.

Just as governments rarely attack the core of the First Amendment openly, they rarely enact any measure arguably impinging on speech without providing some public interest justification. "On balance," then, nearly any speech case can be decided any way. The current Court, like its predecessors, simply gives itself a license to decide each speech case however it pleases.

Federalism. At the outset of this discussion of the Supreme Court's continued tentative, ad hoc style in certain policy areas, we noted that even in most of these some core of consensus existed. When we reach "federalism," even that core disappears. The New Deal Court had effectively announced the constitutional demise of federalism as a limit on the power of the national government. The Warren Court not only approved all congressional and presidential interventions in state affairs but, using the Fourteenth and Fifteenth Amendments, enormously expanded the power of the Court itself over the states, particularly in the areas of criminal justice, education, and voting.

One of the central distinguishing marks of the shift from

the Warren Court to the Burger Court was *National League of Cities* v. *Usery*, a decision that struck down a congressional statute because it violated basic principles of federalism.[25] The decision stood more as a symbol than anything else for a number of years. Then a five-justice majority that contained two of the Republican appointees, Stevens and Blackmun, overruled *Usery* in *Garcia* v. *San Antonio Metropolitan Transit Authority*, an opinion that openly declared that protecting federalism was no business of the Supreme Court.[26] The four other Burger Court appointees wrote bitter dissents openly telling the president that his next appointments to the Court ought to be designed to reconstruct a profederalism majority. The membership of the Court has now changed again. It is unlikely that *Garcia* will be directly overruled, but some drift back toward *Usery* is likely.

The New Style

After this rapid survey of six major areas of the justices' work, it may be difficult to believe that the Court is anything more than a roaming, random, policy intervenor. In fact, however, a new style is beginning to give the Court a distinctive character.

Beginning in the 1890s, the Supreme Court increasingly cultivated a technique that came to be denounced by liberals as "substantive economic due process." The Court proclaimed that no government regulation of economic life was constitutional unless it was reasonable, and the justices would be the final judges of what was and was not reasonable. The Court adopted the standard economic theory of the day, laissez-faire, as the foundation for its reasonableness judgments. Entrepreneurial freedom was the rule, government intervention the exception only occasionally justified by some anomaly in the free market mechanism. In fact, the Court approved a considerable number of wages and hours, industrial safety, antitrust, and rail and utility rate-setting statutes, but it struck down a considerable number, too. Franklin Delano Roosevelt's appointments to the Court in 1937 proclaimed the end of substantive economic due process. Where business regulation was involved, legislatures not courts were to be the ultimate judges of reasonableness.[27]

Reasonableness analysis did not itself disappear. The balancing standard that the Warren Court made central to free speech cases was at bottom a reasonableness standard with free speech the rule and government regulation to be justified by anomalies in the "marketplace of ideas." As the Warren Court became more and more concerned with the rights of the accused, it perforce did more and more reasonableness analysis. After all, the Fourth Amendment does not prohibit all searches and seizures but only "unreasonable" ones.

The Warren Court and its liberal admirers tended to excuse this continued judicial prerogative by saying that it was exercised only when civil rights, not property rights, were involved. In reality, however, the Court was soon back in the property business too, but this time as a protector of the "new property," that is, the right to government employment and benefits. When the Court asked how much process was due to government employees and those receiving government help, it was asking the reasonableness question again.[28]

Thus, in a very real sense the Warren Court had returned to substantive due process and even substantive economic due process. It rarely did so, however, by invoking the general words of the due process clause, and it proclaimed no single all-encompassing economic theory. Instead it usually focused on the specific provisions of the bill of rights or on the equal protection clause, and it proclaimed particular theories or tests or techniques to be used with each of them. If the Court used any kind of theory at all, it tended to be a kind of social democratic theory based in the liberal wings of sociology and political science and, more indirectly, on Keynesian economics.

What is emerging in the Court now is a return to more explicit reasonableness analysis free of the guilt that had been heaped on judicial judgments of reasonableness by the New Deal. Current analysis is more openly based on judicial employment of what the judges regard as the latest and best theories and empirical findings not only in economics but in all the social, and even the natural, sciences. Above all, the new style announces the confidence of the justices that they can manage society. In the following discussion we will concentrate on a few areas that illustrate this new mood most clearly while also providing some reference to its emergence in other areas where the ad hoc style still appears dominant.

Antitrust. This new style is most clearly illustrated by the current Court's antitrust jurisprudence. There are a whole cluster of antitrust laws and major amendments, but for purposes of this discussion we can lump them together. Since their inception in the 1890s, these acts have always been approached in two basic ways. One is to see them as aimed at the dangers of bigness itself. The gathering of a major share of business enterprise into the hands of a few giant corporations may be viewed as a potential threat to small business, to individuals, and to democratic government. Alternatively, the purpose of antitrust laws may be seen not as preventing bigness, but as preserving competition. If competition is preserved, then the irresistible laws of supply and demand in the marketplace will force all business big and small to act in an economically efficient way.

Besides these two fundamentally different ways of looking at antitrust, a further complicating factor is the problem of proof. Large corporations have considerable power to hide their wrongdoings from government. And whether or not a particular business action would reduce competition often depends on *predicting* extremely complex economic behavior by many producers and consumers.

The Warren Court, inclined to the antibigness view of antitrust law, was very sympathetic to antitrust prosecutors' difficulties in proving that bigness actually led to a reduction in competition. The Warren Court thus tended to "per se" rules. Certain business practices—such as tie-in agreements in which a retailer had to agree to sell one of a particular company's products, say tires, in order to get to sell another of a company's products, say gasoline—were held to be per se violations of the antitrust law. If the government could prove that the tie-in agreement existed, that was enough to

69

convict. It did not have to prove that the tie-in actually reduced competition.[29]

A well-financed "law and economics" movement has been busily at work inventing all sorts of "efficiency" defenses. Such defenses try to show that practices that might appear superficially to be monopolistic actually promote competition and economic efficiency under certain economic conditions. Judicial receptivity to efficiency defenses greatly increases the government's burden of proof, thus rendering it far more difficult to gain antitrust convictions. Such receptivity also entails much more detailed and technical economic analyses by the courts.

The Court now tends to view the aim of antitrust laws as preserving competition rather than attacking big business. Following the lead of certain district courts, it has been substituting a "rule of reason" for per se rules.[30] The Court has now made it clear that when it can it will interpret the antitrust laws as forbidding only unreasonable business practices. The touchstone of reasonableness will be economic efficiency. Economic efficiency is to be determined by the best economic theory and analytic techniques of the day. And the Court is to be the ultimate economic analyst. In short, under its authority to interpret the antitrust laws, rather than as a matter of constitutional law, the Court has returned to something startlingly like substantive economic due process. It has based that return on a "neoclassical" economic theory that is startlingly like the laissez-faire economic theory that originally provided the underpinnings for the turn of the century Court's "reasonableness" holdings.

Sentencing. Its antitrust decisions illuminate, as if under an extra bright light, the Court's renewed propensity to employ "reasonableness" as the central standard of legality and its renewed self-confidence in its ability to be the final grand judge of what is or is not reasonable. In antitrust such judgments are at least informed by a highly articulated body of economic theory and analysis. In the Court's jurisprudence about criminal sentences, its return to reasonableness puts it firmly in the role of the Mikado who, for those who remember their Gilbert and Sullivan, is not only to let the punishment fit the crime but whose judgments of what punishment fits what crime are based on nothing but his personal authority.

The early Burger Court struggled with internal disagreements about the death penalty for murder and reached a state of paralysis. In principle it approved the penalty if applied under certain conditions that it refused to clarify. In practice it always reversed or remanded death sentence cases. Then, goaded by Justice Rehnquist, it ended its evasive tactics and in the course of upholding some death penalties made its conditions clearer and easier to achieve.

The Mikadoesque act of the Burger Court was not its challenge to and subsequent regularization of the death penalty for murder, but its truly astounding holding that the states could not impose the death penalty for rape because rape was simply not a sufficiently serious offense.[31] What foundation did the justices offer for such a conclusion? Ultimately, they offered nothing more than their personal moral sentiments. The principle of "proportionality," that the punishment should be proportional to the crime, is an ancient principle of philosophy, a long-held principle of the common law, and a sometimes abstractly announced principle of constitutional law. The Court had never really done anything about that principle, however, for the obvious reason that the principle carries with it no recognized technique for its application. On the basis of what technique of analysis is twenty years or six years or three years the properly proportioned sentence for a second armed robbery? In this situation the justices, who usually believe they need reasons for what they do, left sentencing to legislatures.

In spite of its continued inability to come up with any reasons beyond its own moral sentiments, the Court has now fully accepted the logic of its rape decision. If the Court is to decide whether death is or is not too much for rape, then why should it not decide, indeed how can it avoid deciding, whether life imprisonment is or is not too much for writing a bad check? The Court has now announced that it is going to actively apply the constitutional principle of proportionality to all criminal sentencing.[32]

Religion. If antitrust gives us reasonableness as neoclassical economics, and sentencing reasonableness as moral sentiment, the Court's recent religion cases give us reasonableness as sociology. In such cases as *Walz* v. *Tax Commissioner* and *Wisconsin* v. *Yoder*, the early Burger Court announced a sympathy less for religion as religion than for the stability, social discipline, education, and conventional morality that the traditional, organized religions brought to American social life.[33] In those early days, we could watch the chief justice slowly building precedents and gathering votes for what would have been a major change in the Court's religion policies and one that would have had a substantial impact on American life. That change would have been the bypassing of years of precedent by a Court declaration that public tax monies could be used to support Catholic parochial and other private religious schools. In the *Nyquist* case the chief justice's campaign came to a head and he lost by one vote.[34] Nothing more clearly signaled the matured stage of the Burger Court than the tacit reversal of *Nyquist* in *Mueller* v. *Allen*.[35] In that case the Court finally approved a state tax deduction of tuition and other instructional costs incurred by parents who send their children to private schools, including religious private schools. The Court made no bones as to why it permitted this breach in the traditional separation of church and state. Religious and other private schools, in the Court's view, do an excellent job, often a better job than do the public schools in educating children and instilling in them basic moral values that will make them good citizens.

Perhaps an even more dramatic illustration is *Lynch* v. *Donnelly*, a case in which the Burger Court denied that a violation of the establishment clause had occurred when a city government allowed the display of a crèche on public property.[36] The Court managed in this decision to treat one of the most poignant and specific symbolic statements of the most fundamental Christian belief, that God so loved human beings that he sent his son to dwell among them in human form, as merely a decorative part of the secular national celebration of Christmas. It is hard to say whether true Christians ought to view the war as won or lost when the highest court in the land views the Virgin Mary and the Holy

72

Infant as advertising gimmicks to increase the Christmas rush of retail sales. But the chief justice surely won his point that where religion serves what in the Court's view is a productive social purpose then the state may reach an accommodation with religion that contributes to that purpose. A majority of the justices proposed to engage in the social engineering of the establishment clause to facilitate government support of those activities of the traditional organized religions that in its view contributed to a healthier society.

The Negative Commerce Clause and Company. A number of clauses of the Constitution have always required the Supreme Court to do some economic analysis and, for various reasons, have always resisted the construction of clear constitutional rules. These include the contract clause, the privileges and immunities clause, and the takings clause. One of the most important of these is the "negative" commerce clause—that is, the facet of the interstate commerce clause that is seen to bar state regulations that excessively impede interstate commerce even when the state regulations do not conflict with specific federal regulations governing commerce.

The Rehnquist Court is no more guilty of ad hoc approaches to these areas than earlier courts. It has certainly not responded by being consistently probusiness, or pro-state and antifederal government. What does render these bodies of confused cases relevant to our picture of the current Court, however, is that in a very great many of them the Court openly confronts the policy issues of government economic and social planning that they involve. In doing so the justices boldly proclaim that they are the ultimate judges of whether those plans are reasonable. What is not reasonable is not constitutional. These opinions are full of the justices' own economic and social analysis.

New Property, Old Property, Due Process. Earlier we noted very briefly that the Warren Court had been moving toward constitutionalizing the welfare state. It did so largely through creating a concept of "entitlements." Where federal and state statutes provided certain benefits, such as welfare or disability payments or government employment, those benefits were to be governed by the equal protection clause. They were also to be considered property so that the government might not take them away without due process of law.[37]

The Warren Court said it would decide just how much process was due in relation to each variety of the new property entitlements. At the same time the Warren Court was creating this new property, which was to receive constitutional protection through active judicial review, the justices persisted in the New Deal view that statutes that regulated traditional private property should be presumed constitutional and subject to almost no judicial review.

The early Burger Court also refused to provide any constitutional protection to the old property. It continued the Warren Court's conception of new property entitlements, although it decided in some instances that very little process was due before some of these entitlements were terminated by the government.

The current Court insists even more strongly that it will decide how much process is due in entitlement cases. However, it is beginning to question the distinction between the old and new property and to assert that all government statutes having an impact on any kind of economic interest are subject to careful judicial review to determine whether they are reasonable means of achieving legitimate government ends.[38]

Statutory Judicial Review. The segment of the Court's jurisdiction that probably reveals its new boldness in policy making most clearly is one that is almost entirely ignored by most American politics texts and by most lawyers and political scientists who study the Supreme Court because it does not involve constitutional judicial review (that is, review of whether a statute or other government action violates the Constitution). Instead it involves statutory review: judicial determination of whether a government agency has acted lawfully (that is, in accordance with a statute). In order to understand this segment of the Court's work, we must take a long detour into the kinds of statutes passed by Congress in the 1960s and 1970s and the interactive roles of federal agencies and federal courts in interpreting and administering these statutes.

The New Style in Congressional Statutes. Although Congress passed a wide variety of statutes in the 1960s and 1970s, and frequently amended its initial efforts, the major laws— particularly in the areas of environment, health, welfare, safety, nuclear power, education, and energy—have certain common characteristics. First, they delegate enormous amounts of legislative rule-making power to executive branch agencies and to regulatory commissions. Legislative rules supplement and fill out the detailed meaning of the congressional statutory language and, once validly enacted by an agency, have the same legal authority as the language of the statutes themselves. Congress is actually delegating part of its power to *make* law to the agencies that enforce it.

Congress had been engaging in sweeping delegations of its law-making powers to the executive branch since the beginning of the New Deal. A second characteristic of statutes in the 1960s and 1970s set them apart from most New Deal delegations. By this later time Congress had lost much of its faith in the neutrality and efficiency of the federal bureaucracy. Therefore, in the very same statutes that granted sweeping law-making powers to the agencies Congress would include many extremely detailed commands, such as exactly how many parts per million of airborne lead constituted impermissible air pollution, to ensure that the agencies vigorously enforced the new statutes.

A third characteristic, "technology forcing," was not common to all the statutes. Indeed, there were often vigorous postpassage debates about whether a given statute intended "technology forcing" or not. Technology forcing referred to a statutory requirement that private business achieve some result in the future that was technologically impossible at the time the statute was passed or whose technical feasibility was unknown at the time the statute was passed. For instance, Congress enacted legislation demanding that by specified future dates the exhaust emissions of new cars be reduced to certain levels. At the time, no one knew whether the auto

75

industry could develop new technologies that could reduce emissions that much.

A fourth characteristic was that these statutes almost invariably contained a large number of potentially contradictory and/or extremely ambiguous provisions. The typically liberal democratic proponents of these major statutory innovations would usually specify the name of the statute, dictate the sweeping language of its preamble, and write the general language of its major provisions. Rarely, however, would they have the votes to pass the legislation in the enthusiastic form in which they had introduced it. In order to corral the necessary votes, they would have to write some concessions into the statute.

These concessions took many forms. One was specific exemptions such as the exemption of seniority schemes from the reach of the civil rights statute covering racial discrimination in employment. A second was the statutory empowering of the administrative agency to grant waivers in special cases in which full enforcement of the law would result in undue hardship, such as forcing a polluting factory to shut down and throw a whole town out of work. In still other instances Congress would adopt ambiguously worded commands that would be tough or easy on business depending on how they were interpreted. Both congressional sides could then claim victory. Often Congress would combine two contradictory goals in the same statute. For instance, the amended disability provisions of the Social Security Act command the Social Security Administration to compensate fairly those who have been disabled on the job and to encourage them to return to productive employment as soon as possible. Of course, the better you compensate workers for not working, the less you encourage them to return to work, and the most effective way to get them back to work may be to reduce their compensation. The "compensation" and "rehabilitation" goals of the statute are forever at odds.

Or Congress might introduce "fudge" language that had the same effect. For instance, an amendment to the interstate highways act says that interstates may not be routed through park land, but then it says they may be so routed if there are no "feasible and prudent" alternatives. Behind this language

76

is the goal of saving neighborhood communities and important industries from destruction by interstates even at the cost of park land.

This same highway provision also illustrates two other common sources of contradiction and ambiguity. Congress often hinted that it wanted costs taken into account, that perhaps some of the commands of a statute should not be totally carried out if it would cost much too much to do so. By using words like "feasible" or "practical," however, it refused to say just how much cost was too much or to say explicitly that something should be done only if it yielded more benefits than costs.

Congress often ended up delegating rule-making power to administrators and telling them to weigh a number of factors and arrive at a balanced judgment, but frequently it did not specify what weight or priority should be given to each factor. The highway amendments could be read as telling the secretary of transportation to reach a routing decision by taking into account the importance of preserving parks, the value of preserving long-standing neighborhoods that provide their residents a sense of community, the need to preserve jobs that may be lost if highway construction causes the tearing down of a factory, and the need to get the most highway we can for our money. If the administrators then decide on the route through the park rather than the one that goes over a huge ravine requiring a very expensive bridge and then right through the middle of the old Italian neighborhood, are they obeying or disobeying the law?

The most extreme form of this kind of ambiguity might be called the "lottery" statute. Two or three or ten sides in Congress may be so equally balanced that none of them can win, but each wants to take credit for passing a statute and/ or blocking passage of its "worst" parts. The result may be a tacit agreement among the congressional factions to all vote for a statute that, by resorting to ambiguous language, potentially incorporates all their mutually contradictory preferences. The statute is a lottery in the sense that no one knows how it will be interpreted later by the administrative agencies and courts that must face up to its ambiguities.[39]

A fifth characteristic of many of the major statutes of the

1960s and 1970s is that they contained "rights" language or at least were readily viewed by their proponents as creating rights such as a right to a safe work place or a right of handicapped children to an education. When an interest becomes a legal right it takes priority over all other interests and must be vindicated no matter what the cost. If the inhabitants of a town have a right to clean water, and all work for an old factory that pollutes the local river, the factory may have to shut down and all the people move away so that a clean river may flow through the now deserted town.

A final characteristic of all of these statutes is that they either implicitly or explicitly provide for judicial review of agency implementation.

The New Role of the Federal Courts. Once this statutory background is understood, the increasingly crucial role of the federal courts in public policy is easy enough to understand.[40] If much of Congress's law-making power is delegated to executive agencies in the form of rule-making authority, and if most of the statutes are detailed but ambiguous, then whoever judges whether or not the rules match the laws is an important policy maker. The justices of the Supreme Court, but even more the judges of the federal district courts and circuit courts of appeal, have become important law makers in environmental, safety, health, and a half dozen other major areas of public policy.

The role of the federal district courts has been little studied except in the area of school desegregation. A major study of the role of courts in environmental law does, however, reveal an interesting pattern.[41] The circuit courts of appeal, sitting far away from the local communities affected, tended to see the statutes as rights-creating, technology-forcing, uncompromising, unambiguous assertions of Congress that the environment be cleaned up completely and right now, no matter what the cost. The district courts, sitting in the towns where the factories would have to be shut down, the jobs lost, the small businesses forced into bankruptcy, the local taxes raised, and the building of new housing delayed, tended to allow delays, compromises, exemptions, and variances. They tended to see the various ifs, ands, and buts in the statutory language as far more important, and the sweeping declarations as far less important, than did the higher and farther away courts.

In most of these policy areas the central role has been played by the courts of appeal and most particularly by the one sitting in Washington, the D.C. Circuit. It has been the D.C. Circuit that has heard most of the challenges to the validity of these agency rules. Those challenges typically assert that the agency has not followed the correct procedures for making the rules and/or that the rules made are invalid because they are not in accord with the provisions of the statutes they are designed to implement.

Many of the new statutes contained some special provisions for what procedures were to be followed by the appropriate agency in making rules implementing its program, but basically all rule making falls under a single federal statute, the Administrative Procedures Act of 1946. Passed long before the new statutes, the act is actually very cryptic about rule making. It requires that before an agency makes a rule it must give notice of its intention to do so and must provide an opportunity for outsiders to communicate to the agency their views about the proposed rule although no formal court-like hearing is required. (Thus we speak of "notice and comment," "informal" rule making.) The final rule and a "concise and general statement of basis and purpose" for the rule must be published. The rule must be lawful, that is, in accord with the statute that authorizes it and which it is designed to implement. It also may not be "arbitrary or capricious or an abuse of discretion."

From the very skeletal provisions of the Administrative Procedures Act, the circuits, most particularly the D.C. Circuit, built up an incredibly elaborate set of procedural demands in their decisions reviewing rules. By the 1970s it had gotten so that the D.C. Circuit could always find some procedural reason for knocking out any rule it did not like. In the *Vermont Yankee* case, the Supreme Court finally warned the D.C. Circuit to stop seizing on procedural quibbles to invalidate rules it did not like and to cut back on its procedural requirements.[42] In this very case and in several others, however, the Supreme Court approved the key procedural innovation of the circuits. This was the requirement that for each rule the agency must construct a "rule-making record." The rule-making record must contain all the evidence presented to the agency by all those attacking and defending the rule plus a thorough explanation of the data, analysis, and reasoning supporting the version of the rule the agency finally adopted. The requirement of a rule-making record gave the courts the ammunition to take, as they put it, "a hard look" at agency rules.

As first enunciated by the circuits, the "hard look" requirement meant that courts would review agency rule making to ensure that the agency had taken a hard look at all the data, analysis, and policy arguments for and against a proposed rule before adopting a final version of the rule. Of course, the judges could not tell whether the agency had taken a hard look unless they themselves took a hard look. And once the judges had a big rule-making record to take a hard look at, they could fault the agency any time the judges decided the agency had not done a good job of collecting evidence, conducting empirical analysis, or making policy choices. Thus, in the end the hard look turned into what the judges of the circuits proclaimed as a "partnership" between the agencies and the courts in rule making. In the process the requirement of the Administrative Procedures Act that rules be lawful and not arbitrary and capricious turned into a judicial requirement that, all the facts and arguments considered, they be reasonable—with the judges as final authority on what was and was not reasonable.

If the particular characteristics of the new statutes of the 1960s and 1970s are recalled, it can quickly be seen why the judges became very active partners. These laws called for an enormous amount of rule making so there were lots of rules for the circuits to review. These laws also contained many very specific provisions with which the rules had to accord, so judges could usually find some wording in the statute that they could claim had been violated by the rule being reviewed. When a court thought that an agency had been moving too slowly because it was giving too much credence to business claims that it was technologically impossible to move faster, or worrying too much about the high costs imposed on local communities and businesses by new regulatory demands, the courts could emphasize technology-forcing or rights-creating aspects of the statute under which the rules were made. On the other hand, courts could seize upon any language in the statute that seemed to suggest a concern for costs or cost-benefit analysis to slow down an agency that seemed to be moving too fast. Finally, these laws contained so many potentially contradictory statements, fudge factors, vaguely worded provisions, and just plain lotteries that whether or not any particular rule was lawful under them was always up for grabs, with the judges having the last grab. In short, statutory interpretation became a central means by which the judiciary could impose its policy views on government efforts to regulate economic and social life.

Reviewing courts typically exercised their powers not by totally blocking a new rule or in effect writing their own, but by remanding it to the agency so that it could take a harder look. Agencies thus knew that unless they came up with a rule that would satisfy the courts, they would encounter time costs since they would have to do it over and over again until the courts liked it. Thus, judicial policy preferences and views of reasonableness tended to be incorporated by anticipation in agency rules.

The Court Takes Over Hard-Look Review. The Warren Court exhibited some sympathy for what the courts of appeal were doing, but mostly it blessed their work by doing nothing about it. We have already noted that in *Vermont Yankee* the early Burger Court seemed to be trying to rein in the D.C. Circuit's proliferation of procedural requirements. The mature Burger Court and the Rehnquist Court, however, have resoundingly approved an extremely demanding version of the hard-look approach, have aggressively intervened on the crucial issue of just how much cost-benefit-style analysis should be done for various kinds of rules under various statutes, have entered the technology-forcing thicket, have signaled that they would curb extreme claims of statutory rights, and have showed remarkable skill in creative interpretation of statutes to achieve what they believed to be reasonable results.[43]

The Court has now clearly proclaimed that rather than drastically cut back the judicial review of rule making built up by the courts of appeal, it will join and supervise them in determining when the agencies have used reasonable procedures to attain reasonable results. A large share of this rule making involves just the kinds of government regulation of business, industry, and labor conditions that occupied the turn of the century Court. And although the due process clauses themselves only hover in the background, reasonableness is again the touchstone of judicial approval of regulation of business. Substantive economic due process has returned but in the "other kind" of judicial review: statutory review of rules rather than constitutional review of statutes. There are even strong signs that substantive economic due process is returning in constitutional review. In 1985, the Burger Court actually overturned a city zoning ordinance as applied to a private business on the grounds that it failed to meet the rationality test that the Supreme Court has applied to economic regulations since 1937. This was the first time since 1937 that the Court had flunked any economic regulation under that test.[44]

Conclusion

We have looked at a number of areas in which the mature Burger Court and the early Rehnquist Court have proclaimed most openly the centrality of reasonableness review as a vehicle for judicial engineering. This engineering is based on judicial understanding of economic and social theory and on judicial conceptions of appropriate public policy.[45] This style of reasonableness engineering is increasingly cropping up in other areas as well. Free speech balancing has always been such an approach. The Court has refused to move from de jure to de facto and from intent to impact as constitutional standards of racial discrimination, thus giving itself leeway to uphold some statutes that achieve important social purposes even at the cost of adverse impact on minorities and women. In cases involving affirmative action quotas, it has insisted on maintaining safety valves to protect some white males from reverse discrimination. All this is dramatic evidence of the Court's desire to engineer the elimination of racial discrimination rather than to impose absolute minority rights regardless of the immediate costs to other interests and policies.

The justices are deeply split on federalism, but many of the Republican appointees want to find a balance between federal power and state autonomy that rests on little more than their feel for what a "good" federalism would be like. In the criminal justice area, the central tendency is to use the exclusionary rule as a tool for engineering all sorts of police routines into a reasonable accommodation between individual privacy and good-faith, aggressive police work. In areas involving government employees, beneficiaries, and the inhabitants of government institutions such as prisons and mental hospitals, notions of how much process is due in a particular situation have been used to make the Court the final arbiter of what it is reasonable, and thus constitutional and lawful, for government to do.

In takings, contract, and bankruptcy cases, the justices have exhibited a renewed taste for pre–New Deal style freewheeling economic analysis although not always with pro-business results. In religion cases, the Court has increasingly sought a reasonable accommodation between religious freedom and government support for socially beneficial religious practice. It has tended to view copyright and patent cases more from an economic standpoint and less from the standpoint of defining originality than did the justices of the Warren Court.

In all of these cases, the key seems to be the justices' perception of what constitutes reasonable economic and social policy. Indeed, only in the area of gender discrimination does the Court today seem strongly inclined to the Warren Court's proclivity to get the bad guys, in this instance sexual stereotypes, no matter what economic analysis might show.

Of course, in a sense the notion that only what is reasonable is lawful is such a fundamental building block of Western legal theory that it must crop up constantly in all courts and all areas of law. And some areas of the Court's work, such as the commerce and contract clauses, necessarily involve economic analysis so the Court has had to engage in some analysis of that sort at every stage of its history. Nevertheless, just as we can discern "equality" to be the touchstone of the later Warren Court, we can discern "reasonableness" as the touchstone of the early Rehnquist Court—reasonableness based on a rough analysis that seeks to fit new policies to the traditional principles and values of economic and social life in America. A Court that sees itself as the guardian of reasonableness is likely to be bold but unpredictable. What is predictable is that a Court that numbers Justices Scalia and Kennedy among its members is likely to have a somewhat different majority view of reasonableness than did the late Burger Court in which the crucial vote was often cast by Justice Powell, now retired.

Court Style. Whether one agrees or disagrees with the substantive policy outcomes achieved by the current Court, it is surely fair to say that its style mirrors the reality of its decision making. Few members of the Court today care much about legal scholarship. None seems to combine a sufficiently centrist position with sufficient desire for, and skill at, consensus building to achieve a solid front. We have come to expect five or six opinions in major cases, none of which does more than state the author's policy preferences dressed up in cursory and pro forma legal argument. There is no reason not to say openly what the justices care so little to disguise: that they make their decisions on the basis of seat-of-the-pants predictions of the immediate and direct policy benefits of the various alternatives available to them.

This is not to say that the justices are careless, arbitrary, stupid policy makers—or at least it is not to say that they are more careless, arbitrary, and stupid than other Washington policy makers. From the evidence of the questions at oral argument and from the opinions, most observers would probably agree that the justices prepare themselves pretty well on most major issues. Essentially they follow the normal Washington tactic of letting the issue stew for a while so that there is an opportunity for all to be heard and for the decision maker to absorb what is to be heard. They often make tentative or partial experiments in new areas before going the

84

whole way. They seem to be aware of and responsive to public sentiment and the general political climate, although like other politicians they may occasionally miscalculate. When they miscalculate, they sometimes retreat a bit.

Most of the justices seem to have thought long and hard about the big policy issues that confront the Court. They seem to have made their policy choices on the basis of their own estimates of where the factual data point and their own vision of what the good life in the good state would be.

More than most previous Courts, the current Court openly acknowledges that this is what it is doing. Its reaction to nearly any problem is to enhance its own policy discretion and then wield that discretion case by case to achieve what it believes to be desirable social results. So long as it does not get markedly out of step with the policy preferences of the rest of the political system, there is no reason why this should be an unfruitful or dangerous role for the Court. So far the Court does not seem to be much out of step.

4

Political Parties—Declining, Stabilizing, or Resurging?

James W. Ceaser

Toward the end of the 1970s, political analysts had reached a common diagnosis on the condition of America's parties. The party system was pronounced "the sick man" of American government. The parties themselves, once described by Woodrow Wilson as "our real body politic," were now said to be declining, decaying, or atrophying, with no prospect of recovery. Of the two main parties, the Republicans—whose base in Washington was limited in the late 1970s to a small minority in Congress—would likely be the first to succumb.[1]

Yet just as everyone was preparing a somber face for the funeral, observers began to detect mysterious stirrings. With some embarrassment, the experts began to speak of a miraculous revival of the parties. By the mid–1980s, some were even expressing concern that the national parties were becoming *too* strong—"huge bureaucratic competitors," in Gerald Pomper's words, "torn from their local roots."[2] In an even more unexpected reversal, it was the resurrected Republican party that emerged as the more robust organization, with the Democrats struggling to keep pace.

Anyone relying on the experts for enlightenment can justifiably be excused for feeling bewildered. Has the condition of parties really changed so dramatically, or have the diagnoses, whether of decline or revival, been exaggerated?

Let us leave the doctors of political science to their disputes and turn to the patient. America's parties, it is clear, did decline in the 1960s and 1970s. They were a weaker force in American politics than at any time since their establishment in the 1830s. Party organizations had lost any say in recruiting and nominating candidates for most offices, and they played only a modest role in the campaigns for "their" nominees. The once mighty Democratic machines were subjected to the cruelest modern display of contempt: being featured by the media as relics of American nostalgia. The parties' standing among the citizens also declined. Americans expressed a decreasing regard for the parties as institutions, and a diminishing percentage of citizens identified themselves as supporters of either of the two main parties.[3]

Weak parties had become so much the norm that those who grew to maturity during this period had difficulty grasping what was meant by party decline. Were not the two parties merely the labels under which individual politicians built their own franchises and conducted their private political business? One political scientist, in fact, proposed to resolve this issue by throwing out the traditional understanding of a party as a collective entity and defining it as the sum of the activities of the individuals using the label. So conceived, parties could not really decline as long as the labels remained.[4] This intellectual exercise, however, could not alter the fact that something important had changed. The conduct of politics as it took place under the collective entities once called "parties" was different from the conduct of politics as it took place by individuals under party labels—different enough, in fact, to justify the commonsense reference to party decline.

This decline was most striking in presidential politics. Jimmy Carter won the Democratic presidential nomination in 1976 by publicly running against many of the state and local party organizations. He then went on to govern by ignoring his party. "No modern president," writes David Price, "has made less use of his national party organization than Carter."[5] Carter's chief rival for the 1976 nomination was Governor Jerry Brown of California, who actually bested Carter at this antiparty strategy, but entered too late to win the race. "I knew where I was going," Brown said, and "I was going there myself."[6]

The notion of "going there myself," enunciated by the acknowledged guru of the *Zeitgeist* of the 1970s, may be taken as the motto for political organization of the period. In political science this model is known by the technical term of "candidate-centered politics." In 1980, John Anderson sought to take this model to its ultimate conclusion. After losing a few primaries in the Republican presidential race, Anderson decided that a party nomination was an anachronistic formality. If parties had really lost their grip on the public, if political campaigning was completely individualistic, and if the main link with the electorate was the media, then why not just present oneself to the American people for the general election? After all, that is what George Washington had done.

Today matters certainly appear different. People involved in politics now have at least an intuitive appreciation of political parties as collective enterprises beyond the labels. The commitment of Republicans in the early 1980s showed how a party could be used to help change the political direction of the nation. In running congressional campaigns today, practical politicians—those who know how to count dollars and cents—have suddenly rediscovered the phone numbers of party headquarters. In presidential politics, the party—in the form, for example, of superdelegates to the Democratic convention—has reappeared; the Anderson logic, if it is remembered at all, is regarded as quixotic. Public attitudes toward parties as institutions are less hostile, and there has been an increase in partisan support.[7] Finally, a "reformed" Jerry Brown was elected Democratic state party chairman of California in 1989, singing the praises of "enduring political organization" and emphasizing his conversion from "me" to "we" politics.

The significance of these changes is difficult to assess, coming as they do after an era of decline. Since nothing stands still in politics, a gain in the absolute strength of the parties might not translate into a real gain of influence relative to other forces. And a buildup of parties in certain areas might not mean an end to their deterioration in others. Three possible models suggest themselves: one of *decline*, in which parties suffer a continued loss of influence as previous developments inimical to them work their way through the political system; one of *stabilization*, in which parties marginally strengthen their position and settle into playing a minor role;

or one of *resurgence,* in which parties regain lost functions or acquire new ones that make them substantially more powerful than they were.

Tempting as it is to select among these models, it is impossible to do so. The current situation reveals a complex picture of different tendencies at work at the same time. Each model captures a part of reality; to choose any one of them would only force a crude averaging that conceals more than it explains. There is an additional reason to avoid making sweeping historical predictions. The closer one studies the parties today, the more apparent it becomes that their essential character is not being determined by forces beyond political control, but by such factors as opinion and law over which political leaders have a good deal of influence. Parties exist in an environment to which they must respond and adapt, but the available margin for choice is far greater than most have supposed.

The analysis here stresses indeterminacy in two senses. The current tendencies of party development are not only conflicting and indefinite, but they also do not fully dictate the future. This assessment differs from that of most analysts, who conceive that the highest calling of social science is to make historical predictions. Their accounts of party development accordingly favor explanations rooted in causes beyond practical alteration, such as "the organic change wrought by the electronic revolution" or "the broader social and political system and not the parties themselves."[8] My object in this chapter is far more modest, although not necessarily any easier. Because the character of parties remains in large measure open to choice, the analyst must consider not only what is occurring but also what the consequences would be of promoting a decline, a stabilization, or a resurgence of the parties.

What Are Parties?

America's parties can be thought of in two different, but connected, senses. First, the word "party" refers to an association of citizens who share a set of basic political views that they seek to advance by presenting candidates for elective offices. These associations have generally resulted from the combined energies of popular movements and established political leaders, who from conviction or ambition take up a cause. Parties in this sense are most easily observed when an association emerges and adopts a new label, as with the Jeffersonian Republicans in the 1790s or the Republicans in the 1850s. But associations can also grow up inside an existing party, in which case they take a distinct name, such as New Deal Democrats, conservatives, or members of the rainbow coalition. These associations are nascent parties within parties, seeking to pour new wine into an old bottle.

"Party" in the second sense refers to more enduring institutional arrangements—to the established organizational mechanisms and, in a looser sense, the patterns of partisan behavior connected with the two major parties. These institutional arrangements have been built up in large part by the associations. The original party movements, in the 1790s and the 1830s, devised nominating procedures and laid the foundations for the national committees. Subsequently, associations have often supplied the energy for revivifying the organizations, as in the conservative movement's contribution to the impressive strengthening of the national Republican party in the past decade. The motive in these cases is clear: organization adds effectiveness beyond what any association can generate by itself. It thus offers a way for an association to perpetuate or institutionalize itself.[9]

The parties' institutional arrangements, however, are products of other factors as well. Once the major parties settled firmly into place in the nineteenth century, they became almost official institutions. With a presence in every state and locality, with resources and habitual adherents, and with a recognized role as screening agents for candidates, the parties were able to endure long past the time when the associations that formed them had passed from the scene. Persons connected with the parties had reasons, other than associational ones, to alter the institutional mechanisms. People from outside the parties, generally those who worried that the parties were corrupt and too powerful, used the instrument of law to attempt to dictate their organizational form and limit their activities. This tendency has been so pronounced that American parties today are more closely regulated than those in any other Western democracy.

To describe a party at any given time requires that one analyze it in both senses, as an association—insofar as it may be one—and as an institution. Since institutions endure longer than associations, parties can influence how quickly and in what form new associations come to the fore. Because institutions usually give an advantage to the existing configuration of forces inside them, the relationship between an existing party and a new association that emerges within it is often tense and troubled. The new association will attempt to capture the party, intact if possible, but, if it must, by altering or destroying the arrangements that stand in its way. Failing that, it may attempt to circumvent the party by forming a third party.

In modern American politics, there have been two important associations in the parties: the New Left in the Democratic party from the late 1960s through the mid–1970s and the conservatives or Reagan Republicans in the Republican party in the 1970s and 1980s. New Left Democrats emerged on the national scene during the 1968 presidential campaign. Their movement became a crusade to unseat Lyndon Johnson and his heir, Hubert Humphrey, and to nominate one of the peace candidates: Eugene McCarthy, Robert Kennedy, or George McGovern. The association challenged the dominant public philosophy of liberalism. The major axis of dispute in 1968 was, of course, the Vietnam War and America's place in the world. The old liberalism was internationalist and anti-Communist, while the New Left's position—sometimes called the new liberalism—was more isolationist and shaded into anti-anticommunism. There were other differences as well. The new liberalism was more egalitarian than the old; it celebrated alternative life styles and held in contempt the middle-class values of the old liberals; and finally, it favored a more harmonious relationship with nature—a kind of cosmic passivism that called into question the value of economic development.[10]

After failing to win the Democratic nomination in 1968, leaders of this movement challenged the nation's presidential nomination system, which they believed had unjustly

thwarted their cause. Their effort spawned the reform movement of the 1970s, which dominated institutional discussion
and change for the entire decade. Reformers divided the
world neatly between the forces of the "old" and the "new"
politics. The old politics were undemocratic, closed, and
controlled by special interests; the new politics were participatory, open, and responsive to the "people." The old politics were institutionalized in the practices of the parties; the
new politics lay beyond existing arrangements in a reformed
electoral system, to be brought about either by enacting a
national primary or by changing the parties—in practice,
changing the Democratic party since it was home to the
movement.

Under the pressure of reform, the Democratic party
convention of 1968 agreed to study its delegate selection
rules. Between 1968 and 1972, a party commission, chaired
initially by Senator George McGovern, proceeded to write,
and to a remarkable degree put into operation, a new set of
guidelines for selection of national delegates. The commission report endorsed the general philosophy of reform, down
to the adage that "the cure to the evils of democracy is more
democracy," and, along with eliminating many indefensible
practices, removed most of the prerogatives previously enjoyed by the regular organizations.[11]

Yet no sooner did New Left Democrats capture the Democratic party's nomination in 1972, than the association began
to lose momentum. George McGovern's landslide defeat in
November, with only 38 percent of the popular vote, discredited the movement and provided grounds for a counterattack
by the proponents of the old liberalism, who came to believe
they had been unjustly reformed out of their own party.

Since 1972, no new association has managed to take hold
of the Democratic party. In the 1976 campaign, Jimmy Carter
succeeded in holding together, without ever putting together,
the different elements of his party. His theme of a "government as decent and competent as our people" was peculiarly
personal to him and left no permanent trace on the party.
Since 1976, the Democrats have wandered from a reconstruc-

tion of the party's old ideas under Walter Mondale in 1984, to a flirtation with Gary Hart's "new ideas" in 1986–1987, to Michael Dukakis's profession of no ideas in 1988 ("competence not ideology").

The identity crisis of the Democratic party was especially acute in the early 1980s. Whenever a group of Democratic party strategists met, they would lament that their party was in search of its soul and concede that Republicans—in their own way—had managed to become "the party of ideas." The fact that the Democrats, as the party of the overwhelming majority of academics and intellectuals, should be without ideas was not the contradiction, much less the paradox, many assumed, but it did add to the sense of a party that was drifting. The 1988 campaign revealed the seeds of a possible new association in the party in the form of Jesse Jackson's rainbow coalition. Many Democrats, however, fear this movement would, in the words of Senator Charles Robb, "encourage the public perception that we are dividing the country, [which is] not conducive to the electoral success we are looking for."[12] Indeed, many Democrats are now more cautious about speaking of an intellectual crisis in the party, perhaps in the belief that no viable association is in the offing.

To say that the Democratic party today has no dominant association inside it is not to say that it is more divided than it was from 1940 to 1970. During that period, the liberal association gave direction to the party in presidential politics, but the party also contained a Bourbon Southern wing that defended "segregation now and segregation forever." By the 1970s, the Southern wing had lost its radical, rejectionist character, even though it continues to hold more moderate Democrats. This change led to James Sundquist's prediction in 1976 that "the prospects for interbranch cooperation . . . are brighter than at any time in the memory of anyone now living. . . . Responsible party government under the president as party leader will be possible . . . on a continuing basis."[13] It was not to be during the Carter administration. Removing a source of disunity could not be equated with creating unity. Just when liberals were in a position to take full control of the party, they lost a common understanding of the meaning of liberalism.

The other major association of our era—the Reagan Republicans—emerged in the 1970s. Its roots can be traced to the Goldwater-led conservative movement of 1964. But Barry Goldwater's disastrous defeat, like George McGovern's eight years later, served to discredit the movement before the national public. It continued to grow, however, within the Republican party, and was rekindled by Ronald Reagan in his unsuccessful bid to take the Republican nomination from Gerald Ford in 1976. It gained momentum during the Carter years, when many regarded conservatism as the only alternative to the policies of the Democratic party and of "me-too" Republicanism.

The conservatives' relationship to the Republican party has in many respects been a reverse image of the New Left's relationship to the Democratic party. Although conservatives, too, had to fight to take control of the party, they did so without undermining the regular party organization. Their takeover may actually have been facilitated by the Democratic party reforms, which lowered the threshold for a new movement to capture a party. Yet conservatives by 1980 had already gained control of many state organizations and would clearly have been poised to compete for the nomination under any previous system. Ronald Reagan and his aides viewed the party "as a house" that was "ready to move into."[14] The premises were occupied in 1980, and the party-building that had begun under national party chairman William Brock after 1976 continued in the 1980s, especially under Chairman Frank Fahrenkopf (1983–1989).

With Reagan's election, the conservative movement was largely integrated into the party, with parts of it becoming the party establishment. Under these conditions, Reagan emerged as a staunch "party man"—the modern president who arguably has been the most willing to work on behalf of his political party. Reagan's presidency, according to Sidney Milkis, marked "a significant change in the generally conflictual relationship between the presidency and the party that has prevailed since the New Deal."[15]

Since 1980 the Republican party has become a conservative party. In early 1980 Ronald Reagan was widely viewed in the American populace, and by many within the Republican party, as the leader of the "radical right." By 1988, Reaganism was the party's nominal orthodoxy. In Reagan's words, "conservative thought is the mainstream now."[16] All the candidates running for the 1988 Republican nomination laid claim to being Reagan's heir. Pat Robertson claimed to read his conscience, Jack Kemp his mind, and George Bush his lips. Yet while everyone has professed to be followers of or converts to conservatism, there have been disputes almost from the beginning about what the creed meant in practice.

Conservatives in 1980 generally stood for less government and lower taxes, for a restoration of traditional values, and for a stronger national defense and a staunchly anti-Communist foreign policy. President Reagan pursued these objectives, but not always to the satisfaction of many in the movement who saw conspiracies to prevent "Reagan from being Reagan." Not only was Reagan's own relationship to the creed more complicated than many first thought, but also by 1989 the conservative association's meaning and capacity to sustain itself were being tested by a new situation. Times and problems had changed, leaving many groping to redefine what a conservative orthodoxy meant. This would hardly be the first time that an association lost its original identity by having fulfilled part of its mission. Instead of a philosophy in search of a movement, many now worry that conservatism has begun to resemble a movement in search of a philosophy.

Association developments in the past decade have completely transformed the political landscape of American politics. Party elites in the post–New Deal period (the 1940s to the 1960s) divided mainly on a pro- and antiwelfare state axis, with the center of gravity of the Democratic party being on the Left and the center of the Republican party on the Right. Within each party, however, practically the entire spectrum of American politics was represented: the Republicans had an important liberal wing, and the Democrats a large conservative wing.

The current era has seen a twofold development. First, each party in a certain sense has become less heterogenous. On the Republican side, the old liberal wing by 1984 was scarcely in evidence at the national conventions, and previous moderates or centrists (including Howard Baker, Robert Dole, and even George Bush) were now counted by some as being on the Left of the party. On the Democratic side, the old conservative wing had declined (some of it in fact having passed into the Republican party), which left the party not necessarily more on the Left, but almost all on the Left.

The second development relates to the interplay between the parties. In the post–New Deal period, Democrats (as liberals), being the majority in presidential elections, more or less set the national agenda and exercised a strong pull on the Republican party. In Samuel Lubell's famous analogy, the Democrats were the "sun" and the Republicans the "moon"—a point illustrated by the conscious design of liberal Republicans like Nelson Rockefeller to appear modern and adopt much of the Democrats' program.[17] In recent years, this gravitational pull has clearly diminished. In 1988, Bush won the Republican nomination running as a conservative. He went on, under considerable pressure from within the party, to select a running mate—Dan Quayle—regarded as more conservative than himself.

Whether the Republicans now serve as the sun to a Democratic moon is a more disputable proposition. At a minimum, it can be said that Democrats have felt a stronger gravitational pull from Republicans than they did in the 1960s. Between 1984 and 1988, younger Democrats led by Charles Robb, Sam Nunn, and Richard Gephardt formed the Democratic Leadership Council, which aimed to modernize the party by embracing more conservative ideas. Moreover, Democratic campaign strategists have consciously adopted certain Republican traditionalist symbols such as flag and family; and they have disavowed or played down some of their own symbols, to the point even of their 1988 nominee being reluctant to accept the liberal label. Finally, the Democratic nominee in 1988 decided it was better to move to the moderate wing of his party to select Texas Senator Lloyd Bentsen for his vice-presidential choice. Despite the signs of greater conservatism, however, a moderate force has clearly *not* yet made itself felt in any significant way in the presidential nomination contest. In the 1988 Democratic campaign,

Senator Albert Gore's candidacy was a pale reflection of this sentiment, and Michael Dukakis's stiffest opposition came from the Left, in the persons of Paul Simon and Jesse Jackson, and not from the Right.

A Realignment?

An association that takes over a party aspires not just to win offices, but to become a majority and turn its ideas into the nation's reigning public philosophy. These transformations are known as realignments and have been characterized by four elements: (1) the victory of a president who, as a leader of the association, solidifies support for its agenda; (2) a change in the public's perception of what the parties stand for, including the development of positive symbols for the dominant party and negative symbols for the minority party; (3) a standing advantage for the dominant party in capturing the presidency; and (4) a standing advantage for the dominant party in capturing the Congress.

Has the nation gone through a realignment? Ronald Reagan certainly claimed this as one of his main objectives, and all the talk of the Reagan era suggests that he at least managed to make his presidency the chief reference point of modern politics. For many Americans, Ronald Reagan has eclipsed Franklin Delano Roosevelt, the last president to have led a realignment. As for public perceptions of the parties, the Republicans finally succeeded in shedding the chief negative phrase with which the party had been labeled since the 1930s: the Party of Herbert Hoover and Bad Economic Times.[18] If anything, the most powerful recent negative symbolism has attached to the Democrats' public philosophy of liberalism—which Republicans managed to identify in the presidential campaigns of the 1980s with the economic "misery index" of the Carter administration and with the social and foreign policy views of the New Left. With the help of this symbolism, the Republicans have won three straight presidential elections, all by hefty margins. The election of 1988, run by the heir of the associational leader, was based— very much like the campaigns of 1808 and 1836—on whether the nation wanted to "keep the change."

In modern times, poll data on partisan identification provide a new instrument for helping to gauge whether a

TABLE 4–1
PARTY IDENTIFICATION, 1954–1989
(percent)

Year	Democrat	Republican	Independent
1954	46	34	20
1960	47	30	23
1964	53	25	22
1968	46	27	27
1972	43	28	29
1976	47	23	30
1980	46	24	30
1984	40	31	29
1986	39	32	29
1988	43	29	28
1988[a]	37	35	26
1989	38	34	28

a. Election day poll, *New York Times*–CBS, voters only.
SOURCE: All figures, except the election day reading, come from the Gallup Poll.

realignment has taken place (see table 4–1). These data indicate, at a minimum, a process of alignment *away* from the Democratic party. In the 1960s and 1970s, the Democrats enjoyed almost twice the advantage over Republicans that they do today, and a poll taken at the time of the 1988 presidential election showed the two parties almost on a par.

A more traditional way of considering a party's well-being is to inquire about its base. A base refers first to the social groups that can be counted on to give their support, in a preponderant way, to the party. The Democrats' base once included labor, Catholics, Southern whites, Jews, and other ethnic minorities in large cities. Today, the Democratic base in presidential elections has shrunken to blacks, intellectuals, and Hispanics (in certain states). Since electoral votes are counted by states, a base is also sometimes used to refer to the states (or geographic areas) that can be counted on to support the party. The Democrats once controlled the large urban industrial states and the South. Today, apart from the District of Columbia, the Democratic party has no geographic base, which is apparent not just from electoral results but from the Democratic campaign strategies in recent elections. Ironically, the area in which Democrats have done best in the last two elections—the upper Midwest—is one where their national social base (white Protestant voters) is narrowest.

A movement away from the Democrats is, of course, a considerable relative gain for the Republicans. But it is not quite the same thing as a full-fledged partisan realignment. There are, in fact, two other logical possibilities besides a realignment: (1) "dealignment," or a falling away from partisanship altogether; and (2) ideological realignment, or a change of voters' underlying preference for liberalism or conservatism, without a change of partisan identification. There is evidence for the view that all three of these tendencies—partisan realignment, dealignment, and ideological realignment—are simultaneously at work.

During the 1970s, the major movement in the electorate was toward the "party" of independents, indicating an important dealigning trend. Some of these independents, however, were found to behave very much like partisans, while others may only have been in transition from one partisan affiliation to another. The movement toward independency now seems to have ceased. Today, the number of Republicans is at its highest point since the New Deal, and there have been Republican gains among younger voters, who in time will count for more of the electorate.

In terms of their base, Republicans—in addition to maintaining support in the business community and among the wealthy—have done extremely well with white Protestant voters, especially in the South and West. Republicans have consequently enjoyed a strong geographic base. Yet analysis of this base reveals that it is not strictly partisan, as many of these voters continue to identify themselves as independents or Democrats. They must be mobilized in each election by ideological appeals, even though this process has taken place with remarkable consistency in the past few elections.

The evidence discussed so far, while not unambiguously positive for the Republicans, is clearly unfavorable for the Democrats. But this entire line of analysis is called into question when one looks at congressional elections. For all the Democrats' slippage, they have not lost very much below the presidential level. Democrats now control the Senate—having lost it for a six-year period between 1980 and 1986—and they have held a majority in the House since 1954. Indeed, Democrats today seem to have a firmer grip on the House than Republicans do on the presidency.

The existence of a situation so at odds with the classical model of realignment is one of the more striking facts about American politics today. It has been explained in different ways. One possibility is to regard the Democratic party as still being the majority party, with presidential elections as aberrations. In this view, the Democrats lose the presidency only because they squander their natural majority by their internal squabbling and mode of nomination.

A second possibility is that there has been a "split-level" realignment and that Americans, perhaps for the first time, consciously prefer to balance the government between the parties in order to prevent either party from becoming too powerful.[19] As the more heterogeneous party, Democrats may also benefit at the congressional level from being able to present different kinds of candidates in different districts.

The final possibility is that there is in fact a subterranean trend for a Republican realignment in Congress. If there has not been a realignment, there should have been. But this trend has been largely concealed by another factor: an entrenchment of incumbents that marks one of the major institutional changes of our time. In the 1986 and 1988 House elections, 98 percent of the incumbents seeking reelection won. The irresistible force (realignment) has met the immovable object (incumbency)—and incumbency has won.[20]

If this last possibility is true, analysts should immediately consider why the trend for incumbent reelection is greater today than in the past. Some insist that it is an electoral or behavioral phenomenon. Partisanship among voters has grown weaker, which allows incumbency to be stronger. Others, however, contend that the cause today is institutional rather than behavioral. Incumbency is stronger because the advantages of incumbency are much greater than in the past. The gap between the resources that incumbents and challengers bring to elections is at an all-time high. In this view, the

101

situation today is new, "unnatural," and artificial. It is perhaps remediable—if this is desired—either by reducing the advantages of incumbency or by increasing the resources that can be made available to challengers.

The best way to test whether an artificial advantage exists for incumbency would be to ban incumbents from running and start over. Notwithstanding the generous support Congress has shown for social science research, there has been little sentiment for conducting such an experiment. The analysis of causality in congressional elections must therefore proceed with the help of more primitive techniques.

The Party System as an Institution

Unlike associations, which seem to rise and fall quickly on their own, institutions are more enduring structures, which can be altered by deliberate changes of laws and rules. Institutions are the primary instruments for conscious efforts to control and channel political behavior on a long-term basis. For this reason they have long been the main focus of political science.

Americans have difficulty viewing the party system in institutional terms. Parties were not part of the original constitutional design, and when party competition first developed in the 1790s it was regarded as an unwelcome accident. Yet after parties died out in the early 1820s, it took a deliberate strategy at the end of that decade, engineered by Martin Van Buren, to reestablish party competition. The party system— understood as competition chiefly between two national parties—was at that time founded consciously as an institution and defended on the grounds that it would improve the performance of the political system.

The logic of this analysis, while it can be called into question, still provides the best framework for discussing political parties. The party system, in this view, affects political activity in several key areas. It has a major impact on which political forces are given expression and which, temporarily at least, are held back; on how majorities are put together; on how governing takes place; and on how people are contacted and mobilized to participate in politics. In all the practical activities that parties generally conduct—recruiting candidates, nominating, campaigning, shaping opinion, and governing—there are other entities that can be said to compete with political parties. These entities include personal campaign organizations, ideological movements, interest groups, PACS, and the media. Given this competitive situation, it follows that as parties lose (or gain) strength, the combined influence of their rivals must increase or decrease.[21]

The argument on behalf of parties begins with the claim that their impact in the areas noted above is on balance positive. The party system has helped to organize conflict and prudently manage change; to build more stable and enduring coalitions; to facilitate governance by providing links among different institutions; and to connect citizens with each other and integrate them into the political community as a whole. The entities competing with parties either do not perform these functions at all or not nearly as well as the parties. Parties are the intermediary institutions most conducive to maintaining the broad values of a deliberative republic, and a decline of party influence beyond a certain point means that the political system as a whole will suffer.

The argument for political parties, however, is a qualified one. It does not call for a monopoly of influence for parties or for the strongest parties possible. Moreover, the argument cannot be based on the dimension of party strength alone. Parties can perform their functions only if certain assumptions hold about their nature and character. Not just any kind of parties will do. Finally, like all institutions, parties must be maintained, and certain costs are connected to this task. Parties must be considered realistically, with their advantages and disadvantages weighed in each context.[22]

The Strength of Party Organizations

The organization—formal or informal—is the heart of the institutional party. The resources commanded by the organization constitute one of the most important indicators of party strength, although in the final analysis it is the force that the organization can bring to bear relative to potential competitors that is decisive.

At the national level, both parties have significantly increased their activities since the mid-seventies (see table 4–2). The most notable transformation has been on the Republican side. Under the chairmanship of William Brock (1976–1981), the Republican national party began a program of rebuilding that has altered the role of the national party in American politics.[23] The key to what has been called the "Brock revolution" was financial. Brock took the technique of direct mail fund raising, which had been pioneered in the presidential campaigns of Barry Goldwater, George Wallace, and George McGovern, and adapted it for use by the political party as an institution. Republicans built on Goldwater's lists to become the most successful direct mail fund raising enterprise in American politics. Contributions now come from a broad base, with the typical contributor giving a modest amount. Americans can now be "card carrying" party members and the proud bearers of a piece of plastic resembling an American Express gold card.

Republicans have used their funds in four ways: to provide direct aid to party candidates, first for federal and later for state and local offices; to provide direct aid for the rebuilding of lower-level party units; to create in-house capacities for polling, media production, research, and campaign training, which can be dispersed as in-kind contributions to the candidates and lower-level party organizations; and finally to communicate general party positions directly to the public.

Democrats began their national party building a few years later. By their own admission, Democrats have been attempting to imitate the Republican model, without yet achieving nearly the same success—although very important strides were made under the chairmanship of Paul Kirk (1985–1989). It would be misleading, however, to leave the impression that the Democrats have been poor cousins bereft of all financial support. Although the Democratic party raises far less than the Republicans, Democrats running for Congress—more of whom are incumbents—have easily outraised and outspent their Republican opponents.

Since 1980 temporary committees established during presidential campaigns have also been able to raise funds to give to state and local parties for certain election activities.

TABLE 4–2
STAFF AND RESOURCES OF THE NATIONAL PARTIES,
1976 AND 1984

	1976		1984	
	Millions of dollars raised	Staff	Millions of dollars raised	Staff
Republican National Committee	29.1	200	105.9	600
National Republican Congressional Committee	12.2	8	58.3	130
National Republican Senatorial Committee	1.8	6	81.7	90
Democratic National Committee	13.1	30	46.6	130
Democratic Congressional Campaign Committee	0.9	6	10.4	45
Democratic Senatorial Campaign Committee	1.0	5	8.9	22

SOURCE: Paul S. Herrnson, *Party Campaigning in the 1980s*, pp. 32–39.

These efforts have effectively subverted one of the intentions of the 1970s campaign finance legislation, which was to limit individual contributions for national political offices. The money is collected outside of federal provisions under certain state laws that have no contribution limits. Seen from the viewpoint of limiting contributions, this "soft money" may be an anathema; seen from the viewpoint of providing money for important political activities, it is a boon.

The condition of party organizations today at the state level is more difficult to assess. Measured in strict terms of the resources these units have at their disposal, state organizations apparently reached the bottom in the 1960s and have been improving ever since in funding and staffing (see table 4–2). Yet considering the small sums of money involved, it is difficult to claim that the state parties—until quite recently—made any significant gains during the period as a whole.

Indeed, relative to other entities, their overall activity, and certainly their influence, was decreasing. In the 1980s, however, there has been a noticeable increase in organizational capacity, with the improvement being greater on the Republican side.[24]

Local parties present the most obvious instance of party decline. Although some surveys indicate a nationwide increase of local party capacity in official staff and resources since the 1960s, case studies show that by the 1970s the local parties had become mere shadows of their former selves. The great urban machines are no more. Of course, many states never possessed strong state or local parties, and in these cases it is impossible to speak of decline.[25] The 1980s have seen some revival in local organizations. The Republicans, with the initiative coming from the national party, have begun an ambitious program of local party building, but the results are still uncertain.

Any analysis of the strength of the mass organization at the local level must take into account the diminished value of organization per se in modern politics. In the past, organizations served as a main channel of communication between candidates and the citizenry. This activity was highly labor intensive and had to be carried out ultimately by the "troops" at the local level. Organization for this purpose has been rendered obsolete by the electronic media. "Television," two analysts write, "has supplanted the political party as the main conduit between candidate and voter."[26]

Yet, if organization no longer provides the principal mode of communication, it is still important at the margin for contacting voters—and elections, of course, are often won at the margins. This explains why campaigns, when they have the money, invest in organization to contact voters. Moreover, for activities that integrate citizens into the community, such as registering and turning out voters, communication through the electronic media has never been very effective. Thus, even if the parties may not need the organization for purposes of communicating as much as they once did, a decline of organizational strength can still produce unhealthy consequences for the political system. Since parties are not philanthropic organizations, they must have their own reasons for developing a large organizational base. To counter-balance the lower value of organization as an instrument of communication, the parties may need other incentives, such as greater influence in nominating candidates, for promoting popular participation.

The Strength of Parties in Presidential Nominations

One of the most important developments in American politics over the past two decades has been the loss of the parties' influence in the nomination of presidential candidates. Since 1980, however, the parties have improved their position somewhat, stabilizing their role at a modest level and estab-lishing a base for a possible resurgence in the years ahead.

Parties completely controlled the nomination of presi-dential candidates from the establishment of the convention system in the 1830s until the emergence of presidential pri-maries in 1912. Thereafter, until 1972, a balance of sorts existed between a party-dominated and a candidate-centered model. Hubert Humphrey's nomination by the Democrats in 1968 was the last to take place under this mixed system. Humphrey, who had once remarked that "you have to be crazy to enter a primary," kept his sanity in 1968 by avoiding all primary contests and relying heavily on support by the regulars in the state and local organizations.[27]

Since 1968, no candidate has pursued a pure inside strategy, and for an obvious reason. The locus of decision making has moved from party-controlled delegate selection processes and the national conventions to primaries and open caucuses. The system today consists essentially of a race among individual contenders to win the greatest popular support in a series of sequentially arranged contests. National conventions now serve to register the results of these con-tests. The key to victory in this system is a successful outside strategy of winning support from certain groups or issue activists and, above all, mobilizing a mass following.

The nomination for the presidency was the last major office in which the parties had a decisive say; the nominations for Congress and governor had already passed to direct candidate appeals in primaries. Yet, once presidential nomi-

107

nating politics caught up with the dominant candidate-centered system, its sophisticated campaigns quickly became models for all modern electioneering. Professionals dubbed this style of campaigning the "new politics." They were referring not to the moral themes of reformers, but to the techniques of mass persuasion: media advertising, image building, polling, and rhetorical manipulation. Modern presidential nomination politics has swung between these two poles of the new politics. The candidates express high-minded appeals, but their campaigns are continually accused of being "packaged." Not, perhaps, since the selection of popes in the fifteenth century has a human activity been characterized by so glaring a contrast between professions of idealism and suspicions of cynicism.

The immediate cause of the transformation of the nomination system after 1968 was the new national rules of the Democratic party adopted by the McGovern-Fraser and the Mikulski commissions. The new rules led, often in unanticipated ways, to changes in state party rules and state laws, of which the changeover in many states from caucus systems to primaries was the most important. The previous decay of many state and local parties laid the groundwork for this new system. It was hastened along by three other factors: a rise of antiparty sentiment, which often made it easier to run against rather than with party organizations; the development of modern campaign technologies and consulting firms for hire, which enabled more campaign tasks to be handled centrally by the candidates' immediate staffs; and the federal campaign finance legislation of 1974, which encouraged more candidates to enter the race and centralized campaign spending decisions in the candidates' staffs.

The recruitment and nominating functions, having escaped control by any party mechanism, are performed in what today is known as the nomination process. The use of the word "process" suggests not so much an institution as a loosely structured arrangement. This arrangement, in fact, has done little to constrain or regularize behavior, but on the contrary has produced nomination races characterized by a high degree of unpredictability and volatility. These characteristics result because the forces that have gained at the parties' expense—public opinion, the media, the personal campaign organizations, and interest groups—do not favor structured behavior patterns. Although conventions of the past had uncertainties of their own, on balance they were far more contained and predictable affairs than the modern two-year process.

The center of the modern nomination campaign is the candidate and his immediate national staff. A large personal organization with extensive roots in the communities—such as the organizations possessed by Walter Mondale in 1984 and George Bush in 1988—is clearly an advantage. But it is not essential. A candidate can achieve a position as a significant player without a big organization, as Gary Hart and Jesse Jackson both demonstrated in 1984. A breakthrough in an early primary or caucus can build momentum, which in turn can generate the publicity and money needed to make a serious bid. The recruitment function in this process is essentially self-initiating, with any candidate who can capture a popular following able to become a contender. The logic of this situation would suggest that almost anyone can run. Experience has shown that almost anyone does.

Another entity that has gained at the expense of the parties has been the news media. In the 1970s much was made of the journalists' role during the preprimary stage as a new screening agent, charged by the logic of the system with deciding which candidates are serious. Events have shown that the outcomes of the early contests can upset journalistic efforts to handicap the races. Still, journalists can hardly complain of being completely dislodged from their self-appointed role as the nation's gatekeepers. Their influence derives less from deliberate efforts to assist particular candidates than from the consequences of their interpretation of events. An important factor influencing voting behavior in the primaries is the perception of how well candidates performed, relative to expectations, in the preceding round. The public depends on the news media "to keep score, to define the standards of victory, and to interpret the results."[28] News itself, moreover, tends to play up the unexpected and the new, and media coverage therefore works to magnify short-term campaign developments.

The final competitors to have gained at the expense of the parties have been interest groups and temporary currents and movements, such as the nuclear freeze movement or the evangelical movement. Candidates seek support from groups and movements to help build their organizations, to secure funds, and to win a base of support. Interest groups, of course, have always had an important influence on presidential nominations, but in the past this influence tended to be mediated through the state and local party organizations.[29] The logic of the new system brings the candidates into direct contact with the groups, compelling them to court group support with a promiscuity that often appears excessive, even by modern standards. Walter Mondale's candidacy in 1984 was virtually discredited before it began as a result of this process. Mondale sought support from labor and from the National Organization for Women, only to be attacked by Gary Hart as being the candidate of "the special interests." In certain Democratic campaigns, notably in 1980 and 1984, interest groups bargained with the candidates to have their delegates represented at the convention to press the groups' policy agenda on platform issues. "The activists," Michael Malbin concluded from a study in 1980, "seem able to determine the convention's issue agenda."[30]

Since 1980, there has been an effort at "bringing the party back" into the nomination process. This effort came about as a result of academic criticisms of the reforms and first-hand experience with their consequences. In the late 1970s many in the Democratic party rejected the antiparty aspects of the rules and moved to restore a degree of party influence—without, however, directly challenging the philosophy of the reform movement. This new view was reflected in the party rules adopted by the Hunt Commission in 1982 and the Fairness Commission in 1986. These rules dropped the requirement of proportional representation and, more important, set aside about 15 percent of the convention delegates for party leaders and elected officials who were chosen, unpledged, outside the usual state processes. The Hunt Commission justified this change on the grounds that it would help to "restore *peer review* to the process; put a premium on *coalition building* within the Party prior to the nomination; *strengthen party ties* among officials . . . ; [and] return *decision making discretion and flexibility* to the Convention."[31]

The Democrats' effort to reform the reforms has created difficulties of its own. The reforms of 1972 used national rules to eliminate the selection of ex officio delegates by the states. To bring party officials back in, the party decided not to abolish these rules but to add new rules creating a new category of ex officio delegates, known as "superdelegates." While these delegates have not quite been forced to wear an "S" on their suits, they have been placed in an exposed position. In 1984, the Hart and Jackson forces teamed up at the convention and nearly managed to eliminate the entire category, while in 1988 Jackson publicly warned superdelegates not to deviate from the results as expressed in the primaries. In 1988, at Jackson's demand, the convention voted to reduce their number by more than one-third.[32]

The choice of the nominee is, of course, the key decision of the process, and under current arrangements will ordinarily be determined by the results of the popular contests. Still, the addition of a significant number of party delegates has brought a new element into the system, and in a close or inconclusive race their votes could prove decisive. Moreover, the party's interest goes beyond the choice of the nominee to writing the party platform, deciding matters of party governance, and—not least in a television age—presenting a public image for the party at the convention. On these matters, party delegates have already made a considerable difference by helping to mitigate the contentious nature of platform disputes, to prevent a repeal of the Hunt Commission changes in 1984, and to give the party conventions a more dignified and responsible tone. Finally, the party's greater overall "weight" lent confidence to Chairman Kirk in his insistence that major interest groups not make preconvention endorsements in 1988.

Because the Republicans avoided the revolutionary process of national party rule making, scholars considered it unfashionable to spend much time on their procedures. The Democrats, it was said, had pioneered a major new tool of governance, which Republicans—with old-fashioned scru-

ples about party federalism and a desire to avoid reform—
would not employ. (The difference between the two parties
on national rule making has led, in fact, to a greater degree
of differentiation in the two parties' formal nomination structures than at any time since the Democrats abolished their
two-thirds rule in 1936.) Since 1980, however, the Democrats
have grown less enamored of their new method, and some
Democrats have cast a jealous eye at the GOP's selection
procedures.

There was an interesting development in 1988 on the
Republican side. In prereform years, state and local party
organizations, even when they remained officially neutral,
often served as the nuclei for the campaign organizations of
the national candidates. The Bush campaign in 1988 followed
a similar strategy, relying on the help of certain key Republican governors (and their political apparatus) in New Hampshire, South Carolina, and Illinois. The noteworthy point is
not the endorsements of these governors, but the organizational assistance they provided, much of it drawn from the
cadres of the regular Republican party. The Bush campaign
is one of the first examples of the return of party elites to a
central position in the selection process.

A resurgence of party influence in the nominating process will require, at a minimum, a certain degree of stability in
the basic rules of the game. The nomination rules for every
office in the United States, from dog catcher on up, are
generally known well in advance—with the exception of the
presidency. While the essential character of the system has
remained the same since 1972, the Democrats have altered
their national party rules in an important way for each contest
from 1972 through 1984. This instability has had an unhealthy
effect. The knowledge that the rules could be changed led
prominent contenders to use their influence in the rules-
writing process to adopt rules favorable to their candidacies.
Not only were the politics of the system candidate driven,
but so too were the rules of the system itself. Defeated
candidates like Hart and Jackson in 1984 publicly blamed
their defeat on the rules, which they charged had been rigged
against them.

Aware of how deeply these quadrennial struggles over

the rules were hurting the party, Democratic party leaders resolved to put an end to them. This was an objective they pursued by means that can only be described as worthy of the "old politics."[33] Nevertheless, stability in the system as a whole requires action not only by the national parties, but also by the other major authority responsible for setting the rules—the states. In 1988, the states made important changes, such as the creation of Super Tuesday, in part as a reaction to previous changes in the national party rules. A certain amount of change in state laws is consistent with a stable system, but it clearly cannot continue at the level of 1988.

The strength of the parties in presidential nominations affects how they perform the functions of regulating political change, building coalitions, and (less directly) governing. Party decline since 1972 has made the nominating system more open or permeable. In comparison to earlier party-controlled systems, the reform system fixes a lower threshold for entrance into the political arena of "outsider" candidates and temporary movements or currents, all of which can now more easily affect parties' decisions, even when they do not prevail.

Openness in this sense is at the core of the reform idea of democracy or fairness. Opponents of reform have questioned whether the presidential nominating system is the proper place for so scrupulously indulging these theoretical ideals, when the result is to stimulate the excesses of the new politics and to eliminate any instrument for exercising a prudent control over candidates and movements. Proponents of parties favor giving more weight to the parties' long-term interests over and against the claims of individual candidates or temporary movements. The parties' interests, in this view, are best expressed through institutional mechanisms that allow the party organizations a larger voice in the nomination process.

Party decline in the nominating process has also removed a mechanism once used in building stable coalitions. The loss of this mechanism has been a greater problem for Democrats than for Republicans, because the Democrats, as the more heterogeneous party, stand in greater need of a contrived institutional arrangement to dampen conflict and resolve tensions among the elements of their coalition. A weaker party influence over nominations thus works objectively in favor of the Republicans. Of course, the difficulty that Democrats have recently experienced in running presidential campaigns has associational as well as institutional causes. The story of most modern Democratic nomination races nonetheless has been one of how to put Humpty Dumpty together again before the final election campaign. The modifications of the reforms have sought a way to put the genies of personal faction and temporary movements back into the bottle of party control.

Finally, the party-run nomination served as a point during which the presidential candidate forged ties and alliances with political elites in his party whose support he would need in running the government. In exceptional cases, a strong associational movement can substitute as a base of support for a process of bargaining and accommodation. But a president who has no such association behind him may find that a nomination won by personal means leaves him in a far weaker position for governing, despite having been "liberated" from party constraints.

These consequences of party decline flow from the structure of the "pure" reform system as it existed in 1976 and 1980. That system still substantially prevails. But the modifications since 1980 point in a different direction. How far they will go and how much they will modify the "pure" system remain to be seen.

The Strength of Parties in Presidential Campaigns

It seems odd on the face of it even to conceive of a distinction between the party nominee's own electoral organization on the one hand and the party organization on the other. Yet, beginning in the 1960s, presidential campaigns came to be run mostly by each candidate's personal organization, with the party organization playing a subordinate—and in certain campaigns an insignificant—role. This tendency has been reversed since 1980, and on this score there seems to be a genuine prospect for a resurgence of the parties.

114

In the nineteenth century, the parties ran the campaigns for their candidates. The overall responsibility was given initially to the national committees and later to the national party chairmen, who, by the turn of the century, emerged as important figures in their own right. Their job, however, was largely to energize and coordinate the activities of the state and local organizations, where the parties' effective power resided. The national chairman stood between the candidate and the party, serving in the case of a sitting president as "the party's representative in the presidency and the president's liaison with the party."[34]

The decline of the parties in presidential campaigns has had two aspects. First, in this century presidential candidates (and presidents) came early to have discretion in the choice of the national chairman. In itself, this did not constitute a loss of the party's power. But by the 1960s and 1970s, candidates and presidents began to treat the chairmen as mere subalterns and to consider the national committee staffs as their personal fiefdoms. Senator Robert Dole, Republican National Committee (RNC) chairman from 1971 to 1973, described his summary dismissal by President Nixon after he tried to distance the party slightly from the Watergate affair: "I had a nice chat with the President," Dole quipped, "while the other fellows went out to get the rope." A Carter aide in 1976 proposed "Carterizing" the Democratic National Committee (DNC) by selecting a chairman "willing to take direction from Carter's political and personal staff."[35] The loss of even a semblance of independence for the national chairmen was a clear sign of the parties' weakness.

In a second and further development, the candidates began to subordinate the party mechanism to their personal organizations during the campaign. This practice was a logical result of the modern nomination process, in which the candidates have already built up personal organizations before their nominations. After the conventions, the personal staffs took charge of the campaigns and received most of the credit. The marginal role of the parties was further codified in the campaign finance legislation of 1974, which not only gave public funds directly to the candidates, but also prevented state and local party organizations from spending additional money on behalf of the campaign.

Since the power of any institution cannot be parceled into neat segments, the decline of parties in the electoral sphere naturally carried over into a loss of influence in the counsels of the executive branch. Gone, of course, is the cabinet seat once reserved for the national party chairman; and by the time of Jimmy Carter's presidency, most of the important political functions that the national party once performed, such as liaison with interest groups and building popular support for the president's program, were taken over by the president's own staff and performed in-house.

The parties' role in presidential campaigns, however, has recently increased, especially on the Republican side. This development owes a good deal to the strengthening of some state party organizations. No presidential candidate today can afford to ignore an important resource that is already in place; and the more the regular parties have mechanisms on line, the more weight they carry in national elections. The chances of strengthening the parties were improved by a 1979 amendment to the campaign finance laws, which allows unlimited fund raising and spending by the state and local parties for certain purposes. (It is through this provision that the so-called soft money enters the campaigns.) These changes have led to a situation in which the regular party organizations in certain states actually run the campaigns for their presidential candidates.

Another sign of the strengthening of the parties has been the candidates' acknowledgment of a greater degree of independence for the national chair. This development became evident on the Republican side in 1980, when many in the conservative movement pressed Reagan to remove Bill Brock immediately. Reagan rejected the advice, a decision that Brock later called "a tribute to the party's self-worth."[36] In a less graceful incident, Mondale sought to name Bert Lance as party chairman in 1984; this move met with widespread resistance, and Mondale had to withdraw Lance's name. In a curious way, the Democrats' defeat in three straight presidential elections has provided an opportunity for aggressive party chairmen like Paul Kirk and Ron Brown to build up a partially independent power center. For Republicans, Bush's appointment of Lee Atwater, campaign manager for his nomination campaign, as RNC chairman (rather than to a White House position) indicates the growing importance of the national party, which Bush intends to use as the main instrument for his political activities.

The consequences of the party's role in this area can be seen first in regard to the function of coalition building. Party decline had the effect of favoring the candidate's personal concerns over the party's interests, as illustrated not only in the notorious case of President Nixon's Committee for the Reelection of the President (CREEP), but also in the neglect by Presidents Nixon and Carter of the concerns of congressional candidacies. The rise of split-ticket voting has no doubt been encouraged by the organizational separation of the presidential campaign from the campaigns of the rest of the party.

A second consequence of the place of parties in presidential affairs concerns the function of governing, specifically the president's relationship to the public. Parties in the pre-electronic age served to link the president and the public. Nowadays, this "rhetorical" dimension of the presidency has been largely taken over by the president and his staff on the one hand and the journalistic community in the mass media on the other. Even so, presidents do not consider speeches and news stories to be a complete substitute for continuous contacts with their core constituencies, and they have sought to maintain some forms of organizational communication. Presidents seemed to gain power by bringing this activity in-house. Yet these White House operations, partly because they are so personal, have never matched the parties' efforts. Presidents won a kind of independence from the party and the illusion of power, but at the expense of a source of real support.

As with the nomination process, this description sketches the consequences of party decline a decade ago. The elements of party resurgence that have occurred since 1980 have begun to modify these tendencies, in ways that now can only begin to be glimpsed.

The Strength of Parties in Congressional Races

The decline of the parties' influence in congressional elections has been a gradual process that began early in this century. Developments since the 1970s—the emergence of PACs, for example—accelerated this decline. Yet over the past decade certain kinds of party activity have increased markedly, chiefly in the form of assistance from the national parties. The parties' strengths and weaknesses in this area are thus a portrait in miniature of their overall situation, showing aspects of decline, of stabilization, and of resurgence.

Early in this century, the recruitment and nomination of congressional candidates was handled largely by state and local parties, which underwrote a large part of the costs and part of the personal political risks of running for Congress. The adoption of the direct primary in nearly all of the states early in this century was the main reason for the organizations' loss of influence. In many areas, however, strong organizations were able to maintain control of the nomination by dominating the primaries. As late as the 1960s, congressmen could still say that "in my district and in most of the state, [the organization] every two years designates the whole ticket."[37]

Eventually, however, the logic of the primary system prevailed. Parties lost their power to dictate the results, and they came to consider direct interference in primary elections as illegitimate and inappropriate. By the 1970s, recruitment was performed largely by self-starting individuals with some help from interest groups, and party activity in most congressional races, for both the nomination and the general election, was very limited. The situation was best described as "an every man for himself proposition."[38] In the House districts Richard Fenno studied in the 1970s, he found no instance in which the "local party organizations shape[d] the home style of the members."[39]

As parties lost influence, competitive forces filled the vacuum: the individual and the personal campaign organization; interest groups; and the news media (which have had only a modest bearing on the "invisible" House races, but considerably greater impact on the more glamorous Senate contests). In the absence of party control of nominations, and in an era of weakened partisan voting attachments, each candidate has had to find a way to project his or her name and message. This requires money, especially in an age of the electronic media. Congressional campaigns began to cost more at a time when state and local parties could give less—which forced candidates to go it on their own even more.

In the early 1970s, campaign funds came chiefly from individual contributors (usually within the state or district) followed by some combination of groups and businesses, the candidates themselves, and, to a modest degree, the parties. The campaign finance legislation of the 1970s has had a major impact on congressional elections, not only changing the behavior of existing actors but also stimulating the growth of PACs. Finance legislation establishes four categories of contributors: candidates, individuals, PACs, and parties. All except the candidates face limits on the amount they can contribute to a campaign, and all except the political parties can make independent expenditures for candidates outside the campaign. (There are no overall limits on how much each campaign can spend.)

Fifteen years ago hardly anyone had heard of the curious acronym PAC. Today it rolls easily from the lips of any college sophomore. Much of the recent literature on elections, in fact, has been a laborious description of PAC behavior, in which tendencies were no sooner discovered than they disappeared. A few general points, however, are worth noting. Of the four categories of contributors, PACs have increased the most rapidly since the 1970s. PACs often organize on a national basis, with the result that more funding today comes from outside the state, which has probably increased functional pressures on Congress. In addition, most PACs behave as "rational" actors and therefore do not allow partisan preferences to interfere with their political contributions. Business, after all, is business. PACs seek access or influence, and accordingly they prefer to invest in incumbents—who happen to be mostly Democrats—on the grounds that incumbents almost always win. In 1986, three-fourths of all PAC contributions in House races went to incumbents and only 11 percent to challengers.[40] This pattern no doubt contributes to a self-fulfilling hypothesis: because PACs calculate that incumbents will win (especially in the House), they give them more money, and because incumbents have more money, they win more often and more easily—indeed, they ward off serious challenges in the first place.

Perhaps the most important long-term consequence of the finance legislation, however, concerns the parties, not the PACs. "American political parties," according to David Adamany, "were not mentioned by federal statute until the enactment of political finance reforms in the early 1970s."[41] This law has had the effect of defining and fixing in law the party's status relative to the candidate's. It recognizes the individual candidate's organization as the responsible legal agent of the campaign and limits how much a party can spend to promote its candidates. The legal position of the parties is thus at odds with their actual role during much of American history, when they often contributed most of the relevant resources needed to run congressional campaigns.

The parties, it is true, have a far higher spending limit than any single PAC, which has led some to speak of their "favorable" or "preferred" treatment under the law.[42] Yet it is a curious form of reasoning that begins by adopting the disputed premise. The parties' position is "preferred" only if a party is equated with an interest group, like the National Rifle Association. If parties are considered central to the electoral process, then the limits seem arbitrary. These limits today actually thwart party action, since the parties—unlike a decade ago—now have the resources to give more than the amount permitted. For the moment, however, it is unlikely that the law will be changed because the party with the numerical advantage in Congress (the Democrats) is not the same party with the financial advantage (the Republicans). "The Democrats," according to one congressman, "are not prepared to start every game on the goal line [while] Republicans start every game on the 40 yard line."[43]

The picture painted thus far of parties is one of decline, which best describes the situation in the 1970s. Since then, party activity, especially by the national parties, has increased substantially in congressional races. According to Paul Herrnson, "The political parties are alive and well and

120

the national organizations are more powerful than ever."[44] Along with increased funding, the national parties have provided help for their candidates in campaign planning, polling, and the production of campaign advertisements, including experiments in generic national ads for congressional candidates. Finally, the parties have influenced PAC contributions, serving as coordinators and as clearing houses. As Tony Coelho, the former chairman of the Democratic Congressional Campaign Committee, boasted, "We can turn the PACs off if we don't approve of somebody." Even when the parties have not benefited from these funds, the congressmen directing the campaign committees have managed to move rather quickly into major leadership positions.

As important as this recent growth of party activity may be, it is important to realize its limits. Parties provide more services, but they do not control the key function of nominating. The congressional campaign therefore remains a highly candidate-centered contest, with the parties having perhaps a slightly greater amount of influence on the candidate than before. To refer to the national parties as merely "super PACs," as some analysts have done, does not do full justice to their role, but it does point up that "strong" parties in this area have, at best, a modest role to perform.

There is an even more important sense in which the claims of party resurgence need to be qualified. A party's interest in supporting candidates is not to spend money, but to influence the outcome of elections. The key consideration is thus not the absolute level of spending, but how much party spending counts relative to other factors that affect election results. The overwhelming force in congressional elections today, especially in the House, is incumbency, which is a high-priced "package" of advantages made up of name recognition, franking privileges, staff resources, and leverage with PACs. Despite growing party contributions, challengers are spending less in House races in relationship to incumbents today than in 1980; in real terms, challenger spending between 1980 and 1986 dropped 23 percent while incumbent spending rose 52 percent.[45] To increase the number of competitive races would require an agency willing to underwrite congressional campaigns at a very substantial

121

price—one far higher, incidentally, than permitted by proposals suggesting public financing, all of which carry a spending limit. The only agency with both an interest and the potential capacity to meet this huge price is the political party.

A weakening of party attachment among voters is usually said to have been the major cause of incumbent success in congressional elections. Looking at the situation today, however, it may be that the direction of causality should be reversed. Incumbency now contributes to the low levels of party voting. Incumbents have erected institutional barriers to party resurgence by allowing themselves certain advantages and, even more important, by limiting the opposition party from supplying more resources to assist challengers.

The Strength of Parties in Governing

For many Europeans, the role American parties play in governing is so minuscule as to invite no more than a contemptuous dismissal. As one British observer asked, "How could it [the political party] lose power when it never had any?"[46] Yet, like creatures who inhabit dark regions, American analysts claim to detect glimmerings that go unnoticed by their foreign brethren. And these glimmerings are held to count for a great deal.

Party strength in governing is usually measured by the extent to which elected officials from the same party work together to promote a common program, especially across the divisions of the executive and legislative branches. Strength depends on both the associational configuration of a party and its institutional properties. Both parties today are far more cohesive than they were twenty years ago, as indicated by party unity scores in the Congress. The principal reason for this change almost certainly lies in the associational developments of the decline of radical southerners in the Democratic party and the emergence of modern conservatism in the Republican party.

The institutional component of party strength refers to what party mechanisms and partisan-related norms add to party cooperation beyond the spontaneous associational bond. This dimension is difficult to measure, but the evidence is clear that parties lost institutional influence during the 1960s and 1970s—continuing a trend that stretches back to the early part of this century. In the 1980s there are signs that this decline has slowed down and that we may be entering a period of stabilization.

Admittedly, except for a few brief periods, parties at the national level have never held a dominant position in governing. The Constitution virtually ensures that the will of each institution is superior to that of parties, and constitutional theory has generally encouraged the belief that the individual officeholders should be above parties. The nature of the system, with its separation of powers and staggered electoral terms, militates against hierarchic, programmatic parties that are able to run the government. The party's role, as Henry Jones Ford explained so aptly in 1898, takes place at the margins: "Party organization is compelled to act through executive and legislative deputies, who while always far from disavowing their party obligations, are quite free to use their own discretion as to the way in which they shall interpret and fulfill the party pledges."[47]

The parties' influence as an institutional constraint on elected officials was greatest at the turn of this century, when the parties exercised considerable internal authority over their members, at least separately in each house of Congress. The revolts and reforms of the early years of this century inaugurated a much weaker system of control. Even under this system, however, party leaders were able to "work" the Congress fairly effectively through the 1960s, perhaps because the centers of power in Congress were limited and identifiable.

Almost all observers in the 1970s detected a weakening in the coordinating mechanisms working across the centers of power in Washington. This atomized, disaggregated system, dubbed for a time "the new American political system," lacked the ballast that stronger parties had once helped to provide. The weak integrative capacities of the rivals of parties—individual discretion, constituency opinion, interest group pressure, and the media—created a policy-making process that, in the words of Anthony King, moved "either very sluggishly or with extreme speed."[48]

The parties' decline in governing resulted first from the practice of "going it alone" in the electoral sphere. Members who arrived in Congress as self-starters imported the same individualistic norms into their conduct inside the House or Senate. Second, party decline resulted from a series of major rules changes launched in the House under the banner of reform. Mirroring the party reformers' conflicting ideas of democracy, congressional reformers sometimes conceived of reform as a participatory sharing of power, and sometimes as a "responsible" concentrating of authority at the center. The first view led to decentralizing decision-making authority from a limited number of committees to a much larger number of subcommittees, while the second led to the addition of certain new powers for the party caucus and the Speaker. Of the two tendencies, decentralization has been the stronger and more enduring.[49]

Has the situation changed materially since the late 1970s? The cohesiveness of the Republican party in 1981–1982— which even as a minority in the House helped to push through the budget and tax component of the "Reagan Revolution"—showed that the "new" American political system did not go so far as to *preclude* sustained party action. Yet how much the Republicans' coherence owes to institutional changes is unclear. According to Gary Jacobson, Republicans made some use of their new financial muscle to promote greater discipline and help "overcome the rampant particularism that PACs and other interest groups encourage."[50] On the Democratic side, while the most important legacy of House reform remains decentralization, the centralizing aspects of the reforms have become more evident in this decade, especially in the increased influence of the Speaker (at least until the onset of Wright-gate in 1989). These changes in the parties' institutional role have admittedly been modest, and their effects are still not fully evident. Institutions can be quickly destroyed, but they can only be rebuilt very slowly.

The significance of party strength in governing must be evaluated in the context of what is usually said to be the party system's chief function in this area: serving as a bridge between the president and the two houses of Congress and adding energy and coherence to the policy-making process. What the Constitution separates, parties help to join. Yet today many point out that parties can perform their function of "joining" only when the government is "united," meaning that the same party controls all of the institutions. Where "divided" government becomes the norm—as now appears to be the case—the traditional argument for party strength no longer holds. Indeed, strong parties might even be an impediment to a smoothly functioning system.

This critique of divided government has been extended to a more general charge that the American governmental system today faces a fundamental crisis. In James Sundquist's words:

> The new era [of divided government] has rendered obsolete much of the theory developed by political scientists, from the day of Woodrow Wilson to the 1950s, to explain how the United States government can and should work. That theory identified the political party as the indispensable instrument that brought cohesion and unity, and hence effectiveness, to the government as a whole by linking the executive and the legislative branches in a bond of common interest. . . . [Divided government is] characterized by conflict, delay and indecision, leading frequently to deadlock, inadequate and ineffective policies, or no policies at all. . . . The President and Congress are motivated to try to discredit and defeat each other.[51]

For Sundquist, and for others who endorse his view, the current situation is so fraught with danger that extensive changes in the Constitution are needed to promote, if not guarantee, united government.

Even for those disposed to accept Sundquist's analysis, a few qualifying points are worth noting. First, while united government may be needed ordinarily to enact a major political program, it does not follow that one-party control ensures policy coherence. American parties, in fact, have seldom promoted coherent programs, even when they have held the presidency and have had impressive majorities in both houses of Congress. Second, it is a mistake to be too literal and link coherent policy making completely with the united-divided government distinction. As the 1981–1982 period showed, a party that controlled the presidency plus one house of Congress could enact much of its program when it was united and could find some support from the other party. Finally, if—as Sundquist argues—the recent situation has been characterized by unusual bitterness between the president and Congress, the cause is not divided government per se, but the semipermanent control of Congress by one party (the Democrats) and the advantage in presidential elections by the other party (the Republicans). This situation has led each party to align itself with an institution and to seek to increase that institution's powers and prerogatives. Partisan conflict has not merely made use of, but has become a source of, fundamental constitutional conflict.

The more important issue, however, is not whether there is a difficulty with divided government (most would probably agree that united government is preferable) but what, if anything, should be done to resolve this problem. For certain reformers, like Sundquist and Walter Dean Burnham, divided government offers another reason—or more accurately an excuse—to do what they have always wanted to do: transform the American system into a regime in which elections operate to squeeze out or manufacture not only party majorities, but also coherent (or "responsible") party majorities. These reformers are no doubt correct in saying that if divided government today is the result of the public's "natural" desire under the Constitution, then this problem could be overcome only by a change in the Constitution itself. But one may wonder whether the solution in this case is not far worse than the problem it is designed to solve.

The choice, however, may not be so stark. If divided government today has part of its source in subconstitutional causes, then steps could be taken to resolve the problem short of changing the Constitution. This approach might also be recommended if arrangements have recently developed that give an artificial bias in favor of incumbents. Measures could be considered that might eliminate part of this bias. This approach, however, has a natural limit: it proceeds only to the point of removing artificial barriers *inside* the constitutional system, not to changing the logic or structure of that system.

The Strength of Parties as Institutions

Institutional strength can also refer to the parties' capacity to control their own fate, whether by preventing legislatures and courts from interfering in internal party affairs or by inducing them to act as the parties wish. Without a foundation in the Constitution, parties have never had the same strength as the other major institutions. Nevertheless, for much of the nineteenth century, parties built a wall of support for themselves, grounded in the doctrine that they were self-governing associations beyond interference by ordinary legislation. Parties developed and flourished under this status as private associations.

This wall collapsed near the end of the nineteenth century, when the states began to regulate parties to curb corruption and to limit their power. Largely against their will, parties were subjected to strict legal controls. These were sometimes challenged in the courts, but state controls were invariably upheld. The legal position of parties stabilized until a further decline of institutional strength occurred in the 1970s. In 1976, the Supreme Court virtually declared party patronage unconstitutional and adopted its own views of how parties could best be maintained: "The democratic process," wrote Justice Brennan in *Elrod* v. *Burns*, "functions as well without the practice of patronage, perhaps even better."[52]

In recent years, however, party officials and supporters of parties—many of them from academia—have become far more conscious of the importance of the institutional strength of parties. They have pursued a two-pronged strategy. First, working through state legislatures, they have sought, on the one hand, to secure positive benefits for parties, such as laws giving public funding to the parties to distribute in state elections.[53] On the other hand—and perhaps logically in tension with securing positive benefits—they have asked state legislatures to remove many statutory restrictions on parties that limit their activities and discretion. Some state laws that were once hailed in the Progressive era as salutary reforms are now being widely branded as paternalistic.

Second—and partly as a result of failures in the legislative arena—party officials have begun legal challenges to state laws that regulate parties or limit their activities on the grounds that these conflict with the parties' First Amendment rights as free political associations. The strategy here is to use the courts as the instruments of deregulation. This principle was adjudicated in its most direct form in Connecticut in 1986, when the state Republican party challenged the state's closed primary law—usually considered favorable to parties—on the grounds that it prevented the party from broadening its base. The party wanted a primary that would allow non-Republicans to participate. The Supreme Court ruled in the party's favor in *Republican Party of Connecticut* v. *Tashjian* (1986). The same principle was upheld by the Supreme Court in March 1989, when in *March Fong Eu* v. *San Francisco County Democratic Central Committee*, it ruled in favor of the California Democratic party by invalidating a state statute that banned the party from making preprimary endorsements and that regulated in detail the party's internal governing structure.[54]

Students of parties are divided on whether the legal principle of associational autonomy for parties will be beneficial. One school regards institutional independence as generally favorable to parties, even if in specific instances it works to their detriment. Another school holds that a constitutional principle of autonomy will not only create havoc for state election law and make the courts the final arbiters in this field, but will also in the end harm more than help the parties. Now that parties are enmeshed in the law—receiving, for example, public funding in many states—they can be said to benefit from legal regulations, and only legislatures can intelligently weigh and balance all the conflicting situations.

If no one at this point can say how far the principle of legal autonomy for parties will go, it is certain to have profound implications. Changes in legal status generally work their effects well beyond the immediate cases at hand. Moreover, the efforts to win a new legal status for political parties, whether pursued in courts or in legislatures, affect parties at their base in the states and localities. It is here in the long run that the battle for stronger parties will ultimately be decided.

The Degree of Party Centralization

The emphasis on party decline and resurgence puts a premium on the issue of party strength. There are, however, other important features that describe the character of America's parties. One of these is the degree of centralization. In the 1940s, E. E. Schattschneider described decentralization of power as "by all odds the single most important characteristic of the American major party."[55] In contrast to the parties in most democratic nations, America's parties had their locus of power at the periphery, not the center.

By the early 1980s, this thesis of American party "exceptionalism" was being widely discarded. According to James Reichley: "Both parties are moving toward the model of tightly structured programmatic parties common in other Western democracies."[56] The analogy to European parties might be disputed, but the new financial power of the RNC and the national rule-making authority for delegate selection by the Democrats led to a major new trend of centralization of power within the parties. "Nationalization of the parties," wrote Gerald Pomper in 1984, "is rapidly developing."[57] Moreover, because this process occurred at roughly the same time as the early signs of party resurgence, many scholars argued that nationalization was the cause of party resurgence and that—for better or worse—any further strengthening of the parties would be predicated on a still greater nationalization.

Today, this analysis stands in need of revision. There was, to be sure, a marked centralization of power in the 1970s. Yet since the mid-1980s, there have been clear signs that the movement toward centralization may have reached its limit and even begun to recede. In retrospect, moreover, it is clear that party nationalization and party strength are best regarded as distinct concepts. Almost by definition, nationalization means a strengthening of the central organization. But this is not the same as a strengthening of the parties' overall power. If anything, the centralization on the Democratic side, by introducing rules that enabled outsiders to dominate the candidate selection process, has weakened the party. For Republicans, centralization has strengthened the party so far, but it does not follow that further centralization must be a source of future strength.

Party decentralization traditionally meant three things: that activities related to state and local affairs (including congressional elections) were controlled by the state or local organizations, with no interference from the national parties; that most national functions—such as the selection of national convention delegates—would be carried out mainly by state or local organizations or under state law; and that the collective national decisions that had to be reached—such as the choice of the presidential nominee or decisions on national party rules— would be conducted under procedures in which the state or local organizations were the main actors in any decision-making process.

On the first point, the national parties have clearly become more involved in state and local affairs over the past twenty years. In congressional races, the majority of party contributions of money and technical assistance come from the national parties rather than the state or local organizations; and, as PAC money today is given largely by national interest groups, the national parties today serve more often than they did as "cue givers."[58]

The activism of the national parties has not been limited to congressional contests. Since 1978 the RNC has been involved in funding and assisting candidates for state offices, and in 1983 the party began a program to rebuild local Republican organizations in key metropolitan areas. As James Reichley remarked, "Twenty years ago it is difficult to imagine the leaders of Republican machines in such states as New York, Pennsylvania, Ohio, Indiana, and Illinois agreeing to permit the national committee to work directly with their county units."[59] By the 1980s, state and local organizations had grown so weak that the national party activity was often conducted in a vacuum. Even so, the RNC became involved in state and local affairs in unprecedented ways, and there have been instances of conflicts between the two levels.

The centralization of fund raising has clearly been at the center of this development. Party financing on the Republican side underwent a classic change from a confederal to a national system. In the 1950s, the RNC raised funds by assigning quotas to each state party, which was then responsible for raising the money. In the 1970s, the flow of money began to reverse directions. The states lost important sources for raising funds—such as the "taxing" of patronage workers—while the national parties pioneered direct mail solicitation. The new financial relations within the party have inevitably influenced the overall political relations. With eloquent simplicity, one Republican state chairman recently remarked, "I figure that I should go along with the National Committee as much as possible because I want as much of their money as I can get."[60]

These developments must, however, be put in perspective. Even with more financial power at the center, American parties are nowhere close to being national machines. What the national parties spend on congressional campaigns remains a small part of total campaign expenditures (about 17 percent), and the amounts for state offices are even more modest. More important, centralization has not been the aim of these developments. A large part of the activity of the RNC has been directed not at usurping the powers of state and local parties, but at rebuilding them. Once state and local parties begin to function more effectively—as they have in some cases—they will do more on their own. The nationalizing process thus contains within it the partial seeds of its own reversal. Finally, many of the high-tech computer functions that a decade ago seemed inevitably to favor centralization today can be handled, and handled more efficiently, by the state parties.

Decentralization can also refer to the performance of national functions by state and local units. The prime example here has been the selection of delegates to the national conventions, which had traditionally been considered a prerogative of the state parties or state governments. With the reform movement, however, the Democratic party began issuing national delegate selection rules, stipulating clear dos and don'ts for the states. These have included, at one time or

131

another since 1972, quotas in the demographic composition
of delegates, rules on the timing of delegate selection contests, a proportional allocation of delegates by candidate
preference, and a ban on open primaries. The objective of
this rule-making process, according to Donald Fraser, co-
chairman of the McGovern-Fraser Commission, was "the
creation of a truly national party in which decision-making at
the national level is strengthened and the 50 state parties
become integral parts of that party."[61]

This new assertion of national party authority met initially with only sporadic resistance from the state parties and
state governments, most of which were controlled by Democrats. In one celebrated case in 1972, however, the national
party refused to seat a Chicago delegation chosen under
Illinois state law (*Cousins* v. *Wigoda*). The matter was taken to
the courts, with the practical issue being to decide who had
the final authority to determine provisions for seating of
delegates, the states or the national parties.

The state rested its claim on its legislative power to
determine primary election laws; the national party on its
right as an association to make its own rules and on the
traditional prerogative of the national convention to be the
final judge of its own members. In this case, and in a similar
case later on involving the party's refusal to accept delegates
chosen under Wisconsin's open primary (*Democratic Party of
Wisconsin* v. *La Follette*), the Supreme Court rebuffed the
states' claims to priority. In the immediate aftermath of these
decisions, many began to compare the new national party
rule-making authority to a kind of superlegislative power for
delegate selection.

Today, after several more years of experience with this
process, the Democrats seem to have reached the limit of how
far they can, or wish to, make use of this authority. In fact,
the Court's decisions, while unfavorable to the states, nevertheless left the states with far greater means of legal resistance than most initially believed. The Court, strictly speaking, never ruled that the national party could tell the states
how to choose delegates but only that delegates not chosen
according to national party rules need not be seated at the
national convention. A state can still ignore the party's rules,

putting the national party in the awkward position of punishing a state (as the Democratic party finally did to Wisconsin in 1984 over its open primary law).

The spectacle of a national party imposing its will against a reluctant state, while no doubt gratifying to proponents of the abstract idea of national party power, did little to help the party's electoral prospects. Moreover, members of the state parties and Democratic state legislators began to grow resentful of assertions of national party control and made clear their readiness to resist. Faced with these problems, after 1980 many in the national Democratic party began to look for ways to avoid further confrontations. The 1984 national rules removed more restrictions on the states than they imposed, and the rules for 1988 went further still in this direction by eliminating the ban on the open primary in states where it had once been used.

The outcome of the open primary dispute is revealing of the whole battle over national authority through rule making: the national party won its principle, but the state of Wisconsin has prevailed in practice. This may not be the epitaph for the national rule-making authority, which continues to set important boundaries for the process and which could still possibly be used to make major changes. For legal and political reasons, however, the era of further national party rule making applied against the states now appears to be over.

Decentralization, finally, meant a reliance, in the case of collective national party decisions, on a process that recognized the primacy of the state and local parties. Traditional accounts of decision making in regard to both the national conventions and the national committees emphasize the fundamental role of the state parties. In modern party conventions, however, the state parties have largely been replaced as the real decision-making units by delegate groupings faithful to candidates or to national interest groups. In the national committees, by contrast, the state parties retain a significant degree of the real power and often vigorously promote their organizational interests.

Since 1968, the struggle over the degree of nationalization in the Democratic party has been waged in part as a conflict between the national conventions and the national committee. The first phase of national rule making (1968–1976), which was the most hostile to the state and local parties' prerogatives, worked through party commissions that claimed mandates directly from the convention. These commissions largely succeeded in working around the national committee. In a second phase after 1976, the rules commissions have been kept under much closer check by the national committee and the national party chairman, and the rules have been far less hostile to the interests of the state and local units. The same battle was fought at the 1984 convention. Reformers attempted to work directly by means of a mandate from the convention, while state party officials successfully managed to involve the national committee and national chairman. In 1988, the convention reasserted direct control, although the rules changes this time were more modest.

To summarize, the parties have become more centralized in recent decades, especially since the beginning of the 1970s. Yet in the past few years this movement has been slowed in some instances and reversed in others. American parties will never be as decentralized as they were in the 1940s—but then neither will American politics as a whole. It has long been thought that a decentralized party system is not just a consequence of, but, in William Riker's words, "the main protector of the integrity of the states in our federalism."[62] While this view has been more asserted than proved, it is clear that a decentralized party system with strong state and local parties is at least a sign of a more healthy federal system.

Where the balance will ultimately fall between the national and the state parties depends in large part on what parties are asked to do in the future. If the national parties grow stronger, this could, paradoxically, be a sign that parties as a whole will remain relatively weak. The reason is that there are clear limits to what stronger national parties can do in the context of the American constitutional system. At their strongest, they can help fund campaigns and play some role in generating programs and organizing the government. But they are never going to nominate congressional candidates or run state or local campaigns. If parties are to reassume major responsibilities, such as playing a greater role in nominating candidates, these functions will have to be performed mostly by state and local parties.

The Causes of Party Strength

Parties must be understood in terms of their dual nature as associations and institutions. It is a mistake to ignore this distinction and to attribute institutional results to associational causes. Thus, in the early 1980s the associational strength of the Republican party led some to consider the party in its institutional sense to be stronger than it actually was, just as the associational weakness of the Democratic party in the late 1970s led many to exaggerate its institutional weakness.

Parties in an associational sense are "caused" by a waxing and waning of political issues and ideas. At certain moments, such as the late 1960s or early 1980s, the political climate is charged with debate on basic issues, and people rally to a party as firm advocates of a cause; at other moments, conflict over fundamental issues is absent, and citizens remain with their party more from habit than commitment. Or they recall what they dislike about the other party, it being in the nature of parties, according to Macaulay, "to retain their original enmities far more firmly than their original principles."[63]

A change in the character of parties as associations could occur only if there were a transformation in the way issues and ideas emerge. Certain analysts have posited such a change. In the early 1960s, some theorized that advanced societies were experiencing an "end of ideology," in which material plenty was eliminating the basic sources of political conflict. Parties would wither away from a lack of anything to fight over. In the 1980s, a very different conclusion was derived from the same starting point. Modern society, it was said, had entered a "postmaterialist" era, in which people, free of ordinary material concerns, were becoming more preoccupied with divisive issues relating to "the quality of life." Party disputes would accordingly become more intense.[64]

Those who write about parties have found such theories

135

highly attractive because they purport to explain so much. Yet their accuracy has never measured up to their attractiveness. No one has really proven any *essential* change in the way in which ideas and issues arise in recent American history. For the time being at least, students of parties will have to content themselves with the fact that politics will remain politics.

The analysis of parties as institutions has been far more extensive. In the 1970s, theories were advanced to show how socioeconomic and technological factors were leading inevitably to party decline. In the socioeconomic realm, the emergence of a "new class" of educated citizens was said to spell the doom of parties. New class citizens prided themselves on their independence, avoiding parties in favor of working for specific candidates or of joining single-issue groups like Common Cause. Modern technology added to party obsolescence: the electronic media replaced parties as communicators, and campaign consulting firms set up campaign "boutiques" that could offer candidates all the services needed to conduct a modern campaign.

With some recent signs of party recovery, these deterministic theories seem guilty of overprediction. While citizens have new styles of participating in politics, parties as organizations are not constitutionally incapable of adapting to them. And it strains credulity to think that a blind sociological force is capable of discriminating between an organization like Common Cause and the Democratic party of Santa Monica, California. As for the development of modern technology, its "determinism" may recently have begun to change sides. Many of the high-tech methods that were pioneered outside of parties, and that once worked to their detriment, have recently been put to use by the parties and help explain many of the gains they have been making.

In contrast to such deterministic explanations, the analysis here has emphasized the importance of two factors amenable to influence by political leaders: doctrine and law. Doctrine refers to the prevailing opinion held by elites or the public respecting the proper role of parties. More than any other factor, a change in doctrine in the past decade helps account for the observed elements of party resurgence. During the 1970s, political elites, especially on the Democratic side, were beholden to ideas that, whatever some may have thought, endorsed and promoted the candidate-centered electoral system that had been eroding the foundation of parties for the previous sixty years.

Since then reform sentiment has been subsiding, and party leaders have taken advantage of their new maneuvering room to reinstitute certain party prerogatives. Political leaders are also now more likely to accept the notion that the maintenance of parties as institutions extracts a 'price' in terms of perfect 'fairness' to individual candidates. Yet this movement to reform the reforms nonetheless remains limited and tenuous. While party leaders have pressed this case at the elite level, they have been unwilling to challenge reform openly at the level of mass politics or demonstrate the democratic character of stronger parties. It may be that they will do so only when and if parties gain a greater popular constituency in the states and localities. It is there that the real battle for stronger parties must be waged.

The second cause—the law—refers here to the party rules, federal and state statutes, and court decisions that bear on the arrangement and power of the parties. This factor reflects doctrines about parties, but it develops partly on its own in response to particular circumstances. One way to 'test' the potential importance of this factor is to imagine the consequences that would ensue if someone had the power to alter, in plausible ways, all the rules and laws affecting parties. The change in the position of parties would arguably be far greater than anything likely to result from any imminent developments in the class structure of society or in technology.[65]

A consideration of parties today reveals a number of tendencies and countertendencies at work at the same time. In different ways, parties are declining, stabilizing, and resurging. The fluidity of this situation is reinforced by the forces driving party development, which leave a great deal to human choice. Not everything, of course, is subject to choice, for political limits are often hardly less intractable than physical ones. Nevertheless, there is much latitude for deliberate action. The future of the American political party will depend greatly on what people decide its future should be.

5

From a Partisan to a Candidate-centered Electorate

Martin P. Wattenberg

Nowhere is the impact of the new American political system more evident than in the changes that have taken place in patterns of electoral behavior since the election of John F. Kennedy in 1960. In his last book, *The Responsible Electorate*, V. O. Key wrote, "The voice of the people is but an echo chamber. The output of the echo chamber bears an inevitable and invariable relation to the input."[1] Indeed, as input from the political system has changed since 1960, so has American political behavior.

In the aftermath of the 1988 national election, a comparison with the 1960 election seems particularly appropriate. At first glance the two elections appear to be directly comparable. As in 1960, no single burning issue dominated the 1988 campaign, the focus of each being on the future, not the past, and on who should lead rather than on what specifically should be done. Both involved choosing a successor to a two-term Republican president with high overall approval ratings, and in both the incumbent vice president faced a relatively unknown Democrat from Massachusetts running with a prominent senator from Texas. In fact, one could easily have taken the 1960 cast of characters and placed them into comparable roles for 1988. Yet, with the transformation from party politics to candidate-centered campaigning, it would have been much like casting Shakespearean actors in the frantic chases and slapstick comedy of the 1963 hit movie, "It's a Mad, Mad, Mad, Mad World."

Much about the presidential election process has

changed since 1960. The changes include the decline of political parties, the rise of candidate-centered politics, and the transformation of the nominating process into a wild mass media extravaganza. As *Time* magazine said in a cover story entitled "1988, You're No 1960," "The real meaning of a comparison between the elections of 1960 and 1988 is the vast difference that separates them. The elections of 1960 and 1988 are brackets enclosing a period of astonishing transformation—change that has placed the two campaigns in different eras."[2]

This chapter analyzes the differences with a special emphasis on dealignment and realignment in the electorate together with the consequences of the reformed nominating process. The primary objective is to demonstrate what a tremendous difference candidate-centered politics has made.

The New Nominating System

The most obvious major difference between 1988 and 1960 lies in how the presidential nominees were chosen. What was once a relatively straightforward task conducted largely out of public view has been turned into a long and tortuous media circus. In the 1960s the nomination battle was a test of a candidate's ability to build support among the small cadre of party leaders; in the 1980s building popularity among primary and caucus voters throughout the fifty states has become the key test.

The process has thus moved from smoke-filled rooms to rooms filled with the bright lights of ever-present television cameras. Almost everything a presidential candidate says these days ends up on videotape, as Joseph Biden discovered to his regret. As the Biden and Gary Hart episodes demonstrated in 1987, greater visibility often exposes warts that would otherwise remain unseen by the public. With this greater scrutiny, candidates inevitably end up publicly tainted in one way or another. Because the nomination campaigns of 1988 were aimed at the public rather than at the party leaders, they were far more divisive and therefore damaging to the candidates' images.

More than that of any candidate before 1960, Kennedy's

campaign was boosted by primary victories. Yet his decision to enter seven primaries was seen at the time as an indication of weakness. The conventional wisdom of 1960 held that primary losses would ruin a campaign (for example, Wendell Willkie, 1944) while victories might hardly matter (for example, Estes Kefauver, 1952). Hubert Humphrey expressed this sentiment in 1960, replying to a question about why he was not filing in the Indiana primary:

> Any man who goes into a primary isn't *fit* to be President. You have to be crazy to go into a primary. A primary, now, is worse than the torture of the rack. It's all right to enter a primary by accident or because you don't know any better, but by forethought . . .[3]

Kennedy's decision, however, was by forethought, based on the premise that only by showing his popularity with the voters could he convince the party leaders that he was electable. Indeed, the crucial West Virginia primary yielded no delegates at all, being strictly a "beauty contest." What it did help deliver were key endorsements from such crucial party leaders as Governor Michael DiSalle of Ohio and Mayor Richard Daley of Chicago.

Unlike the primary contests of 1960, those of 1988 were crucial because the overwhelming majority of delegates were chosen through this route. With roughly three-quarters of the delegates now chosen in primaries, these elections have become the main road to the nomination. In contrast to the primary marathon of 1988, only two primary contests drew any attention in 1960—West Virginia and Wisconsin. All told, Kennedy's primary victories (mostly in uncontested races) produced just 18 percent of the delegates he needed for the nomination. Had the party leaders turned against him—as they did against Kefauver in 1952—Kennedy could well have been defeated.

Not only has the nomination process been opened up by the proliferation of primaries, the caucuses are now public events as well. This is most evident in Iowa, where massive efforts are now focused on mobilizing the grass roots for the nation's first test of candidates' strength. Even 1960s' most important contest, the West Virginia primary, merited only ten days of Kennedy's time. In 1988 Iowa loomed so large that nearly a thousand candidate days were spent there, some candidates going so far as to rent apartments in Des Moines. Compare this with the start of the 1960 campaign in New Hampshire, where Richard Nixon did not even campaign and Kennedy was opposed only by Paul Fischer—a ballpoint pen executive from Chicago who ran a campaign on the then revolutionary notion of flat tax rates.[4] Although Governor Michael Dukakis made much out of the idea that he was following in Kennedy's footsteps by winning in New Hampshire, the 1960 contest is little more than a footnote in the history books. Indeed, that is exactly what Theodore White gave it in *The Making of the President, 1960*.

On the Republican side there is no comparison between the hard path that George Bush had to travel and Nixon's 1960 campaign. By the standards of the new American political system, Nixon's road to the 1960 nomination was a breeze. The only Republican who even considered running against him was Nelson Rockefeller. Rockefeller tested the waters in late 1959, found that the party's leaders were solidly behind Nixon, and never went beyond toying with the idea of challenging him. Kennedy could thus taunt the Republicans by saying at the convention that "their ranks are so thin that not one challenger has dared to put his head up in the last twelve months." Bush, however, had to face five strong opponents in Robert Dole, Jack Kemp, Alexander Haig, Pat Robertson, and Pierre ("Pete") du Pont. Although Nixon's easy road to the nomination left him open to taunts from Kennedy, it also left him with a much more positive public image than that enjoyed by Bush. Much damage would certainly have been done to Nixon's image if he had faced comparable opposition—say, from a Senate leader like Everett Dirksen, a House leader like Gerald Ford, a major figure in foreign policy like Henry Cabot Lodge, the Reverend Billy Graham, and a former small-state governor.

With this increased public competition, any ammunition that can possibly be used against a rival will be employed. Even relatively short contests such as Reagan versus Bush in 1980 or Bush versus Dole in 1988 have left memorable scars (for example, voodoo economics and Dole asking Bush to stop lying about his record). Gone are the days when the Kennedy campaign could just sit on material in their possession indicating Lyndon Johnson's continuing support of the antilabor Taft-Hartley Act. Kennedy knew that he would need Johnson's support in the end and thought it would be counterproductive to attack Johnson if he could avoid it. Indeed, at the famous Kennedy-Johnson debate during the week of the convention Johnson called Kennedy one of "the ablest leaders in our party" and unequivocally promised to support him if he were nominated. Johnson did refer to Kennedy's lackluster attendance record in the Senate but stopped short of criticizing him by name. Kennedy, for his part, easily sloughed off this indirect reference and said that he was "full of admiration for Senator Johnson, full of affection for him, and strongly in support for him for Majority Leader."

Now, of course, we have "attack videos." Furthermore, the endless debating that takes place until one candidate has locked up the nomination also serves to weaken the eventual nominee. Dukakis's thirty-nine television debates during the primaries frequently made the Kennedy-Johnson debate look like a love feast.

Candidates' Popularity in Decline

It is thus no wonder that our presidential nominees are so much less popular than they were before the nominating process went public. No politician can endure opposition from a wide array of opponents in numerous contests without alienating a significant proportion of voters. Public competition also forces the candidates to take stands on a host of controversial issues. While voters may get a better sense of what the candidates will do in office, such specific stands typically divide public opinion far more than the generalities that constituted the old, brokered convention platforms. In addition, more public focus is now placed on a candidate's competence for the presidency, as judged by his campaign. Few mortals can go through thousands of public appearances without erring from time to time. Because misstatements and gaffes break the monotony of the long campaign, they receive

FIGURE 5–1
DECLINE IN PRESIDENTIAL CANDIDATES'
POPULARITY, 1952–1984
(voters only)

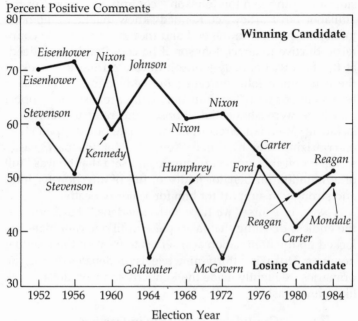

Percent Positive Comments

SOURCE: 1952–1984 SRC/CPS National Election Studies.

a great deal of attention in the news media and make lasting impressions on the public. As Bush said only partly in jest at the 1988 Al Smith dinner, he had learned that "a slip of the tongue is a gaffe, and a gaffe is a two-day story, and a two-day story is a trend."

The result has been a steady decline in the popularity of presidential nominees since 1960, as shown in figure 5–1. Although Nixon lost the 1960 election, he was nevertheless an extremely well-liked and respected candidate in that year. When a national sample of voters were asked what they liked and disliked about him, over 70 percent of the comments were positive. Nixon's popularity was unprecedented for a losing candidate in the era of survey research, but Adlai Stevenson also received high marks while losing in 1952 and 1956. Since then, however, losing candidates for the presidency have usually generated far more negative than positive remarks.

More consequential than the decline in the popularity of losing candidates has been the decline in the popularity of those who have won the opportunity to govern in the new American political system. Voters' open-ended comments regarding Dwight Eisenhower were over 70 percent positive in the 1950s. In contrast, when Reagan was elected president in 1980, voters had more negative than positive remarks to make about him and his candidacy. Even in 1984, when his popular vote margin equaled Eisenhower's in 1956, positive comments barely outweighed negative ones.

Although comparable data from 1988 were not yet available when this chapter was written, there is little reason to expect that Bush and Dukakis reversed this trend. One of the most common findings among the plethora of journalistic polls in 1988 was that many people felt dissatisfied with the candidates and the campaign. Most notably, a *New York Times* poll in late October found that nearly two-thirds of the probable electorate wished they had choices other than the two major party candidates—a much higher level of dissatisfaction than the *Times* had found in 1984 or 1980.

In sum, in an electoral era centered on candidates, it is fascinating to note that the candidates themselves have become less and less popular. With the decline of partisanship in the electorate in recent years, the influence of evaluations of candidates has become less mediated and more direct. No longer are voters likely to support a candidate unequivocally just because he is their party's nominee—particularly given the internal party criticism nominees now face during the primary season. It seems that the more the public comes to know about the candidates, the less it likes them. Familiarity breeds contempt.

Dealignment in the American Electorate

As in 1960, the absence of an incumbent from the race in 1988 made it inevitable that far more attention than usual was placed on candidates' images. In contrast to 1960, however, the candidate with the most favorable personal image did not

TABLE 5–1
CORRELATIONS WITH PRESIDENTIAL VOTE, 1900–1980

	Senate	House	Governor
1900	—	.97	.94
1920	.80	.70	.55
1940	.76	.66	.61
1960	.43	.55	.36
1980	.24	.06	.00

SOURCE: Walter Dean Burnham, "The 1984 Elections and the Future of American Politics," in Ellis Sandoz and Cecil V. Crabb, Jr., eds., *Election 1984: Landslide Without a Mandate?* (New York: Mentor, 1985), p. 235.

lose—as Nixon did. In the closest presidential election ever, Kennedy managed to squeak out a victory based on the Democratic advantage in party identification. In contrast, the Bush victory in 1988 had relatively little to do with blind party loyalty.

Mountains of survey evidence attest to Americans' declining concern with partisanship and the role of political parties in U.S. government. The belief is pervasive that one should vote for the man, not the party. Even in 1956, when most voters were in fact voting straight tickets, 74 percent of respondents in a Gallup poll agreed with this general belief; by 1968 this figure had risen to 84 percent.[5] Most recently a 1986 survey by Larry Sabato found 92 percent agreeing with the statement, "I always vote for the person who I think is best, regardless of what party they belong to."[6]

Since 1960 voters not only have increasingly said that they vote for the man rather than party but have actually done so with great frequency. Analysis of American voting patterns over the course of the twentieth century clearly reveals a steady trend away from straight party voting. As Walter Dean Burnham has shown, the shared variance between a state's vote for president and its vote for Senate, House, and governor has declined continuously throughout this century.[7] The squared correlations (R^2) with the presidential vote for every fifth election year from 1900 to 1980 are as shown in Table 5–1. What this means is that at the turn of the century one could predict almost perfectly how a state would vote for Congress and governor by its vote for president. By the time of Kennedy's election states would often follow the same pattern in voting for president as for other offices, but with a substantial number of exceptions. In the 1980s, however, knowing a state's presidential vote has been of virtually no help in predicting its vote for other offices.[8]

It would be an overstatement, though, to infer that even a majority of voters are now splitting their tickets between major offices. Rather, ticket splitting between presidential and House voting has risen from 14 percent in 1960 to a high of 34 percent in 1980. Some have argued that such behavior is simply due to the nomination of presidential candidates whom many party identifiers cannot support. Yet secular increases can also be found in measures that do not involve presidential voting. For example, in 1960 only 9 percent of voters split their tickets between House and Senate candidates of different parties; the figure in 1980 was 31 percent.

The results of such patterns are far from academic. They can clearly be seen in the unprecedented level of split party control of both the federal and state governments in recent years. In 1984 only twenty-two states had one party in control of both houses of their legislatures and the governorship, and after the 1988 election this figure dropped even further to eighteen states. Not since the formation of the Republican party in the 1850s can one find anything like this in the history of state politics. Similarly, from 1981 to 1986 different parties controlled the federal House and Senate for the first time since 1916. Most visible, of course, have been the divisions in partisan control of the presidency and the Congress since 1952. By the end of Bush's first term, the same party will have controlled the presidency and the House for just fourteen of the past forty years. When Eisenhower was re-elected in 1956 with a Democratic Congress, it marked the first time in a century that the voters had split control of the two branches; by the time of Bush's election, such an outcome had become commonplace.

Given current public attitudes concerning the desirability of voting the man rather than the party, such split-ticket voting may well reach even higher levels in the future. The attitudinal potential for ticket splitting has consistently been greater than its incidence, and one can reasonably interpret recent trends as reflecting the tendency for behaviors eventually to come into line with attitudes.

Accompanying the trend toward greater split-ticket voting has been a decline in party identification. With the development of the candidate-centered mass media campaign, long-term party loyalties have atrophied substantially. Election studies from 1952 to 1964 consistently found that approximately 75 percent of the electorate identified themselves as either Democrats or Republicans. By 1972 the percentage of respondents identifying themselves with one of the parties had dropped from 77 to 64 and the proportion of strong partisans from 38 to 25 percent.

What once appeared to be a continuing downward spiral now no longer seems to be such, but rather a limited period effect in which a rapid decline was followed by the development of a new, somewhat lower level of stability. Since 1972 the proportion of the population identifying with one of the parties during presidential election years has held steady at 63 to 65 percent. In retrospect, it seems that the period of weakening party loyalties, 1964 to 1972, was an unusually tumultuous era in the history of American politics, which may never again be duplicated in the severity of the shocks—Vietnam, racial unrest, and so on—that the electorate felt.

In contrast to the decline of party identification, the dissipation of party images has occurred over a much longer period and has been far more pronounced. The proportion of the electorate that can be classified as having a neutral view of both parties increased gradually from 13 percent in 1952 to 36 percent in 1984.[9] Virtually all these people exhibit the following response pattern to the four standard open-ended questions about the parties:

Q: Is there anything in particular that you like about the Democratic party?

A: No.

Q: Is there anything in particular that you dislike about the Democratic party?

A: No.

Q: Is there anything in particular that you like about the Republican party?

A: No.

Q: Is there anything in particular that you dislike about the Republican party?

A: No.

In Eisenhower and Kennedy's era, such a response pattern typically reflected general political ignorance. Most of these people had little to say about the candidates, and few voted. For instance, 84 percent of them in the 1960 National Election Study (NES) sample were classified as "no issue content" on Philip Converse's classic measure of levels of conceptualization.[10] In contrast, in 1984 only 44 percent of those who had nothing to say about the parties failed to mention an issue when they were asked about the candidates. In the 1980s such people have tuned out the parties but often not the candidates and the issues. Indeed, they are often considered the most important group in American electoral politics—the floating voters.

In sum, evidence of dealignment is readily apparent almost everywhere one looks in public attitudes and behavior. The belief that one should vote the man rather than the party has now become part of the American consensus, and split-ticket voting has risen markedly. Fewer people now identify themselves with the parties, and the percentage of those who have neither likes nor dislikes regarding the two parties has more than tripled since the 1950s. (See table 5–2 for exact figures on these trends from 1952 to 1984.)

The wealth of time series data indicates that most voters now view parties as a convenience rather than a necessity. Yet, regardless of whether the public recognizes it, parties are necessities for structuring the vote. The major question raised by recent trends, therefore, is not whether political parties can survive in an atmosphere of dealignment but rather whether they can still perform many of their key functions in such an atmosphere. If many voters no longer pay much attention to party labels, what reason do elites have to pay more than lip service to the concept of party unity either in campaigns or in governing? When Eisenhower was first nom-

TABLE 5-2
KEY INDICATORS OF DEALIGNMENT, 1952–1984
(percent)

	1952	1956	1960	1964	1968	1972	1976	1980	1984
Identify with a party	75	73	75	77	70	64	63	64	64
Strongly identify with a party	36	36	36	38	30	25	24	27	29
Split their ticket between president and House	12	16	14	15	26	30	25	34	25
Split their ticket between Senate and House	9	10	9	18	22	23	23	31	20
Neutral toward both parties	13	16	17	20	17	30	31	37	36
Positive toward one party and negative toward the other	50	40	41	38	38	30	31	27	31

SOURCE: 1952–1984 SRC/CPS National Election Studies.

inated in 1952, he told the Republican convention that to achieve their aims there must be a "total victory." As he put it, "We must have more Republicans in our state and local offices; more Republican governments in our states; a Republican majority in the United States House of Representatives and in the United States Senate; and, of course, a Republican in the White House." Now candidates rarely utter the name of their party, and the past two elections have seen recriminations from disgruntled congressional leaders, Robert Michel of the House (1984) and Dole of the Senate (1988), about the lack of help from the top of the ticket.

The Era of Party Disunity

Although political parties are now much less of a factor in shaping political attitudes, they remain crucial to the outcome of presidential elections in one respect—the candidate with the most united party behind him won every presidential election from 1964 to 1988. Given the periodicity of American political realignments, many scholars expected a realignment to take place in the mid-1960s. In retrospect Burnham argues that the realignment "actually happened around that date, but in the 'wrong' place." Instead of producing a new majority, "parties themselves were decisively replaced at the margins by the impact of the permanent campaign."[11] I would add that a crucial feature of the permanent campaign has been the increasingly difficult task of unifying any political party after a hotly contested struggle for the nomination. Thus I believe that an appropriate label for party politics since Kennedy's death is "the era of party disunity."

From the viewpoint of the 1980s, it is striking to note that Kennedy won in 1960 even though his party had the more divisive of the two nomination campaigns. The same was true of Eisenhower in 1952. With the weakening of partisan attachments in recent decades, it has become increasingly difficult to rally partisans around a newly anointed nominee: internal animosities stirred up by the nomination race are now more likely to continue to haunt him in November. Such animosities hurt a candidate not only with his own party's voters but with independents and the opposition party's

151

supporters as well. After all, if members of his own party find fault with a candidate, why should those outside the party view him favorably?

Numerous studies have shown that a nominee's chances in November are adversely affected by a tough fight for the nomination. Party activists who invest their efforts in losing campaigns for the nomination are often reluctant to continue their campaign involvement during the general election. For example, Emmett Buell's study of New Hampshire primary activists in 1984 found that about half the supporters of Hart and Walter Mondale's other opponents more or less sat out the November campaign.[12] Thus, just when Mondale needed all the activist support he could get, he found it difficult to overcome the divisions of the spring. Such a phenomenon can best be understood as primarily due to personal loyalty to the losing candidates rather than to ideological differences. As Walter J. Stone found in his study of Iowa activists in 1980, nomination preferences in both parties had a significant effect on participation, independent of the effects of ideology, past levels of political activity, and attachment to the party organization.[13]

Similarly, one can hardly attribute the defection of 41 percent of Democratic voters who preferred Hart to Mondale in 1984 to their preference for a conservative like Ronald Reagan. Given Hart's biting criticism of Mondale during the primaries, many Hart supporters (whose party loyalty was weak to begin with) apparently had difficulty in seeing how Reagan could be any worse. Mondale said at the outset of his nomination acceptance speech:

> Behind us now is the most wide open race in political history. It was noisy but our voices were heard. It was long but our stamina was tested. It was hot but the heat was passion and not anger. It was a rollercoaster, but it made me a better candidate.

Yet he was a battered and bruised candidate whose image had been irrevocably tarnished. While Mondale asserted that he did not "envy the drowsy harmony of the Republican party" in 1984, he had good reason to.

Throughout the history of presidential primaries divisive

primaries in individual states have seriously hurt a party's chances of winning those states in November.[14] In the most comprehensive study to date, Patrick Kenney and Tom Rice use the percentage of the primary vote received by both nominees in each state from 1912 to 1984 to assess the relative effect of divisive primaries.[15] They find that for every percentage point that one nominee does better than the other in a given state, he gains an additional 0.07 percent of the general election vote than would otherwise be expected. The effect is analogous to that of becoming a favorite son candidate; having done well in the state during the primaries, a nominee begins the general election campaign there with the image of a winner—both well known and well liked. In contrast, when a candidate makes a poor showing in a state primary, he starts his general election campaign there with a serious handicap.

The national results from 1964 to 1988 are also consistent with the notion that one can predict a candidate's strength in the fall from his showing in the primaries. The greater the margin a nominee accumulates over his closest rival in the primaries, the better he does in the general election (table 5–3). Candidates who ran virtually even with their closest challenger throughout the primaries, such as Barry Goldwater, George McGovern, and Mondale, ended up on the losing side of landslide elections. On the other side of the coin, candidates Jimmy Carter in 1976 and Reagan in 1980—both of whom far outdistanced their primary rivals—unseated incumbent presidents who faced relatively close nomination contests. Of course, incumbent presidents who were scarcely challenged in the primaries fared best of all.

Therefore, on Super Tuesday, March 8, 1988, Bush was in a nearly ideal position to win the presidency. Aside from his weak showing in Iowa and his tough battle to win New Hampshire, Bush rode along a smooth trail to the nomination. His Super Tuesday sweep left the contest all but over barely a month after it had begun. In contrast, Dukakis did not even emerge as the clear front-runner until a month after Super Tuesday. Furthermore, he continued to face opposition from Jesse Jackson throughout the primaries and the preconvention maneuvering. Although Bush had made peace with

TABLE 5–3
NOMINATION AND GENERAL ELECTION POPULAR VOTE MARGINS OVER CLOSEST OPPONENT, 1964–1988
(percentage points)

	Nomination Margin	General Election Margin
Bush 1988	48.5	7.7
Reagan 1980	37.5	9.7
Carter 1976	23.5	2.1
Carter 1980	14.1	−9.7
Dukakis 1988	13.2	−7.8
Ford 1976	7.4	−2.1
Mondale 1984	1.7	−18.2
Goldwater 1964[a]	1.0	−22.5
McGovern 1972	−0.5	−23.2

a. Based on the three contested primaries between Goldwater and Rockefeller in New Hampshire, Oregon, and California.
SOURCE: *Congressional Quarterly*.

Dole by May, Dukakis had to struggle to deter the Jackson camp from waging major floor fights at the convention. Thus it should not be surprising that when the fall campaign began Bush was the candidate who most effectively mobilized the various groups in his party's coalition.

The Decline of Turnout

Getting one's coalition to the polls is becoming an increasingly difficult task in American electoral politics. In 1960 the turnout of the eligible voting population was 62.8 percent, in 1988 just 50.2 percent. Thus, although Bush won a substantially higher percentage of the vote than Kennedy, he received the support of considerably less of the eligible population. Indeed, the 26.8 percent of the eligible electorate that voted for Bush is the lowest such total this century in a two-man race.

As the puzzle of low U.S. turnout has been unraveled in recent years, scholarly focus has come to center on the problem of voter registration. Because the United States is the only Western democracy to place the burden of registration entirely on the citizen, the costs of voting are much higher. This unique feature of the American system certainly explains a good portion of the consistent difference between turnout in the United States and in Western Europe.[16] Registration procedures cannot be held accountable for the decline in turnout since 1960, however, for such procedures have been made easier. Many states have enacted postal registration and permitted deputy registrars to go out and register people rather than have the people come to them. Furthermore, as a result of the Voting Rights Act, states can no longer set their deadlines for registration earlier than one month before the election.

The most conclusive evidence that registration barriers are unrelated to the decline of turnout comes from states where there are no such barriers. In sparsely populated North Dakota registration was never deemed necessary to prevent voter fraud. Yet turnout in the state declined from 77 percent in 1960 to 60 percent in 1988. Similarly, in 1976 Minnesota and Wisconsin established election day registration to facilitate participation, but turnout in each was lower in 1988 than when registration requirements made participation more difficult.

While changes in registration procedures might lead us to expect an increased turnout, changes in public attitudes toward the candidates and parties are consistent with the actual trend of a declining turnout. Because of the unique impediments to voting in the American political system, it is particularly important that political attitudes be conducive to overcoming these barriers. A public that increasingly does not care about the political parties or like the candidates for office is one that finds the benefits of voting frequently outweighed by the costs. Thus, even though registration barriers have been reduced since 1960, fewer citizens in the 1980s can be mobilized to overcome them.

The Rise of Interest Groups in Electoral Politics

Nevertheless, the mobilization of diverse social groups into a broad coalition remains crucial to electoral victory in the new American political system. Indeed, this is especially true in the candidate-centered age, as many functions formerly performed by the political parties have been taken on by groups. Social groups increasingly define substantive political goods, serve as objects of symbolic politics, and provide the instruments for political action.

With the decline in the salience of political parties to the electorate since 1960, group identifications have become increasingly important to voters as alternative political reference points. Where once the political function of social groups was primarily to guide party identification, they now take on the more direct role of influencing members' opinions on candidates and issues. Such a transformation was foreseen in 1960 by Angus Campbell and his colleagues as being probable under conditions of party decline. They wrote in *The American Voter*:

> If there were no parties, but only a flux of candidates and issues, it does not follow that there would be no political influence exerted by other membership groups. The psychological economy of the individual demands parties as an organizing principle, and if bereft of this, there might be much more straightforward dependence on other groups for guidance.[17]

As political parties have lost much of their relevance over the past several decades and hence their ability to mobilize the public, interest groups have acquired resources that have made them more powerful than ever before. Direct-mail strategies have enabled groups to organize potential members better, to communicate with them about key issues, and to raise money for campaigns. Furthermore, the expansion of the federal government's scope and power since the Great Society has provided new policy areas (namely distributive benefits and regulatory issues) for groups to mobilize around. Many social groups have therefore gained additional reasons, as well as resources, to engage in group political activity.

If the relationship between various social groups and the political sphere has in fact become closer and more prevalent, it can be hypothesized that the role of group identifications in individual political behavior will also be greater. *The American Voter* postulated, "As proximity between the group and the world of politics becomes clearer, the susceptibility of the individual member to group influence will increase."[18] To test this hypothesis, it is necessary to examine subjective measures of group identification, since objective identifications are not likely to fluctuate much over time.

Beginning in 1972 the NES has attempted to measure just such subjective group identifications. At the end of the postelection interview, respondents are given a list of groups that have been discussed during the interview and are asked to list the groups that they "feel particularly close to—people who are most like you in their ideas and feelings about things." Although this question fails to make a clear reference to political ideas and feelings, the context of the interview is so overwhelmingly political that it seems reasonable to infer that most people answer it with politics in mind.

Table 5–4 displays the percentage of those interviewed in each year who stated that they felt close to each of the various social groups. These data provide substantial support for the hypothesized recent increase in group identification. Of the nine social groups for which the wording is identical from 1972 to 1984, the data show an average increase of twenty percentage points in the proportion of identifiers, ranging from a low of twelve points for southerners to a high of twenty-six points for women. Increases in perceived closeness are also evident for all the social groups that were asked about in only some of the election years. It is clear that the rise in identification with social groups is a major trend in American public opinion, encompassing greater psychological ties to religious, class, occupational, racial, gender, and age groups. This is consistent with the general theory that groups are replacing parties as organizing objects for political life in the United States.

The New Republican Coalition

As the gap between Democrats and Republicans in the electorate has narrowed in recent years, the task of mobilizing a winning coalition of groups has taken on increasing importance. In 1960 the Republican party had such a narrow base

TABLE 5–4
IDENTIFICATION WITH SOCIAL GROUPS, 1972–1984
(percent)

	1972	1976	1980	1984
Middle-class people	52.1	65.8	65.4	77.3
Workingmen	42.1	55.5	—	—
Workingmen and workingwomen	—	—	62.9	72.9
Young people	43.7	48.7	51.4	61.9
Elderly people	40.7	50.8	57.0	59.0
Whites	39.2	46.0	46.5	62.2
Women	33.1	44.6	41.7	58.7
Farmers	26.3	32.9	40.5	46.9
Poor people	25.2	32.6	41.5	46.9
Men	—	—	—	41.5
Businessmen	16.3	19.7	—	—
Businessmen and businesswomen	—	—	28.4	43.5
Southerners	15.0	18.4	19.9	26.8
Blacks	14.6	12.9	18.4	27.6
Protestants	29.9	32.3	—	—
Catholics	18.1	20.1	—	—
Jews	7.4	8.9	—	—
Evangelical groups, such as the Moral Majority	—	—	5.9	16.4
Labor unions	—	—	14.3	18.4
Hispanics	—	—	7.4	16.7

SOURCE: 1972–1984 CPS National Election Studies.

that holding onto it was neither difficult nor sufficient for victory. Indeed, Nixon received 73 percent of his vote from Republican identifiers, as did Reagan in 1984. The difference, as can be seen in the party identification figures shown in table 5–5, is that among the white majority there were far more Republicans after Reagan's election. The Democratic advantage among white voters, which averaged fifteen percentage points from 1952 to 1980, was nonexistent in 1984 and just three points in 1986. Only the bedrock support of the black electorate, which has been evident since the passage of the landmark Civil Rights Act of 1964, has kept the Democratic party from slipping to dead even with the Republicans nationwide.

TABLE 5–5
PARTY IDENTIFICATION, 1952–1986
(percent)

	1952	1956	1960	1964	1968	1972	1976	1980	1984	1986
Whites										
Democrats	56	49	51	54	51	49	47	49	44	45
Independents	6	9	9	8	11	13	15	14	11	12
Republicans	35	39	38	32	37	33	37	36	44	42
Apoliticals	2	2	1	1	1	1	1	2	2	2
Democratic advantage over Republicans	21	10	13	22	14	16	10	13	0	3
Blacks										
Democrats	62	55	51	82	92	75	84	81	77	84
Independents	4	7	16	6	3	12	8	7	11	8
Republicans	13	20	20	8	3	11	5	8	9	7
Apoliticals	17	18	14	4	3	1	1	4	2	2
Democratic advantage over Republicans	49	35	31	74	89	64	79	73	68	77

SOURCE: SRC/CPS National Election Studies.

159

Thus, unlike Bush's chances in 1988, Nixon's in 1960 hinged greatly on how well he could penetrate the large Democratic base. One of his toughest strategic choices was whether to take a conservative line on civil rights to attract white southerners, thereby risking losses among blacks and northeastern liberals. His moderate stance helped him hold on to 29 percent of the black vote but enabled him to win just 50 of the South's 162 votes in the electoral college. In contrast, Bush started with a solid base in the South and quite rightly felt that he had little to lose regarding the black vote. The Republican strategy for presidential elections has therefore changed dramatically from needing to win Democratic and independent votes to simply maintaining their own base.

Of the social groups that strongly supported Republican candidates in the 1980s, three are particularly interesting to analyze in detail: Christian fundamentalists, upper-income voters, and white southerners. Fundamentalists constitute a new force on the conservative Republican scene, upper-income voters the major traditional source of such support, and white southerners the long-time core of the conservative wing of the Democratic party. Thus fundamentalists can be labeled the New Right, upper-income voters the Old Right, and white southerners the Former Democratic Right. Each of these three wings provides a unique asset to the Republicans. The New Right supplies grass-roots enthusiasm, the Old Right money, and the Former Democratic Right a solid regional base. Together they now constitute a potent force on the conservative side of American politics.

The New Right. In 1960 the issue of religion in politics was one of Catholic versus Protestant. Although both Kennedy and Nixon sought in public to minimize their church affiliations, religious denomination was nevertheless strongly related to voters' choices.[19] Since 1960, though, Catholic-Protestant tensions have lessened considerably, and the voting patterns of the two groups have converged.[20]

In the 1980s, however, the emergence of evangelical groups active in politics raised the possibility of renewed religious influence in the political arena. Groups such as the Moral Majority represented the potential development of a

TABLE 5–6

POLITICIZED FUNDAMENTALISM AND THE VOTE, 1980 AND 1984
(percent)

| | Fundamentalism Scale | | | | |
	0	1	2	3	4
White voters					
1980	43.1	29.0	17.8	6.3	3.9
1984	42.5	27.0	16.8	7.9	5.8
Whites voting for Reagan					
1980	50.1	56.0	60.5	74.1	81.8
1984	56.8	64.1	65.4	71.9	91.5

SOURCE: 1980 and 1984 CPS National Election Studies.

new religious cleavage—one that cut across traditional denominations, dividing the electorate according to the extent
of the fundamentalism of their religious beliefs. Christian
fundamentalists can best be defined in surveys as having an
unquestioning view of the Bible and considering themselves
"born again." In the 1984 NES, 43 percent of the white
electorate agreed with the statement that "the Bible is God's
work and all it says is true," and 25 percent stated that they
had undergone a religious experience of being "born again in
their life." Beyond these objective criteria, 30 percent had a
positive feeling-thermometer rating of "evangelical groups
active in politics, such as the Moral Majority," and 15 percent
expressed an identification with these groups.

Combining these four indicators into an index of politicized fundamentalism, table 5–6 displays the distribution of
white voters on the scale and also the percentage at each level
who voted for Reagan.[21] In both 1980 and 1984 the relationship between the fundamentalism index and the vote is linear
and of moderate degree. All told, the proportion of voters
who met all the criteria for politicized fundamentalism was
small. Only 4 percent in 1980 and 6 percent in 1984 considered themselves born again, expressed complete faith in the
Bible, rated evangelical groups active in politics favorably,
and said they felt close to such groups. Their voting, however, was solidly Republican—81.8 percent in 1980 and 91.5
percent in 1984.

What has been surprising to many scholars about this relationship between fundamentalism and voting behavior is not its current existence but rather its dormancy for so long. If politics is concerned with the allocation of values, as David Easton suggests, it is hardly avoidable that one of the key sources of values, that is, religious beliefs, should guide political choices.[22] The answer to this enigma in the past was that fundamentalist views were only weakly related to the basic value conflict between egalitarianism and individualism, on which the New Deal party system was largely based. For example, among whites in 1984 the correlations between fundamentalism and the issues of jobs programs and cutting government services were only .03 and .02, respectively.

It took the influx of new policy issues dealing with matters of morality and traditional family values for fundamentalist attitudes to make their impact. Whereas there is little relationship between the fundamentalism index and economic issues among white voters, on the issues of abortion and school prayer the correlations are quite high (.39 and .34, respectively). New Right Christian ministers and leaders have taken their firmest stands on these issues, arguing that they are related to the moral fiber of the American family.

While vocal evangelical pronouncements on social issues like abortion have increased national media attention to such matters, only a small fraction of the population ever mentions a social issue as one of the most important problems facing the government. Yet those at the extreme end of the fundamentalism scale mention a social issue six times as often, indicating the heightened salience of social issues to these voters. Some 23 percent of these people spontaneously mentioned Reagan's opposition to abortion as a reason for voting for him in 1984, but just 3 percent of the rest of the white electorate did so. Similarly, 13 percent of strong fundamentalists but just 1 percent of other white voters mentioned Reagan's support for school prayer.

In sum, we can isolate a significant subset of the electorate for whom fundamentalist religious beliefs have become politicized. These politicized fundamentalists now form a group of such size and voting cohesion that they have come to play a role in the Republican coalition equivalent to that of blacks in the Democratic party. Indeed, the 1988 *New York Times* exit poll found that white fundamentalist or evangelical Christians made up 9 percent of the electorate and voted 81 percent Republican; blacks constituted 10 percent of the 1988 electorate and voted 86 percent Democratic.

The cohesiveness evident in evangelical political attitudes and voting behavior suggests an effect attributable to shared religious interests and the mobilizing influence of the New Right Christian leadership. Employing television and other means of mass communication, the leaders of this movement have been successful in institutionalizing a new link between religion and politics. With the continued political activity of religious broadcasters such as Robertson and Jerry Falwell, Christian fundamentalists appear destined to form a crucial conservative voting bloc for some time to come, thereby forcing Republican candidates to address the social issue agenda of the New Right.

The Old Right. What will no doubt remain the central element on the Republicans' agenda for the foreseeable future, however, is their support for conservative economic policies. The image of the Republican party as the party of big business and the upper middle class has shaped the feelings of many voters toward it throughout the twentieth century. When the 1960 NES asked which party would be the most likely to leave things to private business to handle, people picked the Republicans over the Democrats by 42 to 15 percent. Similarly, in December 1985 a *New York Times* poll found that 66 percent of the electorate considered the Republicans the party that cared most about the needs and problems of big business; just 17 percent said the Democrats. It should therefore come as no surprise that those who identified with business people were among Reagan's and Bush's strongest supporters. Whereas fundamentalist Christians constitute the New Right, voters of high economic status form the Old Right.

Rather than being diminished as a determinant of the vote by relatively recent social cleavages such as religious fundamentalism, the effect of economic status grew to new heights during the 1980s. Certainly the relationship between

TABLE 5-7
REPUBLICAN VOTERS BY FAMILY INCOME, 1960 AND 1988
(percent)

Family Income	1960	1988
0–10 percentile	54	37
11–30 percentile	56	49
31–50 percentile	45	56
51–70 percentile	49	56
71–95 percentile	49	61
95–100 percentile	76	65

SOURCES: 1960 SRC National Election Study; and 1988 *New York Times* exit poll.

income and the vote was much stronger in 1988 than in 1960, as the vote totals by family income shown in table 5–7 demonstrate. Whereas income lines sharply divided Democrats from Republicans during the New Deal era, by 1956 and 1960 such a pattern had dissolved to the point where income made virtually no difference, the only exception being that people in the top 5 percent in family earnings were notably pro-Republican. It was the Kennedy administration that instituted one of the largest tax cuts in history up to that point. In the 1980s, though, the Republicans clearly became the party of lower taxes, with Reagan's 1981 tax cut, Bush's call for a cut in the capital gains tax, and his famous "Read my lips, no new taxes."

Another key difference accounting for the greater relationship between income and the vote is the increased effect of income tax rates on voters' financial status. As Thomas Edsall documents, "In the early 1960s, the progressivity of the system—sharply higher rates for those with higher incomes—was concentrated almost entirely in the top 5 percent of the population."[23] With the rapid inflation of the 1970s and the resulting bracket creep, a rise in income triggered a substantial rise in tax rates for the majority of Americans. Thus voters at the middle as well as the top of the income ladder came to pay close attention to the economic policies of the candidates and to relate their own financial status to governmental policies. In both 1988 and 1960, for example, approximately 40 percent of the population said they were better off financially than a year ago, but 70 percent of this group voted for Bush in 1988 and just 60 percent for Nixon in 1960.

Thus, just as the New Right was coming onto the political scene, the Old Right was being reinforced, and its key issues were being expanded so as to affect a greater percentage of voters. Whereas the former group has been attracted to the Republicans on the basis of social issues, the latter have been most influenced by the party's handling of the economy. It is worth noting, however, that the Old Right's support for conservative policies is substantially less than the New Right's, income typically being less related to policy positions than religious fundamentalism. Only 52 percent of those in the top 10 percent of family income labeled themselves conservatives, compared with 74 percent of strong fundamentalists. The only issues on which income is more highly correlated with policy stands than fundamentalism are economic questions such as government services and jobs programs.

Family income is indeed related to stands on social issues, but on these topics high income is associated with more liberal rather than more conservative views. Thus the New and the Old Right are at odds with each other on the issues of abortion, an equal role for women, and school prayer. Should these questions become more generally salient in electoral politics, Republican candidates will find the task of holding the two groups together extremely difficult.

The Former Democratic Right. The delicate job of holding a diverse coalition together has historically been much more of a problem for the Democrats than for the Republicans. Ever since the beginning of the New Deal, the Democratic party has been split regionally between its northern and southern wings. Only by sidestepping the most divisive issue of all, race, could it hold the coalition together. In 1948, however, the Democratic platform on civil rights seriously called into question whether the party could be held together on this basis. The defection of many southern Democrats to Strom Thurmond's States' Rights ticket demonstrated that the

South would not vote so solidly Democratic given the right issue appeal.

As Converse wrote in the early 1960s, "It has long been obvious against the backdrop of national politics that the historical link between the South and the Democratic Party has become quite implausible from an ideological point of view."[24] Conservative southerners, however, had insufficient incentives to deviate from their century-long commitment to the Democratic party as long as the Republicans remained so visibly tied to northeastern business interests and differed little from the Democrats on civil rights and the fight against communism.

All this began to change with the passage of the Civil Rights Act in 1964 and the nomination of Goldwater. Goldwater was a new kind of national Republican leader, one more in tune with southern and western concerns about governmental interference from Washington as well as southerners' more hawkish views on foreign policy. The polarization between Goldwater and Johnson on civil rights was a rare case in American politics where the differences were crystal clear on an issue of great importance. Three-quarters of the people interviewed in the 1964 NES said they had heard that the Congress had passed a civil rights bill in that year. Of those who were aware of the bill, 96 percent knew that President Johnson had favored its passage, and 84 percent knew that Goldwater had opposed it. The result was that, while the Goldwater candidacy was a debacle for the Republicans nationwide, he managed to carry a row of five states from South Carolina to Louisiana, none of which had voted Republican since Reconstruction.

Learning from the Goldwater experience, Nixon adopted the so-called southern strategy in 1968. The crux of Nixon's bargain with Thurmond was that, if elected president, he would find a way to ease the federal pressures forcing school desegregation—or any other aspect of civil rights. After making good on this promise, in 1972 Nixon succeeded in pushing the Republican percentage of the southern vote above the national average for the first time in history. Nevertheless, the unusual relationship between ideology and party in the South was slow to change. Conservative Democrats continued to outnumber conservative Republicans in the South throughout the 1970s. In 1972, for example, 63 percent of all conservatives living outside the South identified as Republicans compared with just 44 percent of conservatives inside the South.[25]

The presence of the Georgian Carter on the Democratic ticket helped return the South to above-average Democratic support in 1976 and 1980. With Carter gone from the scene in 1984 and the first unabashedly conservative Republican president in office, the South voted 4 percent more Republican than the national average in both 1984 and 1988. Whereas white southerners split their vote evenly in 1960 between Kennedy and Nixon, in 1988 they went for Bush over Dukakis by 67 to 32 percent, according to the *New York Times* exit poll.

Most important, it is now clear that a major transformation has taken place in the partisanship of southern whites. In 1988 survey data could be found for the first time that clearly showed the predominance of Republicans over Democrats among white southerners. The NES Super Tuesday survey, for example, found that the Republicans and Republican leaners outnumbered Democrats and Democratic leaners by 51 to 41 percent in the white south.[26] Among those under thirty years of age, the Republican edge was an astounding twenty-nine percentage points in 1988. That those under thirty are by far the most Republican while those over sixty-five are the most pro-Democratic should benefit the Republican party for a generation to come, as population replacement takes its toll.

For the Republicans to capitalize on this new regional base, a somewhat different policy emphasis will be required from a straightforward appeal to either the New or the Old Right. While fundamentalists are especially conservative on social policies and higher-income voters on economic issues, the white South is most notably conservative on aid to minorities and foreign policy. There is little doubt that civil rights questions were the straw that broke the back of the once-solid Democratic South. As Johnson remarked to an aide after the 1964 act was passed, "I think we just delivered the South to the Republican Party for a long time to come."[27] Since the passage of the civil rights legislation of the 1960s, however, southern and nonsouthern views on such questions have gradually converged.[28] The decline of sectional differences on this central question has proceeded largely through the nationalization of the attitudes of white southerners.

As regional differences continue to narrow on racial issues, taking hawkish stands on military and foreign affairs appears to be the best basis on which Republicans can mobilize conservative sentiment in the white South. Since 1960 the parties have traded places on military spending and national defense in a way that has been to the advantage of Republicans in the South. In 1960 it was Kennedy who warned of a missile gap and Eisenhower who cautioned against the danger of the military-industrial complex, and in 1964 Johnson boasted in his nomination acceptance speech that the Democrats had "carried out the greatest peacetime buildup of national strength of any nation at any time in the history of the world." The Democratic party of McGovern, Mondale, and Dukakis, however, turned this issue into a liability in the South when faced with the peace-through-strength appeals of Presidents Nixon and Reagan.

Holding the Three-headed Coalition Together. In sum, since 1960 the Republicans have substantially expanded the scope of their social group support. Yet the diversity of conservative policy interests may cause some internal friction and constrain the Republicans' flexibility in governing. The New and the Old Right are clearly at odds with each other on social issues such as abortion, school prayer, and equal rights for women. When economic times are not particularly favorable toward the Republicans, the social issue agenda of fundamentalist Christians may prove to be a significant source of alienation to upper-income voters. And should the budget situation worsen, the Republicans will find themselves with little maneuvering room. The power of the Old Right has made the prospect of a tax increase untenable for any Republican president, and the hawkish white South will make it difficult to cut into defense spending.

In short, only a candidate who is unequivocally conservative on economic, social, and military policies will be able to hold this coalition together effectively. Bush succeeded in this task by (1) giving pledges against new taxes for the Old Right, (2) labeling Dukakis a liberal and choosing Dan Quayle as ambassador to the New Right, and (3) deftly playing up the issues of patriotism and national defense to win the support of southern whites.[29] One can only marvel at the change from 1960, when a tax cut was advocated by the Democrats, ideological labels were scarcely ever referred to, and the South was still a Democratic bastion.

A More Conservative Electorate?

While the parties are now more ideologically polarized than they were in 1960, it does not necessarily follow that the Republican victories of the 1980s can be traced to the existence of a more conservative electorate. That governmental policies have shifted to the right as a result of Republican successes in presidential elections is beyond doubt, but the evidence for a movement toward conservatism amongst the voters is almost nil. The key assumption in spatial models of voting is that voters cast their ballots for the candidate who is closest to them in ideology. Yet in the candidate-centered age presidents get far more of both the credit and the blame for the country's condition than they did previously. With this increased focus on short-term results, when ideological preferences conflict with performance assessments, the latter are more likely to take precedence in voting decisions. Indeed a key to understanding the elections of the 1980s is to recognize that a large percentage of voters had contradictory attitudes toward Reagan and Bush on policy versus performance criteria. All too often political observers and commentators assume that people have relatively consistent attitudes and are therefore tempted to draw the erroneous inference that any major shift in voting behavior must have been the result of a shift in the public's ideological preferences.

The proportion of self-identified conservatives in the 1980s increased only slightly, and feelings toward liberals and conservatives remained virtually unchanged (table 5–8). Among the 60 to 70 percent who had thought enough about the question of ideology to place themselves on the scale, conservatives increased from 36.8 to 44.1 percent between

TABLE 5–8
TRENDS IN POLITICAL IDEOLOGY, 1972–1986
(percent)

Self-Placement Scale	1972	1976	1980	1984	1986
Strong conservative	16.0	19.7	23.1	20.8	19.3
Weak conservative	20.8	18.5	21.0	20.1	20.1
Moderate	37.4	37.7	30.6	33.4	36.9
Weak liberal	13.7	12.0	13.5	12.9	14.2
Strong liberal	12.1	12.1	11.8	12.7	9.4
Conservative plurality	11.0	14.1	18.8	15.3	15.8

Mean Feeling-Thermometer Ratings	1964	1968	1972	1976	1980	1984	1986
Conservatives	56.8	56.9	61.4	58.9	62.7	59.9	58.6
Liberals	53.4	51.1	53.8	52.3	51.7	55.9	53.4
Mean conservative edge	3.4	5.8	7.6	6.6	11.0	4.0	5.2

SOURCE: 1964–1986 SRC/CPS National Election Studies.

1972 and 1980. Yet most of this change came from a decrease in the moderate category and not from any substantial decline in the number of self-identified liberals. Most important, both the 1984 and the 1986 data show a slippage of over three percentage points in the conservatives' gains and continuing stability in the size of the liberal bloc. Finally, the General Social Survey—using a nearly identical question—found that the gap between conservatives and liberals had closed from twelve to seven percentage points between 1984 and 1988.

Another method of measuring ideological attitudes is through voters' feeling-thermometer ratings of liberals and conservatives, which were first introduced into the NES in 1964. Even as Goldwater was being defeated by a wide margin, ratings of conservatives were nevertheless more positive than those of liberals. As the only major democratic country without a significant left-wing Socialist party, the United States has long had a tradition of favoring the conservative label, and the 1964 data are an excellent indication of this. Given that 1964 is the least likely year for feelings toward conservatives to be high, we would expect any change since then to be in a rightward direction. This is indeed the case, with the mean rating of conservatives rising from the 1964 low of 56.8 to 62.7 in 1980. As on the self-placement scale, liberal attitudes have been more constant, declining only 1.7 points over the same period. Yet also matching the pattern of the ideology scale is the noticeable decline in conservative preferences after 1980. The mean rating of liberals reached a new high in 1984, and the average respondent in that year rated conservatives only four points higher than liberals. In sum, except for a small, short-lived surge in favor of conservatism in 1980, there is little support for the thesis of fundamental ideological change. The picture is far more one of stability than change on liberal-conservative attitudes among the electorate.

Similarly, examining the public's stance on specific issues over time does little to confirm the notion of a rightward swing in public opinion.[30] There have been small changes in both liberal and conservative directions, the only indication of a mandate for Reagan occurring in 1980 when a rapid rise in public support for defense spending took place. While the data on ideology indicate consistently higher support for the conservative label, more voters felt closer to Mondale's issue positions than to Reagan's on many of the crucial policy questions of 1984. By fairly substantial margins those with opinions disagreed with Reagan's willingness to commit military help to Central America and his desire to increase defense spending further. By somewhat smaller margins people saw Reagan as wanting to cut government services too deeply, not providing enough government aid to minorities and women, and being too tough with the Soviet Union.[31]

Political Polarization in the Candidate-centered Age

In 1960 a frequently voiced concern among students of American elections was the lack of a sufficient choice for the voting public. This was seen as symptomatic of the absence of "responsible party government." The electorate was faced with a choice between two centrists, and the most discussed issues of the 1960 campaign were Kennedy's Catholicism and his youth, whether there was a missile gap (there was not), and what to do about the tiny islands of Quemoy and Matsu. Although subsequent history demonstrated profound policy differences between Kennedy and Nixon, few voters could have inferred them from the 1960 election campaign.

As Anthony Downs wrote in 1957, political parties have a rational incentive to converge toward the center when public opinion is distributed in a unimodal fashion—as in the United States. To the degree that parties succeed in placing their candidates at the optimal position to appeal to the most voters, they thus obscure the issues. As Downs stated, "Apparently the more rational political parties are, the less rational voters must be."[32] The 1960 election represents the last gasp of the old era, when party leaders had the power to ensure such elite rationality.

As control of the nomination process has devolved from the party leaders to issue activists in the primaries and caucuses, centrist candidates have come to be the exception rather than the rule. As Byron Shafer notes, nomination activists are especially likely to "lean away from the political center due to their lack of concern for a geographically based electorate" and their "dedication to a particular group or cause as their principal motive for participation."[33] Thus it has been the parties, rather than voters, that have acted contrary to Downs's notions of rationality in many elections since 1960. By nominating candidates substantially outside the mainstream, both Democrats and Republicans have offered clear choices in spite of the electoral risks.

The 1988 campaign offers every reason to anticipate that the pattern of offering the voters a choice rather than an echo will continue. While the congressional delegations of both parties are still fairly diverse, each party's would-be presidential candidates in 1988 showed little divergence of views. Howard Baker was the only Republican who even considered running who was not firmly associated with conservative causes. On the Democratic side, the creation of a southern regional primary offered an additional incentive for a conservative to enter the presidential race. Nevertheless, such a notable conservative as Senator Sam Nunn stayed on the sidelines, leaving only the moderate Albert Gore to represent the Democratic party's nonliberal faction. The result was that for the second election in a row the electorate was presented with a fairly clear choice between a liberal and a conservative—something that would have seemed inconceivable three decades ago.

In sum, in recent elections advocates of responsible party government have finally got the clear choice and decisiveness of action that they have long desired. Yet many of the worst fears of opponents of responsible party government have been realized as well. These critics have generally preferred the more consensus-oriented, pluralistic model of democracy that was practiced in 1960. A key point in this line of argument is that, given the diverse and multifaceted American political culture, precipitous change should not be based on a single choice between ideological extremes.

With the decline of parties, attention has increasingly been focused on candidate-centered issues. Such issues can be broadly categorized as policy decisions (that is, the specific actions a candidate will take or has taken) or performance judgments (that is, the results expected or produced). The former may polarize the electorate more than ever around assessments of candidates, but the latter are likely to take precedence in voting decisions. We are therefore left with the seeming paradox that, although the elections of the 1980s produced profound ideological changes in government policy, voting behavior was not very ideologically determined. Whereas the increasing politicization of group affiliations has fostered a more conflict-ridden and polarized electoral process, the prominence of economic considerations led the elections of the 1980s to be decided on consensual performance factors.

It could of course be argued that governmental outputs have always taken precedence in voting behavior. The key difference in the candidate-centered age is that the likelihood that policy factors and performance factors will push the electorate in opposite directions is far greater. In the past, policy and performance were tied together in the public's mind through the central role of partisanship in political behavior. Some may initially have chosen their party on the basis of their upbringing, others on its performance during a

173

crucial period of history such as the depression, and some no doubt on key long-term policy issues such as civil rights. Yet, whatever the explanation, partisanship provided the psychological guidance necessary to interpret the political world in a consistent fashion. The conflict between policy and performance evaluations experienced by many voters during the 1980s was unlikely to occur at a time when partisanship greatly influenced how people felt about both.

Such a conflict was therefore probably inconceivable to members of the Committee on Political Parties of the American Political Science Association, which in 1950 advocated a more responsible two-party system. It is thus crucial to note that, although proponents of responsible party government got the kind of programmatic choice and decisive action they had always sought during the 1980s, they did not get it in the kind of partisan-dominated environment they had envisioned. The responsible party model can hardly work in an atmosphere in which individual candidates dominate the political scene, with political parties struggling to maintain a modest degree of relevance amid rampant split-ticket voting.

Without a solid base of continuing partisan support, it is not surprising to find the secular decline in presidential candidates' popularity shown in figure 5–1. The more the public has come to be polarized by the candidates rather than by the parties, the lower its opinion of the candidates has fallen. Thus presidents in the new American political system can expect an environment increasingly lacking in dependable partisan support within both the Congress and the public at large. Greater visibility and freedom of action may well, paradoxically, yield less power for the president and less effective government.

6
Broadcasting, Narrowcasting, and Politics

Austin Ranney

The mass communications media play a critical role in all modern democratic political systems but nowhere more than in the United States. It could hardly be otherwise for since the late 1960s the media, more than any other agency, have filled the vacuum left by the steady erosion of the mediating institutions that once bridged the gap between the understandings and desires of mass publics and the actions of government.[1]

Other chapters of this book detail many of the causes, manifestations, and consequences of this erosion, but the central role of the mass media is especially apparent in what has happened to the presidential selection process. Before 1968 the presidential candidates of both major political parties were typically chosen by coalitions of national, state, and local party leaders cobbled together at, or just before, the national nominating conventions. But the many changes in party rules and state laws since 1968 have effectively transferred the power to choose presidential candidates from party leaders to ordinary citizens voting in presidential primaries (a total of 35 million participated in the selection of Republican George Bush and Democrat Michael Dukakis in 1988).[2]

Since those citizens no longer leave the screening of aspirants to party leaders, and since only a fraction of them

I am grateful to Norman J. Ornstein and Percy H. Tannenbaum for their comments on an early draft of this chapter. They do not, of course, agree with everything it says.

can possibly have any firsthand knowledge of the aspirants' ideas, records, and personal qualities, they have to make their choices on the basis of secondhand information and images provided almost entirely by the mass media.[3]

There was a time when most social scientists believed that the political information and images dispensed by the mass media were filtered to most members of the general public indirectly through the mediation of opinion leaders in a process known as the two-step flow of communications.[4] In step 1 the political content of the mass media was absorbed by only a handful of citizens especially interested in politics. In step 2 these opinion leaders passed on their versions of the media's information and images to their associates in such primary groups as families, work associates, and friendship circles. Accordingly, most students of political behavior believed that while the messages from the mass media no doubt affected most people's preferences and activity somewhat, they were far less influential than messages from their parents, spouses, friends, and workmates.[5]

Since the 1970s, however, scholars of communications have been impressed by the fact that most Americans now spend far more time watching television than discussing politics with other people, and as a result most people get their political information and images directly from the mass media, particularly television, rather than through mediation by other people.[6] And scholars of American politics have come to agree that the mass communications media, especially broadcast television, are one of the most important forces (many would say the most important force) shaping the American political system today.

In 1983 I ventured a commentary on the special nature of mass communications in the United States and their central role in changing the political system so much since the advent of television.[7] For the 1990s, however, even that analysis is obsolete in several respects: the mass communications media are changing in ways that are altering the nature of their impact on the political system. In this chapter, accordingly, I propose (1) to outline the role of the media in the present network era; (2) to describe the emergence of a new communications system in the late 1980s, leading to what might be called the era of narrowcasting; and (3) to speculate about the impact of the new communications structure on the American political system.

Politics in the Network Era, c. 1960–c. 1990

The Structure of Mass Communications. Media analysts generally say that the television age began in the United States in the late 1940s and has shaped every aspect of American society since the early 1960s. There are indications that the period, more accurately labeled the network era, is now coming to an end as the nation moves into the narrowcasting era. The two eras have some similarities: being launched by basic changes in communications technology, with each technology creating a particular kind of mass communications system and each system distinctly affecting the political system. Let us consider first the main features of the age that is passing.

The dominance of the networks. The network era was based on a technology in which more than a thousand television stations throughout the nation literally broadcast signals that were plucked out of the air and converted into pictures and sound by receivers in people's homes. Each station was licensed by the Federal Communications Commission (FCC); each licensee was assigned a particular channel (frequency band) for transmitting its signals; the political contents of each licensee's programs were regulated by rules laid down by Congress and the FCC; each license had to be renewed every five years; and nonrenewal was the main sanction enforcing the rules governing the political contents of programs (though in fact only a handful of licenses were not renewed).

Radio broadcasting operated under the same legal conditions, but television plays so much greater a role in the American political system that I concentrate on it in this chapter.

Television broadcasting was dominated by privately owned and operated stations: in 1988, 968 such stations were licensed, compared to 303 publicly owned stations.[8] The commercial stations charged their viewers no fees and received no revenues from the licensing of receivers. Broadcasters' incomes came almost entirely from the sale of air time to businesses for broadcasting advertisements. The stations attracted audiences to watch their programs and sold access to those audiences to advertisers. Particular programs were frequently targeted at particular demographic groups inclined to purchase particular products: sports programs, for example, were aimed mainly at men and were especially attractive to advertisers of beer and automobiles; daytime soap operas were aimed mainly at housewives and drew many advertisements for detergents and cosmetics. Especially in the prime-time hours (week nights and Sunday nights from 8 P.M. to 11 P.M.) the larger the audiences were, the higher the rates that advertisers were willing to pay. Accordingly, each broadcaster aimed at attracting and holding the largest possible audience; the periodic ratings of the audience sizes for various programs issued by the A. C. Nielsen and Arbitron audience-survey organizations largely determined which programs survived and which were dropped.

Developing the kind of programs that attracted and held large audiences was both expensive and chancy, and most commercial station owners decided that, rather than going it alone, they would affiliate with one of the three national commercial networks: the American Broadcasting Companies (ABC), the Columbia Broadcasting System (CBS), or the National Broadcasting Company (NBC). (There were two other networks, Fox and Westinghouse, but in 1984 more than 83 percent of all commercial television stations were affiliated with one or another of the three major networks.) Each affiliate negotiated a contract with the network (usually a two-year, renewable contract) in which it agreed to air network programs (the affiliate could, however, choose not to air particular network programs); the network paid the affiliate a fee for each network program it broadcast; and in return the network received the money advertisers paid for airing their commercials while network programs were broadcast.

The principal feature, then, of the period from the late 1940s to the mid-1980s was the overwhelming dominance of the three major commercial networks. More than 80 percent of the commercial stations affiliated with them; network programs regularly attracted more than 90 percent of viewers. Thus, it seems appropriate to label the period the network age rather than the television age.[9] In the 1990s, television remains as important as ever, but the networks are losing their dominance.

Political programming and the "inadvertent audience." Throughout the network era, all television broadcasters were required by an FCC regulation known as the fairness doctrine to "devote a reasonable percentage of . . . broadcast time to the coverage of public issues" even though such programs might be unprofitable for the broadcaster.[10] The FCC never spelled out precisely what percentage was reasonable, but it was generally understood that at least 10 percent of a licensee's programs had to be nonentertainment and at least 5 percent had to be informational.[11]

Broadcasters were convinced that large portions of their mass audiences were bored by politics and would tune out if their favorite situation comedies and police shows were pre-empted by coverage of political events such as national nominating conventions or congressional committee hearings.[12] Indeed, some analysts believe that most broadcasters would have aired little or no nonentertainment programming if it had not been for the FCC requirement.[13] This belief is reinforced by the fact that cable stations have no such obligation: while a few present a great many public affairs programs, most present none at all.

Since over-the-air broadcasters were forced to meet the requirement, however, most did so mainly by regular local and national news programs (only a handful of political documentaries were broadcast, and almost all lost money). No radio or television station has ever lost its license for airing too few public affairs programs. Since they all have conformed to the informal "ten and five" rule, it appears that the mere possibility of losing their highly lucrative licenses (some say that owning such a license is like owning a license to print money) has been enough to make them observe the rule.

Most people who watched the network newscasts constituted what Michael J. Robinson aptly calls an "inadvertent audience" for political information.[14] That is, most viewers did not actively seek political information and tune in programs they knew would provide it. Rather, they watched television for entertainment and relaxation and occasionally happened to be watching television (usually news programs) when political information was broadcast in a mix with information about weather, sports, fires, floods, entertainment personalities, and the like. Ordinary viewers, however, did not ignore or reject the political information they happened upon—quite the contrary.

Television as most people's main and most trusted source of political information. Surveys of Americans' television-viewing habits in the network era consistently showed that about half of the viewers said they watched some part of a national network newscast every day, and another 30 percent said they watched at least a few times a week.[15] Moreover, most people said that television was their main source of information about world events and that they trusted the accuracy of the information from television more than from any other source (table 6–1).

Political and structural bias in network news. The fact that network news broadcasts have been the most important and also the most trusted source of political information for most people has led many politicians and scholars to ask whether those broadcasts were and are biased. A number of commentators have charged the networks with political bias, that is, with deliberately slanting political news so as to promote the causes of particular candidates, parties, or ideologies. Some, notably former vice president Spiro T. Agnew, Edith Efron, Joseph Keeley, and Reed Irvine and his Accuracy in Media organization, have denounced the networks for slanting the news to favor Democrats over Republicans and liberal and radical causes over conservative ones. Others, notably Robert Cirino, David Altheide, Nicholas Johnson, and Lance Bennett, have charged that newscasts are tilted to defend the privileges of the broadcasters' capitalist bosses.[16]

I concur, however, with many scholars that while the networks' presentation of political information has indeed been biased, that bias has been structural rather than politi-

TABLE 6–1

Television as a Source of Information

"I'd like to ask you where you usually get most of your news about what's going on in the world today—from the newspapers or radio or television or magazines or talking to people or where?"

Source of Most News	Percentage[a]
Television	64
Newspapers	40
Radio	14
Magazines	4
People	4

"If you got conflicting or different reports of the same news story from radio, television, the magazines, and the newspapers, which of the four versions would you be most inclined to believe?"

Most Believable	Percentage[b]
Television	53
Newspapers	24
Radio	8
Magazines	7
Don't know, no answer	8

a. More than one answer permitted.
b. Only one answer permitted.
SOURCE: Burns W. Roper, "Public Attitudes toward Television and Other Media in a Time of Change" (New York: Television Information Office, 1984).

cal. That is, "it arises not so much from the newscasters' desire to promote particular causes as from some special constraints on newscasting."[17]

The principal constraints, according to this view, have been four:

• *Economic.* The broadcasters' vital need to attract and keep large audiences of people mostly bored with politics has prompted them to make political news entertaining by keeping it short, visual, and focused on conflict.
• *Time.* The networks' nightly newscasts have had only twenty-two minutes (thirty minutes of total air time minus

eight minutes of commercials) in which to cover news of all kinds; hence, as longtime CBS news anchor Walter Cronkite put it, they could offer only a headline service.

• *Legal.* The manner in which the networks present political information has been governed by a number of laws and FCC regulations.

• *Journalistic.* Most American television newspeople, like most of their colleagues in the print media, believe that they have a professional obligation to act as the people's watchdogs. It is their special duty as journalists to ferret out what people in high places are really doing and to disclose fully their misdeeds. The journalist's duty, they avow, is not to make it easier for the government to carry out its policies but to keep the people fully informed about what government is doing—especially what it is doing wrong. Hence bad news is more important and gets more coverage than good news. Good news, after all, requires no action and serves only to make citizens complacent, but bad news provides the information and stimulus that citizens need to want to make things better.

As a result of these constraints, it is argued, the networks have portrayed the political world quite differently from the way most political scientists see it. According to Paul Weaver, the networks have presented politics as

> essentially a game played by individual politicians for personal advancement, gain, or power. The game is a competitive one, and the players' principal activities are those of calculating and pursuing strategies designed to defeat competitors and to achieve their goals (usually election to public office).[18]

Thus the networks have focused mainly on personal conflict and competition among politicians. They have presented more information about which politicians are winning and which are losing than about the complexities and merits of their behavior in office or about their positions on issues. Their newscasters have been tough on front runners and easy on underdogs. They have glorified "the people" and taken a dim view of all political organizations, especially large and powerful organizations such as political parties, lobbies, and political action committees. The newscasters have suggested that any secret negotiation or agreement is probably a cover-up of some transaction discreditable to the politicians who made it. And they have presented unflattering portraits of all politicians, especially all powerful and successful politicians, whether they are Democrats or Republicans, liberals or conservatives.

Whether the bias of network television has been political or structural, the networks' position has been regarded as so special and their power so great that the political content of their programs has been subject to far greater government regulation than the contents of newspaper stories, magazine articles, or books.

The "scarcity doctrine" and government regulation of television. What newspapers, books, magazines, and pamphlets say about politics in the United States is protected from government regulation by the stipulation in the Constitution's First Amendment that "Congress [and, by judicial extension, other national, state, and local government agencies] shall make no law abridging the freedom of the press." By judicial interpretation the only restrictions on the print media that are not prohibited by the First Amendment are the few imposed by laws against libel, slander, and obscenity.

Almost from their beginnings, however, radio and television have been in a different position. The political content of their programs is regulated by Congress in the Federal Communications Act of 1934 and its subsequent amendments and by a series of administrative rules imposed by the FCC as part of the conditions broadcasters must observe to qualify for renewal of their licenses.

The Supreme Court has consistently upheld the constitutionality of these special restrictions. The main jurisprudential basis for doing so has been the scarcity doctrine: while there is no limit (other than economic) on the number of newspapers and books that can be published, it is impossible for two broadcasting stations to broadcast signals on the same frequency at the same time without jamming each other. Accordingly, an extensive system of public broadcasting is clearly in the public interest, and such a system is possible only if the government allocates particular frequencies to particular broadcasters. Thus broadcasting is a kind of public resource, analogous to the national park system or navigable rivers. And this status not only allows but requires the government to allocate the frequencies and to set standards for their use that promote "the public convenience, interest, or necessity."[19]

During most of the network era, the FCC, acting on the basis of the scarcity doctrine and with the Supreme Court's full approval,[20] imposed four main rules governing the political content of radio and television programs. (Three of the four rules remain in force, but the fairness doctrine was rescinded, perhaps permanently, in 1987.)

1. *The fairness doctrine.* The fairness doctrine first emerged in a series of FCC rulings in the late 1940s; the commission's power to make such rules was later confirmed by Congress in several 1959 amendments to section 315(a) of the Federal Communications Act. The first part of the fairness doctrine requires all broadcast television stations to devote "a reasonable percentage" of their air time to the presentation of news and programs dealing with public issues of interest. The second part requires that in presenting such programs the broadcasters must "operate in the public interest and . . . afford reasonable opportunity for the discussion of conflicting views on issues of public importance." A voluminous and complex body of administrative law has grown up over the interpretation and application of the doctrine's second part; on the whole broadcasters have satisfied the FCC by portraying political issues as conflicts between a pro side and an anti side and presenting the statements of at least one advocate for each side. As Steven J. Simmons points out:

> Although the [FCC] sensibly declared in its 1974 *Fairness Report* that for many issues a variety of contrasting viewpoints may need broadcast coverage, it has never found a licensee unreasonable for presenting only two viewpoints. In fact, the Commission has reinforced the "two viewpoint" perspective by frequently referring to the licensee's obliga-

tion to present "both" sides of issues instead of "contrasting sides."[21]

Thus, the view of political conflict that emerges from network news programs is that every issue has two, and usually only two, sides—a proposition that would not command the universal agreement of epistemologists but seems to satisfy the FCC, which is the broadcasters' main concern.

2. *The personal attack rule.* This rule provides that if, during a program presenting views on a controversial issue of public importance, an attack is made on the honesty, integrity, morality, or other personal qualities of an identified individual or group, the station must, within a reasonable time, notify the individual or group concerned of the attack and offer a reasonable opportunity to use the station's facilities to reply. The rule does not apply, however, to attacks on foreign individuals or groups, to personal attacks made by legally qualified candidates for elective offices or their representatives, or to bona fide coverage of political matters in newscasts, interviews, or on-the-spot broadcasts of political events.

3. *The equal opportunities rule.* Section 315(a) of the Federal Communications Act stipulates:

> If any licensee shall permit any person who is a legally qualified candidate for any public office to use a broadcasting station, he shall afford equal opportunities to all other such candidates for that office in the use of such broadcasting station.

Thus, if broadcasters give free candidate-controlled air time to a candidate, they must give equal free time to all other candidates for that office. If they sell time for political advertisements to a candidate, they must sell comparable time at the same rates to all other candidates who wish to buy. All programs, such as regular newscasts and interviews with candidates, in which the broadcasters and not the candidates control the programs' contents, are exempt from the equal opportunities rule, however.

4. *The reasonable access rule.* It might appear that a broadcaster could avoid the constraints of section 315(a) simply by refusing to air advertising by political candidates, but section

185

312(a) of the act stipulates that one of the grounds on which the FCC can deny a station's application for renewal of its license is "willful or repeated failure to allow reasonable access to or to permit purchase of reasonable amounts of time for the use of a broadcasting station by a legally qualified candidate for Federal elective office on behalf of his candidacy." This has been interpreted to mean not that stations must sell advertising time to political candidates whether they want to or not but that if they do not air political ads, they must fulfill their access obligations by presenting their own debate or discussion programs in which all candidates are invited to participate on an equal basis.[22]

In the network era, then, the networks' power over the presentation of politics was significantly restricted by the legal constraints on how they covered politics. What was the impact of the network-dominated mass media on the American way of politics? In what ways is that impact likely to change now that the networks no longer dominate mass communications?

The Impact of the Network Era on the Political System. The first version of *The New American Political System* considered many ways in which American political processes and institutions had changed from the election of John F. Kennedy in 1960 to the late 1970s. In the concluding chapter, the editor Anthony King summed up the changes thus:

> [In the textbooks of the 1950s] there is one word that keeps recurring in all kinds of different contexts. That word is "coalition." American politics is almost universally seen as the politics of coalition building. . . . Coalitions presuppose blocks—or, more precisely, blocs. Yet, if one message emerges from the pages of this book, it is that fewer and fewer collective blocs are to be found in the American polity. . . . American politicians . . . are no longer, or at least not very often, in the business of building coalitions. The materials out of which coalitions might be built simply do not exist. Building coalitions in the United States today is like trying to build coalitions out of sand. It cannot be done.[23]

King's analysis remains an accurate account of the basic changes in the American political system since 1960. And it calls to mind an interesting juxtaposition: most students of mass communications believe that two events marked the beginning of the network era. The first was the series of nationally televised presidential campaign debates between Richard Nixon and John Kennedy in 1960; the second was the 1963 increase in the air time of all three networks' nightly national newscasts from fifteen to thirty minutes.[24] Thus, the fragmentation of politics that King points to took place when network television came to dominate the presentation of political information and images. The synchronism of the two developments strongly suggests that they were connected.

I have set forth elsewhere my impressions of what that connection was.[25] Since this chapter is concerned more with the present and future than the past, I will review the connection briefly and summarily. While network television was not the only factor producing the fragmentation of which King wrote, it certainly hastened and intensified it in at least the following four ways:

1. The networks' coverage of politics weakened most of the traditional coalition-building agencies, especially the political parties. Whatever the political desires of its producers may be, television is at its best picturing the concrete and at its worst explaining the abstract. Political leaders are much more telegenic as tangible, individual faces, voices, and personalities than as members of abstractions such as political organizations or coalitions. In portraying politics, network television therefore focuses naturally on individual politicians, on the way they look and sound when they are doing and saying things. Political parties, however, are abstractions; they consist of certain kinds of similar behavior abstracted from the total of unique behaviors of many individuals. Accordingly, network newscasts were irresistibly drawn toward portraying parties either as individual leaders saying things or as mobs of party followers cheering at a rally or hordes of delegates milling about on a convention floor.

This tendency was reinforced by the well-documented belief of network news producers that their viewers wanted to see "horse race" coverage of politics, by their celebration of participatory mass politics as manifested in presidential primaries, and by their suspicion of secret meetings and private deals as the supposed essence of caucuses and brokered conventions.

Moreover, the post-1968 party reforms transferred the selection of presidential candidates from dozens of party leaders to thousands of activists voting in caucuses and conventions and to millions of voters voting in presidential primaries. All but a handful of the new "selectorate" got most or all of their information about the aspirants from the mass media, especially network television. Horse race journalism required the networks to focus their coverage on aspirants who had a chance of winning and to declare the winners and losers (that is, the candidates who had done better and worse than expected) in each primary. In deciding which aspirants to cover and which to ignore, and in building momentum for the winners they declared and its reverse for the losers they declared, the network newscasters effectively took over the candidate-screening function that had been performed by party leaders.[26] Thus, the networks became important participants in, as well as reporters of, the selection of presidential candidates—and therefore of presidents.

2. The networks' focus on individuals rather than parties also encouraged ticket splitting. For generations high school civics instructors have taught that the good citizen votes for the best candidate for each office regardless of party labels, but ticket splitting has increased significantly only in the network age. Norman H. Nie, Sidney Verba, and John R. Petrocik estimate that in the 1960 presidential election, just at the beginning of the network age, only about 35 percent of the voters split their tickets and voted for Democrats for some offices and Republicans for others. The figure rose to 57 percent in 1964, 66 percent in 1968, and 67 percent in 1976. It remained at about that level in 1980, 1984, and 1988 and seems to have become a permanent feature of American politics.[27]

3. Network television intensified the fragmentation of power in Congress. As Norman J. Ornstein points out, in the 1950s Congress was a closed system in which the rewards

and punishments for individual members of both chambers were provided, first, by their constituents and, second, by their party leaders. In House Speaker Sam Rayburn's famous words, "To get along you have to go along"—that is, success in a congressional career was built by serving on important committees and rising to positions of official leadership; ambitious young members could achieve such success only by convincing their parties' leaders of their reliability and good judgment through complying with the leaders' wishes. But things changed in the network age. The newscasters found that stories about rebels and mavericks who defied the congressional establishments were far more telegenic than stories about leaders making deals out of the camera's range; the dissenters got a lot of coverage. Thus, according to Ornstein, in the network era many members followed quite different routes to quite different kinds of success:

> As media coverage expanded, the number of members of Congress who were brought to public attention mushroomed, and more and more of the publicized members came from the rank and file. . . . This trend toward personal publicity provided, in contrast to the Rayburn era, a range of tangible and possible outside incentives. No longer did a member have to play by inside rules to receive inside rewards or avoid inside setbacks. One could "go public" and be rewarded by national attention; national attention in turn could provide ego gratification, social success in Washington, the opportunity to run for higher office, or, by highlighting an issue, policy success.[28]

While congresses in the network era may not have had more or better leaders than in the Rayburn era, they certainly had fewer and less compliant followers. To get something done, many more members had to be bargained with on a one-on-one basis than before, and congressional coalitions consequently became harder to build and harder to sustain.

4. Finally, network television contributed heavily to a political culture increasingly hostile to the kind of negotiation and compromise among political leaders that builds coalitions. Network newscasters typically believed that their prime objec-

tive was to satisfy the public's right to know. Accordingly, any politician's effort to do public business in private was not only a violation of that right; it was probably also a cover-up of something immoral or illegal. Moreover, the networks' idea of truly admirable political leaders was those who stay resolutely faithful to their personal convictions regardless of what their colleagues and leaders think; the least admirable were the party hacks who always go along with their paymasters, the party bosses.

Then, too, public confrontations among opposing politicians made great material for mass television audiences, while "talking heads" discussing issues were boring, and cutting deals behind closed doors could not be televised at all.

Moreover, if the main political business of network newscasts was to keep viewers up to date on the state of play in the great game of politics, between as well as during elections, then merely reporting occasional election results was not enough. There had to be other ways of keeping score so that new standings could be broadcast every few days. Thus the nightly newscasts were filled with the latest poll results, stock market indexes, inflation rates, unemployment rates, currency exchange rates, international trade balances, gross national product levels, and the like. For all of these reasons,

> [while] all of the ways in which the American way of government has changed [in the network era] certainly cannot be blamed (or credited) solely or perhaps even mainly on the advent of television, . . . it seems clear that the glare of television's attention has helped significantly to weaken the ability of presidents and congressmen to govern.[29]

Politics in the Era of Narrowcasting, 1990–?

The thesis of this chapter is that in the late 1980s the network era was coming to an end in the United States, that the era of narrowcasting was beginning, and that the changes in the media are likely to change the nature of politics in the 1990s and beyond.[30]

Let us be clear about the terms. The network era, as noted, was based on a broadcasting system in which most television signals were transmitted over the air, aimed at mammoth and heterogeneous audiences, and taken from the air by viewers on wireless home receivers. Narrowcasting, on the other hand, is a system in which television signals are transmitted either by air or by direct wires to people's homes and are aimed at smaller, more narrowly defined, and more homogeneous audiences. Each system has arisen largely as a response to a particular technology.

The New Technology of Narrowcasting. The emerging American mass communications system is based upon the technical development, lowered costs, and rapidly increasing use of five main devices:

1. *Cable television.* Cable television began in the United States in the early 1950s as a way of improving the quality of broadcast reception by enhancing the strength of signals for viewers living in fringe areas remote from broadcasting transmitters. Private companies in such areas constructed large antennas on high towers, received broadcast signals on those antennas, amplified them, and passed them on by cables directly wired to the home receivers of viewers willing to pay modest fees for the service. For the most part the companies were locally franchised and locally operated, and the FCC paid little attention to them.[31]

It soon became clear that cable television could provide much more than the mere transmission of sharper images of broadcast programs. New cable systems were soon established all over the country, many of them in urban areas with good over-the-air reception. By 1987 cable was available to more than two thirds of the population, and more than 39 million households (43 percent of all households) subscribed.[32] In 1984 revenues of all cable systems (including payments by subscribers and purchases of cable TV advertising time) totaled about $7.8 billion; revenues of the three commercial broadcast networks, $7.9 billion (revenues for cable and broadcast were projected to exceed $13 billion apiece by 1990). Cable television had already become as big a business as network broadcast television.[33]

2. *Direct-broadcast satellite television.* In this technology, as for regular broadcast television, signals are broadcast by a ground transmitter and reflected off an earth-orbiting satellite. Unlike network television, the signals are received by individual homeowners using high-gain dish antennas set up in their backyards or on their roofs. The industry has grown more slowly than its investors hoped, but it remains an important alternative for viewers who are weary of network television programming and prefer an even wider range of alternatives than those offered by the available cable systems.

3. *Low-power television broadcasting.* In the network era most television broadcasting stations had transmitters powerful enough and antennas high enough to send signals reaching line of sight to the horizon. There is no technical reason, however, why stations cannot broadcast weaker and shorter-ranging signals aimed at much smaller markets (viewing areas). In 1982 the FCC announced that it would receive applications for licenses to operate stations limited to radiuses of ten to fifteen miles each. Within a few weeks more than 5,000 applications had been received, but the established stations and networks pressed the FCC to go slowly in unleashing so many new competitors. By the end of 1986 only two low-power stations had been licensed on an experimental basis. There is no technical reason, however, why low-power television stations cannot become significant alternatives to the established high-power stations.[34]

4. *Videocassette recorders.* Since the early 1980s there has been a great boom in the sale and use of home videocassette recorders: in 1980 only about 10 percent of the nation's households had VCRs, but by 1987 more than 50 percent had at least one. VCRs are used for two main purposes: time shifting, the recording of programs for viewing at a later time, and showing rented or purchased cassettes. Both uses are a major threat to network television. Viewers who are watching movies on rented cassettes are not watching network programs. Even when they are viewing network programs recorded earlier, many viewers take advantage of their VCRs' fast-forward controls to zap (speed through) advertise-

ments. There is no definitive information on just how much zapping takes place, but as Geoffrey Colvin observes, "the prospect of 'zapping' on a mass scale chills advertisers' blood, and the prospect of disaffected advertisers chills network bosses' blood. " [35]

5. *Remote controls.* The absence of remote controls on most of the receivers sold during most of the network era underlay the networks' standard programming strategies of audience flow. Their producers believed that most viewers were couch potatoes who turned on their sets, set their channel selector to the channel with the first show they wanted to see, and then slumped on their couches the rest of the evening and watched programs only on that channel rather than get up to change channels. General programming strategy followed especially strong shows with weaker shows so that the large audiences drawn by the strong shows would stay tuned for the weaker ones. As one result, Edward Jay Epstein points out that the relative popularity of the networks' national newscasts in particular markets was determined less by their own merits than by the popularity of the local newscasts that immediately preceded them. [36]

In the 1990s, however, perhaps the most widespread of all the new technological developments are the remote controls with which most television receivers sold in the United States are now equipped. They allow viewers to switch channels merely by pressing buttons while remaining comfortably on their couches. This gives viewers a more easily exercised and therefore a greater control over what they watch and thus minimizes the importance of the order of programs on any particular channel. Together with the other technological changes, remote controls have created a mode of television viewing significantly different from that of the network era.

The advent of narrowcasting. The main respects in which television broadcasting is changing are already clear. For one, it is becoming cheaper to broadcast and receive signals. Increased competition and greater manufacturing efficiency are steadily reducing the cost of both transmitting and receiving equipment. Moreover, low-power television stations cost less to build and operate than the higher-powered stations characteristic of the network era. Cable systems require considerable initial capital investment to install, and there are also sizable maintenance costs. But once the startup costs are amortized, the main costs, as for network television, come from creating programs.

The new technologies dramatically increased the number of alternative programs available to most viewers. In most areas at the peak of the network era, even viewers in the large markets could tune to no more than 8 or 9 channels: affiliates of the three networks, three or four unaffiliated commercial stations, and one or two public stations. In smaller markets viewers typically had only four or five alternatives. In the new era, most cable systems are technically capable of providing up to 108 channels, and in the late 1980s the systems in many major markets were providing between 40 and 50 channels in addition to the 8 or 9 available over the air.[37] The final numbers are unknown, but the new era will give most viewers four or five times as many alternatives as they had in the network era. This is likely to have a major impact on the nature of television programming.

The past and present of radio give powerful clues to the present and future of television programming. When radio was the dominant form of electronic mass communications from the 1920s to the early 1950s, the national commercial radio networks, like the television networks that overtook them, broadcast programs to attract the largest possible mass audiences. The larger the audiences were, the higher the rates that advertisers were willing to pay for access to those audiences; the object was to appeal as strongly as possible to all listeners. Since the 1950s, however, radio broadcasters have lost most of their mass audiences to television. They have responded not by going out of business but by converting to an entirely new type of programming that has become known in the trade as narrowcasting. For each station the object of the new programming strategy is not to try to attract all kinds of listeners but rather to target a particular segment of the public (children, adolescents, young adults, blacks, Hispanics, Asians, born-again Christians, and so on), broadcast only programs calculated to attract that segment, and sell advertising time to firms that sell products especially appealing to such people. [38]

Narrowcasting has become the basic strategy of just about every American radio broadcaster—so much so that in their lists of the principal local radio stations, most newspapers present in parentheses after the call letters and frequencies of each station the kind of programming in which it specializes: all-news, talk, hard rock, soft rock, country and western, classical, golden oldies, and (evidently to distinguish it from all other kinds) beautiful music. This programming strategy has worked so well that, far from being driven out of business by the prime-time dominance of television, more AM and FM radio stations were operating in the late 1980s than in the presumed heyday of radio in the 1940s. [39]

Cable television also follows the narrowcasting strategy. A number of national syndicates have been established to develop specialized programs for local cable systems that cater only to particular demographic groups. The Christian Broadcasting Network, Eternal World Television Network, and National Jewish Television, for example, provide only religious programs. Black Entertainment Television produces programs targeted for blacks, and the Spanish International Network produces programs intended for Hispanics. The ESPN and USA networks produce only sports programs. Cable-Satellite Public Affairs Network (C-SPAN) and Cable News Network (CNN) provide only news and public affairs programs.

The networks and their newscasts are already feeling the impact of the new era. For one thing, the networks' share of the audience has declined sharply. In the 1960s the three networks together regularly attracted more than 90 percent of the viewers in prime time, but in the mid-1980s their share had fallen to slightly more than 70 percent. Most industry analysts expect it to fall to 50 percent or less by the turn of the century.

Audiences for the networks' nightly newscasts have also fallen off sharply: in the 1980–1981 period those newscasts had a collective Nielsen rating of 41.4 (41.4 percent of all homes with television sets were tuned to them), but in 1984 their collective rating had fallen to 36.5. [40] In a growing num-

195

ber of major cities such as New York and San Francisco, some national newscasts have been displaced from their traditional time slots (7 to 7:30 P.M.) by popular game shows such as "Wheel of Fortune."

By the end of the 1980s, in short, the network television era had about run its course, the era of narrowcasting had begun, and by the year 2000 it should be firmly established.

Narrowcasting and the Presentation of Politics. As noted, in the network era the main legal constraint on political broadcasting was the FCC's fairness doctrine, which imposed two major constraints on broadcasters. The better known required broadcasters, in broadcasting information about controversial public issues, to provide "reasonable opportunity for the presentation of opposing viewpoints." Broadcasters found it easiest to comply with this rule by treating every issue as having two sides, no more and no less, and by following coverage of one side's case with coverage of the other side's. Thus, a Republican president's state-of-the-union address was followed routinely by a half-hour rebuttal from Democratic congressional leaders; interviews with conservative advocates of a constitutional amendment mandating a balanced budget were routinely followed by interviews with liberal opponents of the amendment.

Broadcasters have always vociferously objected to this constraint because, they say, it denies them the First Amendment freedom enjoyed by the print media to publish the truth as they see it. As Edward Jay Epstein puts it:

> This model of "pro and con" reporting is perfectly consistent with the usual notion of objectivity—if objectivity is defined, as it is by most of the correspondents interviewed, as "telling both sides of a story." It can, however, seriously conflict with the value that journalists place on investigative reporting, the purpose of which is "getting to the bottom" of an issue or "finding the truth," as correspondents put it. Since a correspondent is required to present contrasting points of view, even if he finds the views of one side to be valid and those of the other side to be false and misleading (in the Fairness Doctrine, it

196

will be recalled, truth is no defense), any attempt to resolve a controversial issue and find "the truth" can become self-defeating.[41]

The fairness doctrine's other requirement may well have had an even greater impact on political broadcasting in the network era. It required broadcasters "to devote a reasonable amount of broadcast time to the coverage of public issues." Throughout the period many industry analysts believed that most broadcasters would broadcast many fewer news and public affairs programs without such a rule. Audience surveys showed that most of their viewers much preferred entertainment programs—game shows, situation comedies, movies—to programs about politics. Local news shows, to be sure, attracted larger audiences, cost relatively little to produce, and were generally quite profitable. But during much of the period national newscasts lost money; political documentaries drew small audiences and few commercial sponsors and almost always lost money. Hence it was widely believed that broadcasters could attract larger audiences, charge higher advertising rates, and make more money if they cut public affairs programs to a minimum. Without the fairness doctrine, they would have done just that.

During most of the network era the fairness doctrine was under sharp attack, first from broadcasters and then from the FCC itself, especially from Mark Fowler, who was appointed chairman of the commission by President Reagan and served from 1981 to 1987. Fowler argued that broadcasting stations should be as free as newspapers to publish what they wish, and market forces (that is, the preferences of viewers) rather than government regulators should determine what kinds of programs are broadcast. If deregulation means that most broadcasters will present no news or public affairs programs at all, he said, so be it; a few broadcasters will always cater to the hunger of politics junkies for programs about politics. And if viewers think that particular broadcasters are trying to promote their pet causes and candidates by slanting the news, they can always switch channels.

In 1986 the U.S. Court of Appeals for the District of Columbia ruled that Congress's 1959 amendments to the

Federal Communications Act had not written the fairness doctrine into law but had given the FCC only congressional permission to make such regulations if it wished. This decision gave the FCC the opportunity to rescind the rule. In early 1987 Congress tried to prevent that by passing legislation directing the FCC to retain and enforce the doctrine. But President Reagan vetoed the bill and declared the rule "antagonistic to the freedom of expression guaranteed" by the Constitution. "In any other medium besides broadcasting," he added, "such Federal policing of the editorial judgments of journalists would be unthinkable."[42] In August 1987 the FCC voted unanimously to abolish the rule, although some members of Congress spoke of making it a rider to some future bill a president could not afford to veto.[43]

Whatever its ultimate fate, almost all of the controversy over the fairness doctrine has focused on its mandate to present opposing viewpoints; there has been little discussion, pro or con, of the mandate to broadcast news and public affairs programs. Those most concerned about political bias in broadcasting seem much less intent on requiring that all broadcasters broadcast such programs than on ensuring proper political balance in whatever programs are broadcast. Moreover, cable systems are bound by the doctrine only in presenting programs they themselves originate, not in those they merely pass on from other sources.[44]

As a result, many of the most profitable cable systems and networks—for example, ESPN, HBO, Disney, and MTV—broadcast no political information at all. It seems likely that in the era of narrowcasting an increasing proportion of broadcasters will be free to avoid all political programming if they so choose. And most of them will do so.

In the new era as in the old, the great majority of television programming will be produced by private broadcasters trying to make profits by selling air time to advertisers and by charging subscription fees to viewers. If broadcasters have no legal obligation to broadcast public affairs programs, each company will decide for itself whether to broadcast them. They are likely to decide mainly on the basis of whether the programs will attract and hold audiences that will yield substantial subscription revenues and attract advertisers.

On the basis of hundreds of audience surveys, most broadcasters already think they know how the viewing public feels about public affairs programming. They believe that only a small minority of potential viewers, perhaps 10 to 15 percent, are much interested in politics and eager to see many news shows and other programs about political topics. The great majority of the viewers are usually uninterested in politics. They find it complicated, confusing, repetitive, and boring; most of the time they will pass up public affairs programs in favor of entertainment shows. To be sure, viewers become more interested in politics in times of political scandal and crisis, such as the Watergate hearings of 1974 and the Iran-contra hearings of 1987.

The only political events that regularly interest most viewers are elections; the main things of interest about elections are the horse races. That is, viewers follow election contests in much the same way and for most of the same reasons that they follow sports contests. They want to know who is ahead, who is gaining, who is falling behind, and what the candidates' game plans and tactics are. The minority of politics buffs are interested in the horse races as well as in the loftier matters of issues and ideology.

Political narrowcasting. Accordingly, when the object in covering politics is to attract the largest possible audiences as in the network era, that is, attracting both the politically bored majority and the politically interested minority, the best programming strategy is to focus on the one aspect of politics that interests both groups: the horse races.[45] In the era of narrowcasting, however, each broadcaster will try to attract certain segments of the audience by programming only materials calculated to have special appeal for the targeted segment. That logic seems likely to yield four main programming strategies for political coverage:

1. A few outlets, such as C-SPAN and CNN, will broadcast nothing but news and public affairs programs and will have extensive political coverage including gavel-to-gavel, live coverage of congressional hearings and floor debates, national

nominating conventions, and political candidate debates. These broadcasters will probably have small but loyal audiences that are disproportionately upscale demographically and active and influential politically.

2. A much greater number of outlets will broadcast no public affairs programs at all but will focus exclusively on entertainment programs of one kind or another.

3. The national broadcast networks will continue to aim their programs at relatively wide segments of the viewing public. They will operate on the premise that while the great majority of the viewers do not want a lot of political coverage, they do want enough to give them the electronic equivalent of skimming the front page of newspapers, that is, a short program every night, preferably just before the prime-time shows come on, that will provide brief and visually interesting news bytes on the day's major events—enough to make them feel they are keeping up with what is going on in the world but not enough to bore them or tax their attention spans unduly. These programs will emphasize horse race coverage, try to make sense of each day's events by presenting them as episodes in a series of continuing stories, and, above all, do whatever is necessary to be nonboring. Newspaper journalists, political scientists, and other media critics will probably disdain these programs, but mass audiences will find them acceptable as long as they do not intrude too heavily on the evening's electronic entertainment. The networks' financial officers will continue to appreciate their low production costs.

4. A few outlets on cable and low-power television will be owned and operated by political interest groups, such as feminists, born-again Christians, and labor unions, whose programming will be heavily political. But their programs will be designed not to make money or even to attract and convert mass audiences but to keep true believers faithful and indignant so that they can be more readily mobilized for political action when the need arises.

In short, in the era of narrowcasting, much more than in the network era, any and all viewers who keep punching the buttons on their remote controls are likely to find among the sixty or seventy alternatives available at least one and perhaps more that have just about the right amount and type of political programming to suit their tastes. How is that kind of television likely to affect the changing American political system?

The Future

In the era of narrowcasting, people who are already highly politicized are likely to become even more so. Not only will the all-news, all-public affairs, and all-political-advocacy channels pour out many more reports, hearings, debates, discussions, and other political talk to feed their addiction, but a certain amount of channel hopping will yield an even higher proportion than formerly of the kind of politics they find congenial.

People who are not very politicized—which is most Americans—are likely to become even less so, however. The new communications cafeteria will offer them a much larger variety of nonpolitical items, and it will be easier than ever to ignore politics if they do not find it entertaining even as a spectator sport, for example, during political campaigns.

This may or may not make for more viewing pleasure or a better political system. But this much seems clear: it is likely to make political interest groups even less inclined and less able to make coalitions, and to make mass publics even less concerned about whether they do.

7

The Paradox of Interest Groups in Washington— More Groups, Less Clout

Robert H. Salisbury

One of the most startling events in the history of public policy in the United States was the Tax Reform Act of 1986.[1] It was startling not so much because of its content or its possible impact as, first, because it happened at all, contrary to the forecasts of all knowledgeable observers and, second, because it was fashioned and passed while virtual armies of lobbyists looked on in distress and frustration, unable to intervene to affect the outcome. The "Battle of Gucci Gulch" was fought by members of Congress, mindful, to be sure, of the needs and concerns of organized interests but operating in a context shaped mainly by broader policy, partisan, and institutional considerations. It seemed a heavy irony indeed that, just when the number and variety of organized interests represented in Washington were at an all-time high—with unprecedented numbers of lobbyists using high personal skill supplemented by elaborate modern technologies of analysis, communication, and mobilization—and in a policy area, taxation, that had acquired many of its bizarre existing contours from the pressures and demands of narrowly based interest groups, the ultimate decision process should largely screen out those interests.

This paradox of more interest groups and lobbyists wielding less influence over policy results does not manifest itself all the time, to be sure. The paradox, however, is substantially valid, if not in quite this stark form, then at least in more nuanced forms. In this chapter I argue the case that the growth in the number, variety, and sophistication of interest groups represented in Washington has been associated with, and in some measure has helped to bring about, a transformation in the way much public policy is made and, further, that this transformed process is not dominated so often by a relatively small number of powerful interest groups as it may once have been. I certainly do not want to be understood as saying that interest groups as a whole have weakened in the way, say, that party organizations have lost control over the nomination of candidates. Nor would I deny that in particular instances the old ways are still intact—the "veterans' system" comes to mind—with triangular symbioses linking groups, congressional committees, and executive agencies in nearly impregnable policy success. Moreover, policies such as social security may be quite rigid and largely beyond amendment, not so much because of organized group pressure as such as from the fear among policy makers that such pressure is potentially mobilizable and would soon follow any adverse policy revision. Still, I contend that a great many interest group representatives seek information more than influence, that in many ways they have become dependent on and are sometimes exploited by government officials rather than the other way around, and that much of what contemporary lobbyists do is to be understood as a search for order and a measure of predictability in a policy-making world that has been fundamentally destabilized by developments of the past twenty years.

Changes since 1960

The Explosion in Numbers. The number of organizations directly engaged in pursuing their interests in Washington, D.C., has grown dramatically since about 1960. We have no reliable base line of observation, but the following items suggest the magnitude of expansion in the interest group universe.

- The number of registered lobbyists increased from 3,400 in 1975 to 7,200 in 1985.

- The annual publication *Washington Representatives* managed to find and list more than 5,000 people in 1979; by 1988 it listed nearly 11,000.[2]
- The proportion of U.S. trade and professional associations headquartered in and around Washington grew from 19 percent in 1971 to 30 percent in 1982.[3]
- The number of lawyers belonging to the District of Columbia Bar Association (a requirement for practice in Washington) increased from 10,925 in 1973 to 34,087 in 1981.
- The number of business corporations operating offices in Washington increased from 50 in 1961 to 545 in 1982.[4]
- Some 76 percent of the citizens' groups and 79 percent of the welfare groups in Washington in 1981 had come into existence since 1960.[5]

The Shifting Composition. From Tocqueville to Truman and beyond, interest group scholarship focused almost exclusively on voluntary associations, organizations of members who joined together to advance some common purpose. Mancur Olson showed that the simple fact that people share some political values is not a sufficient basis for collective action.[6] But Olson and other scholars have identified a variety of factors, including the presence of political entrepreneurs, selective benefits, social pressure, philanthropic motives, coercion, and sheer uncertainty, that can account reasonably well for the substantial numbers of voluntary associations that exist and are active in the political arena. This large set exhibits considerable variety, however. Thus trade associations composed of corporations operate quite differently from citizens' groups, especially expressive groups where the problem of free riders is more difficult to control. Important changes have occurred among voluntary associations in both composition and relative importance. In addition, however, three other, rather different kinds of interest organizations inhabit the Washington community, each of which has attained a larger and more consequential place in recent years.

First are institutions. Individual corporations, universities, state and local governments, and religious denominations are active on their own behalf as well as often belonging to voluntary associations of similarly situated entities.[7] Some of these institutions are profit seekers while others are in the nonprofit sector, but they share the condition of being affected by public policy and hoping by their presence in Washington to turn policy to their advantage. Although some have long been influential—large oil companies, for example—it seems likely that in the past two decades individual institutions have been of greater importance in affecting national policy and certainly have devoted greater effort to keeping track of the policy process than they did before the 1960s.

A second category of interested participant, once not nearly so important, is the think tank. The American Enterprise Institute, the Brookings Institution, the Heritage Foundation, the Urban Institute, the Institute for Policy Analysis, the Cato Institute, and a good many others have come to play a significant role in national policy making. Some of these organizations have been havens for out-of-office politicians who remain in Washington in the hope that the next election will return them to office. The principal mode of think tank operation, however, is to publish and publicize policy analyses and recommendations.[8] Think tanks do not usually insist that policy makers adopt their recommended positions to placate some organized constituency they represent. Rather, they depend on the logical power of their arguments or the persuasiveness of their evidence and analysis. They often seek more to shape the broad agenda of policy action than to push for specific decision outcomes. These are only tendencies, to be sure, and there is considerable variation among these organizations; but it is important to include them in any comprehensive picture of the nongovernmental participants attempting to influence the policy-making process. Moreover, it is important to recognize not only that they are more numerous than, say, in 1960 but that they have become considerably more visible. Their ultimate effect may be difficult to determine precisely, but policy institutes and other such think tanks are in no sense merely academic enterprises.

Third, Washington lobbying is carried on not only by organizations on their own behalf but by agents of various kinds retained to advance their interests. Thus many of the lawyers in Washington do not pursue much conventional law practice but concentrate on representing client organizations before federal regulatory agencies, assisting in the presentation of testimony before congressional committees, arranging for a discussion between a client and a high-ranking White House staff person, or approaching potential sources of campaign contributions to help a senator's reelection campaign. This last example highlights an important feature of the lobbyist-agent. Such figures often operate as go-betweens, building symbiotic connections between client organizations and public officials so that each can advance its own interests by helping the other. Some of the living legends of contemporary Washington lobbying—Thomas Boggs, Clark Clifford, Charls Walker—have served a wide range of clients in this manner, and as a consequence a considerable mythology has developed around the notion that Washington lawyers are formidable power brokers whose impact on the policy process is vast, largely undesirable, and sometimes scandalous. To the roster of Washington lawyers in private practice must be added the very considerable number of consultants, of whom Michael Deaver, Lyn Nofziger, and a good many other peddlers of influence are notorious though perhaps unrepresentative examples, and public relations firms, a few of which, such as Hill and Knowlton, have become large enterprises offering clients a broad array of services, including lobbying but extending to many other forms of contact with the public.

Inasmuch as these agents are free-standing rather than organizational employees, they must often hustle for clients, persuading them that policy expertise or connections with officials will yield payoffs more than matching the fees charged. It is understandable that, as the ranks of such agents expand, the competition for business may sometimes tempt people into actions that exceed the bounds of legitimacy. Of all the people engaged in interest representation in Washington, however, only a minority—20 percent according to the one major study, by Robert L. Nelson and others—are free-standing agents, "guns for hire," so to speak.[9] The remainder are employed by the organizations whose interests they represent; and although they must often keep their members happy, they do not have to be so anxious about obtaining clients, arguably a major source of legal or moral corruption in the process of interest representation.

The Fragmentation of Interest Sectors

In the "old days"—the 1950s, say—it was characteristic of many policy sectors for a few organizations, sometimes only one, to have hegemony. The American Medical Association (AMA) dominated health policy, the American Farm Bureau Federation (AFBF) was far and away the most influential group on agricultural matters, the American Petroleum Institute led the list of energy interests, and so on. In the late 1980s these are still substantial organizations, actively involved in making policy pronouncements and using the tactics of influence, but in most policy domains such quasi-monopoly power has been undermined by a process of interest fragmentation that has greatly changed the distribution of influence.

This fragmentation process has two distinct components. First, the self-interested groups have increased in number, variety, and specificity of policy concerns. In agriculture the National Farmers Union gained a position as liberal Democratic rival to the conservative Republican AFBF, only to be challenged on specific issues by the National Wheat Growers Association, the Soy Bean Association, the Corn Growers Association, and dozens of commodity-based trade associations. Some, like the National Milk Producers Federation, had been around for decades but as relatively peripheral players. Others, like the corn growers, were newly organized, drawing on more self-conscious and, because of changes in farming technology, more differentiated groups of producers. But not just producers. Many of the groups now active in agricultural issues include corporations engaged in other stages of the chain linking the farmer to the consumer. The Grocery Manufacturers Association is one example, but there are scores of others in which farmers play little or no role. Commodity organizations and trade associations have been joined by numerous individual corporations, including giant agribusiness firms like Cargill or Archer-Daniels-Midland and firms like Coca-Cola or Pizza Hut, concerned about the prices they must pay for commodities they use.

In the mid-1980s William P. Browne identified well over 200 interests involved in shaping farm legislation.[10] With this massive expansion of private interest group participants, it has been necessary since at least the late 1950s to construct quite elaborate coalitions of these groups to get the support necessary to enact major farm legislation. In agriculture the farm bills still take broad multipurpose form and are enacted for terms of three to five years, after which there is another round of negotiation. The complexity of these negotiations defies quick summary, but it is clear that the peak associations no longer guide the process.

A similar story can be told of the health policy domain.[11] There no single legislative enactment brings into focus the full extent of interest fragmentation, although efforts to achieve national health insurance and sometimes medical cost containment issues have come close. Issues concerning hospital construction, medical research, veterans' health care, and drug regulation, however, have long been treated separately. Whatever the question, the AMA, once so imperiously powerful, is no longer the dominant voice even of organized medicine. The hospital associations now speak with quite independent voices. So do many organizations of medical specialists. Medical insurance interests, medical schools, corporations engaged in medical technology research and manufacturing, and of course the drug companies all get involved. Again, complex coalitions among diverse interests are necessary to enact legislation and secure its continued funding.

An alternative approach to the building of broad interest coalitions so that groups can secure stable and supportive policy attention is to carve out a small but vital slice of the total policy pie and try to insulate it from invasion by competing interests. Medical schools succeeded for a time in keeping medical student subsidies from rival claimants. Veterans' interests have successfully protected their hospitals. Tobacco growers have maintained their benefits separate from broader farm policy questions. Quite large numbers of examples of such cozy programs could be cited where at least for a time a program and its interest group constituency have been effectively isolated from broader entanglements. But the fragmentation process has a second component in addition to the proliferation of self-interested groups just described, which puts even these narrowly bounded islands of policy stability at risk. This component may be called the "invasion of the externality groups."[12]

A major category of growth among interest groups has been citizens' groups. This label is attached to a broad array of motivating concerns and points of view, but it applies to all those groups for whom self-interest, narrowly defined, is not the primary organizing appeal. Members of taxpayer groups and animal rights enthusiasts may thereby express some private desire to save money to protect their pets, but even for them the collective purposes of the group bear only an indirect connection to their personal situations. In any case, the rapid growth of citizens' groups has affected the policy process in important ways.

Many of these groups are primarily expressive, or what Byron Shafer has called "issue organizations," formed around specific causes or categories of policy and mobilizing support on the basis of appeals to the deeply felt value commitments of some segment of the public.[13] It may not be accurate to call the right-to-life activists or the National Gay Rights Organization ideological if that term implies a comprehensive structure of articulated principles from which particular policy positions are deduced, but the emotional intensity and resistance to compromise and broker politics of these expressive groups are in sharp contrast to the pragmatism associated with more self-interested organizations. Moreover, some of these citizens' organizations employ quite encompassing language to articulate their guiding principles. Common Cause distributes its efforts across a wide range of issues under a broad banner of "reform in the public interest," and some of the think tanks, especially politically conservative operations like the Heritage Foundation (whose recommendations to the incoming Bush administration ran to more than 900 pages), speak out on practically every item on the public agenda.

The central importance of the newly prominent externality groups is that they further destabilize the policy-making process. The proliferation or fractionation of interests in particular policy domains has undermined the hegemony of peak associations in those domains, pushing some groups into small policy niches and forcing others into much more complicated coalitional efforts to secure their policy desires. To this has been added this further assortment, differing from one policy domain to another in their specific concerns but similar in their tendency to appeal to high moral principle as the only proper criterion for deciding who gets what, when, and how. Many of these groups have dubious political muscle in the usual sense, as measured by membership size, money, or even social status, although some are impressive in one or more of these respects. Regardless, however, of their ability to affect electoral prospects directly, these groups are assertive in their use of mass media and thereby make themselves felt regarding which items get on the agenda, forcing the recognition of values and concerns that might, if left to the traditional cozy triangles, receive little attention. Further, the externality groups often call into question the legitimacy of otherwise stable cozy relationships among self-interested groups and officials. The attacks on the so-called cozy or iron triangles have been mounted by reformers of both left and right, by think tanks and citizens' groups of diverse motives and persuasions; as these groups have grown more numerous, the arrangements they have challenged have become less cozy, less stable. Not only are policy processes more uncertain, they are more often contentious. Externality groups attract considerable hostility from the more self-interested institutions and associations, which doubt the seriousness of purpose or understanding of real world effects on the part of citizens' groups and assorted do-gooders.[14]

A major exception to the tendency for established patterns to be overrun by newly emergent specialized interests and externality interests occurs in the field of labor policy. There too we find conflict, but in the form of bipolar struggles between two self-interested coalitions, the American Federation of Labor–Congress of Industrial Organizations (AFL-CIO), supported by assorted individual unions, and the U.S. Chamber of Commerce, the Business Roundtable, and the

National Association of Manufacturers, backed by a miscellany of corporate firms and trade associations. Externality groups seldom intrude, and policy concerns that might cut across the dominant dimension—affirmative action in hiring, for example—tend instead to be drawn into the basic oppositional structure. That structure has strong partisan overtones too, of course, which make it all the more difficult to transform labor policy issues into less contentious language. One result, as Terry Moe has shown, is considerable stalemate with neither side able to prevail over the other.[15] This does not mean that labor and business never cooperate on issues, of course. Rapport was good between trucking firms and the Teamsters Union in opposition to truck deregulation, for example, and between automobile manufacturers and the United Auto Workers on trade policy. It is on labor policy itself that the basic conflict exists, and this pattern, while hardly a conventional interest triangle, has not been destabilized by the developments at work in other policy domains.

Uncertain Structures of Power

The destabilization argument I have been developing affects the pattern of policy outcomes at two levels. In the formulation of legislation and the implementing of regulations it means that it is no longer accurate to account for outcomes by reference to the familiar metaphor of iron or cozy triangles wherein interest groups, congressional committees or subcommittees, and executive agencies operate in symbiotic interdependence. For some time, indeed, attentive observers have doubted the validity of the triangle interpretation. Charles O. Jones suggested that "sloppy hexagon" might come closer to expressing the shape of the policy subsystem.[16] Hugh Heclo abandoned geometric tropes entirely in favor of the notion of "issue network."[17] The quest for a suitably evocative phrase will no doubt continue, but it will be difficult indeed to capture in simple terms the shifting, almost kaleidoscopic configurations of groups involved in trying to shape policy.

At a more highly aggregated level, destabilization challenges the value of what for two decades has been the dominant conception of most U.S. policy, interest group liberalism. Theodore Lowi's view, embraced in at least substantial part by most observers, was that in the United States, since the 1930s at least, the major thrusts of policy decision reflected the demands of particularistic groups, opposed weakly if at all by competitors and enacted without much reference to standards of judgment drawn from outside the interest-dominated arenas of politics.[18] In a destabilized world of fragmented interests and multidimensional challenges from externality groups it becomes impossible for policy makers to identify which interests, if any, they can succumb to without grave political risk. They find themselves with choice and discretion, able to select policy alternatives and take positions knowing that almost any position will have some group support and none can prevent opposition from arising. We can easily carry this interpretation too far, denying all policy effect to organized groups, and this would be quite unwarranted. Nevertheless, as was illustrated by the Gucci Gulch example I began with, the presumption has been significantly altered: where interest groups were seen as the prime motive force pressing politicians to make policy decisions in their favor, now the officials very often exploit the groups.

This partial reversal in the flow of influence is not simply a product of the expansion in size and fragmentation in purpose of interest sectors. It is also closely linked with changes in the institutional configurations of Congress and the executive branch. I need not detail these developments here but merely identify those that have especially affected the position and practice of interest group politics.

First has been the diffusion of power in Congress. The weakening of seniority, the empowering of subcommittees, and the expansion of congressional staffs have all contributed to the result that many members are in a position to participate actively and meaningfully on a much larger number of issues than once was possible. Specialization is not so much required to gain substantive expertise—and not so much deferred to by others in any case. On any particular set of policy concerns there are multiple points of potentially relevant access as groups seek support in the Congress, but the depressing corollary for the groups is that none of them is likely to carry decisive weight in shaping policy. Indeed, the position-taking and credit-claiming competition among these many focal points may well mean that ultimately no action is possible in any direction.

Diffusion of power within Congress has been accompanied by the widely remarked increase in the electoral success of incumbents. Incumbents' electoral safety further undermines dependence on interest groups. As John Mark Hansen has shown with reference to the growth of interest triangles in agriculture, the influence of farm groups developed in the late 1920s as members of Congress gradually learned that farm issues were a perennial part of the legislative agenda and farm organizations were therefore continually active and more reliable sources of electoral support than the political parties.[19] Farm belt Republicans therefore defected from their party and forged independent, mutually supportive links with the farm groups. But what was learned can be unlearned. As members of Congress today find themselves increasingly secure beneficiaries of pork, casework, and name recognition, they learn that they can afford to stand aloof from many interest groups. There are important exceptions, but my argument is that in the Congress of the late 1980s interest groups are virtually awash in access but often subordinate in influence.

In the executive branch the most significant development affecting established interest triangles has been the centralization of policy initiatives within the Executive Office of the President and particularly the White House staff. Interest group access in the past has been greatest and most productive with line agencies and independent commissions. The White House is a much more difficult target for lobbyists to reach, and even though White House decisions will necessarily favor some interests over others, it will rarely be, in any direct sense, because of the groups' skill or power. The groups report regular contact with the White House only about one-third as often as with the leaders of their most significant cabinet departments; this reflects a difference in accessibility, not power.[20] The groups go where they can; but ever since Franklin D. Roosevelt executive authority has been brought more and more fully within the White House orbit, and most organized interests have been disadvantaged accordingly.

Interest Group Adaptation

Strategies and Tactics. Despite repeated efforts to reform them, the legal rules constraining the behavior of organized interests in Washington have remained essentially stable for several decades. Only in the area of campaign finance has the law undergone major revision since 1946. Yet the world in which interest groups must operate has changed profoundly. Growth and the changing composition of their ranks are part of this transformation; diffusion of power in Congress and concentration of initiative in the executive are another part; the increase in incumbents' security against electoral defeat has likewise been a factor. The result is that from the perspective of the private interests old patterns of access and influence cannot be depended on to suffice for policy representation needs. Relationships are often friendly but generally unstable, with new groups and new coalitions appearing and reforming while the officials become stronger, wealthier in campaign funds, and as autonomous as they choose to be vis-à-vis the multitude of supplicant interests. Given these changes in their environments, how have organized interests responded and adapted? I consider two levels of adaptive action, tactical and strategic. The tactical question is this: how do lobbyists allocate their time and energy so as to be effective in this uncertain setting? At a more strategic level, what organizational techniques and means of action do interests employ to maximize their impact?

For interest groups as for candidates for presidential nomination or party leader in Congress, fundamental choices of strategy must be made. One option is to go "outside," seeking to shape political agendas and policy outcomes by arousing public opinion, using mass media and indirect marketing techniques to attract attention and broad support for their causes. A significant part of their effort may be directed toward the electoral process, for if they can alter the composition of Congress or significantly affect the result of a presidential election, their influence thereafter may be very considerable. As Kenneth Godwin has shown, however, the appeals needed to arouse sufficient mass support must be vivid, even sensational, and they tend therefore to be both extreme and negative.[21] Such appeals may work well in the short run, but they often fade nearly as rapidly as they flowered. What we call political movements tend especially to display these characteristics: rapid growth in numbers, fueled by extensive publicity, with a penchant for extravagant language and various forms of direct action, followed by an equally rapid decay.[22] The movements of the 1960s—civil rights, antiwar, student empowerment, and even environmentalism to some extent—displayed this pattern, and it seems that many of the causes generally referred to as the New Right, having flourished in the late 1970s and early 1980s, have fallen on hard times in the past few years.

Outside strategies, like inside straights in draw poker, can sometimes work, but the odds are generally against them. Godwin suggests that this was especially characteristic of the many citizens' groups, of diverse persuasions, that came into existence after 1960 to mobilize broad public support. Given the tendency for their appeals to decay swiftly, any particular configuration of citizens' groups might therefore be expected to have only a short-term effect on policy. To revert to the terms employed before, this means that externality groups, by reason of the basis on which their organization rests (mass appeals couched in vivid but ephemeral political imagery), will destabilize relationships between officials and interests. In other words, it is not simply their numbers but their organizational dynamics that make citizens' groups so troublesome to the long-term players in the Washington community.

I am painting this picture with a broad brush, of course. Some citizens' and externality groups have managed to solve their membership mobilization problems well enough to achieve a stable and significant presence in Washington.[23] Nevertheless, those groups whose interests are predominantly material rather than expressive have a strong tendency to be the more numerous and consequential participants in policy subsystems (however unstable some of those have become) and to work primarily in a framework of "inside" strategy and tactics.

The inside strategic options for interest groups have crystallized in recent years as the principal means of action have become more clearly differentiated and better documented. I will look in some detail at several of these options as they have been used by business corporations.[24] Since some of the data reported are nearly ten years old and corporate organization has been extremely volatile in many respects, changes have surely taken place in the use of these strategies. Nevertheless, these data allow us to examine systematically not only the frequency with which business firms employ one method or another but the factors that help explain their strategic selections.

A time-honored method of securing representation in Washington is to hire an agent. Washington has no shortage of people with formal credentials as lawyers, public relations advisers, or consultants with substantive policy expertise to whom groups can turn for assistance. Indeed, the supply of independent lobbying agents has increased massively in recent years. Nearly every really large manufacturing firm engages at least one such agent (98 percent of the leading 100 firms in sales volume do so), and organizations that can afford to often employ ten or a dozen for various purposes. Nevertheless, only about one-fifth of the interest representatives examined by Nelson and his colleagues were independent agents, and many of these are used for specialized tasks—litigation, for example—that are on the periphery of the interest group's policy agenda.

Despite the very sizable hourly rates charged by many Washington representatives, it is generally cheaper for a group to employ them ad hoc than to staff a Washington office all year round. The rapid growth of corporate offices in Washington therefore signifies a major increase in the investment that firms have found it useful to make in the tasks of policy representation. To be sure, some companies, often under pressure from Wall Street, have decided that a permanent D.C. establishment is too expensive and have closed down, but especially among the larger firms the proportions with Washington offices remains very substantial.[25]

Coalitions. As the relatively secure relationships of the 1950s were destabilized by the developments of subsequent years, a wide range of efforts ensued, in Burdett H. Loomis's phrase, to "build bridges in a Balkanized state" with more or less explicitly designated coalitions.[26] Coalitions of interests are generic components of the political process, of course, and not a recent invention. Moreover, there have long been relationships among interests, cutting across the lines of party, region, and economic sector, that mobilized in cooperative political effort the resources of disparate groups, sometimes on an ad hoc basis, sometimes in more enduring fashion. What is striking about the most recent period, however, is how numerous are the coalitions designated as such and also how many counterpart coalitions, generally called caucuses, have been formed in Congress. In each case the fragmentation of interests and the breakdown of older patterns of connection have made it attractive to construct so many new combinations.

A major form of interest coalition, which has been with us for more than a century, is the trade or professional association. There have been several spurts of growth in the number and variety of these organizations over the course of American development, and their number continues to increase as new specializations and new combinations of functions emerge. Nearly 2,000 such organizations are represented in Washington, and their effect on the commercial real estate and restaurant facilities of the nation's capital has been profound.

The most striking change, however, in cooperative interest representation strategy reflects the inherent limitation of nearly every trade or professional association. More and better coalitions are required by the complexity of effects of federal policy on the institutions of society.[27] Not all widget-making corporations or banks or universities will be affected in the same way by what the government does. Peer-reviewed research grants from the National Science Foundation are greatly admired by large research universities but are not much help to the colleges; the leading dozen or so private universities have somewhat different concerns from the public institutions, and so on. Some of these differences are reflected in different voluntary associations, of course; the Association of American Universities (AAU) is distinct from both the National Association of State Universities and Land Grant Colleges and the National Association of Independent Colleges and Universities. In addition, however, several smaller working groups of university lobbyists exchange information and try to orchestrate their actions for maximum, highly targeted effect.

Other universities may not possess the resources or be sufficiently affected by federal policy to invest in deploying their own lobbyists but may still see possibilities in being represented in Washington outside the framework of the formal associations. For such interests a lobbyist broker can be a useful intermediary, bundling a collection of organizations together when it is useful but serving each one's specific interests without being troubled by having always to represent all its "members" in the way that leaders of voluntary associations like the AAU or the American Council of Education (ACE) must try to do. Thus, in the quarterly report filed under the Regulation of Lobbying Act and published in the *Congressional Record* for November 10, 1988, Cassidy and Associates, a public relations and lobbying firm that specializes in such matters, listed forty-four college and university clients.

The growing numbers of coalitions and alliances cutting across the boundaries of formal associations are made possible because so many more individual business corporations, universities, and other institutions have established Washington outposts. While they continue to pay their association dues (often to several associations), they operate independently as well when necessary. Some of the independent action is aimed at affecting public policy. For example, eighteen large firms in the financial sector organized a group to push for banking reform legislation opposed by the American Bankers Association and the American Council of Life Insurance.[28] Quite often, however, a major purpose of the new coalitions is informational. At weekly breakfast meetings and the like, similarly situated interest representatives can share information and interpretation that would come more slowly, if at all, through the more bureaucratic channels of a trade

TABLE 7–1

CORPORATE USES OF STRATEGIC FORMS OF ACTION,
1982 AND 1983
(percent)

Sales Rank	With PAC (1983)	Using Agent (1982)	With D.C. Office (1982)
1–100	89	98	85
101–250	73	77	63
251–500	44	32	17
501–1,000	15	16	3
Total	39	38	24

SOURCE: Craig Humphries, *The Political Behavior of American Corporations*, Washington University, 1989.

association serving a larger and more diverse membership. One other feature of many of these new coalitions is that the groups and organizations that participate must spend considerable time lobbying one another, trying to persuade colleagues concerning the policy stance that the collectivity should adopt.

Groups vary a great deal in the forms of action they employ in Washington, and while it would be rash indeed to claim to know precisely how much variation exists or what factors affect it, we can examine the behavior of manufacturing firms in some detail. Table 7–1 presents the proportions of the largest 1,000 companies that employ independent agents (1982), have created political action committees (PACs) (1983), or have established Washington offices (1982).[29] It is obvious that firm size and the resources that go with size are of decisive importance. Big business is far more fully represented in Washington than smaller firms. But that is by no means the end of the story.

Are big firms more actively represented simply because they can afford it, or are other factors involved? A number of possibilities come to mind. Craig Humphries finds that the extent of government regulation of a firm's industry strongly affects whether the firm establishes itself in Washington.[30]

Among regulated industries, those that are more concentrated (that is, with a smaller number of firms) are more actively represented. So also are firms with more diversified product lines. The threat of imports has some effect, but the degree of unionization is not very important, at least not for the entire array of 1,000 firms. Having government contracts is associated with establishing a Washington office but not with the hiring of an independent agent or the creation of a PAC.

A significant relationship exists among those three strategic forms. That is, if a firm has a Washington office or uses independent agents, it is likely also to create a PAC. Using agents is strongly related to establishing a D.C. office. The forms of action go together, reinforcing one another and to some extent creating the necessity for one another. A company needs a Washington office in part to supervise its agents and direct its PAC's selection of the candidates it will favor. But the office can seldom cover all the politically relevant bases it can identify; hence the agents. And without a PAC to finance attendance at fund raisers, a corporate presence in Washington may be dismissed by officials as worthless. This interdependence among strategic forms of action leads to the recognition that interest group representation is a dynamic phenomenon, driven not only by the "objective" needs of rational actors affected by what the government does to them or for them but also by the internal logic of the association or the institution. It also points up the importance of examining such highly publicized matters as PACs in the context of other forms of interest group action.

The Tactical Repertoire. I turn now to the more specific activities in which business corporations and other groups engage, in which the organizational means discussed above are employed. As I have done throughout the chapter, I emphasize those aspects that appear to have changed in recent years. The emphasis on change is tricky to implement because, as with so much else about interest groups, we lack good historical base lines. Nevertheless, whereas Kay Schlozman and John Tierney concluded that contemporary group

221

practice mainly involved "more of the same," some quite important changes have occurred in the things groups do.[31]

Groups must first make choices regarding the political arenas in which they will invest money and effort. A plausible expectation would be that, as relative power to determine policy outcomes shifts within a governmental institution or from one institution to another, the lobbyists will follow. Thus it was said that as policy-making dominance in Britain moved from Parliament to Whitehall, the lobby shifted its efforts accordingly. There is a competing hypothesis, however, to the effect that lobbyists go anywhere they can, using the authority of any institutional arena that they are able to penetrate in the hope that, because in the United States authority to shape policy is shared by so many separate institutions, some influence on their objectives can be exerted. On the whole the latter argument is more persuasive. Accessibility of an institution is a key element in shaping the decision of a group to seek access.

Interests differ considerably in the ease or difficulty with which they can penetrate a particular institution, and these factors also vary over time. Obviously, what groups try to do depends not only on the relevance to their concerns of an institution's authority and its accessibility to their efforts but on the group's resources as well. Not all tactical options to gain access and influence are available to every group. Choices must be made, and we need to examine some of them.

Byron Shafer has recently described a major shift in the process of nominating presidential candidates beginning in the 1960s, whereby interest groups of various kinds came to play an increasing part in sponsoring delegates, lobbying on the platforms, bargaining over the nominations, and mobilizing support in the election campaign.[32] The strong support of the National Education Association for Jimmy Carter and of groups from the religious right for Ronald Reagan in 1980 illustrate a development of long-term importance. Shafer contends that in this process mainly the ideologically motivated groups are active, not the more pragmatic interests that are willing to bargain and compromise; as a result, the presidential campaigns are more radicalized than in "the old days" when party organizations were stronger and could play a more effective brokering role.

In the electoral process generally, the PAC phenomenon, so often denounced in the media and by reformers everywhere, has seemed to move from one tack to another with little assurance of where, if anywhere, a stable equilibrium may be found.[33] Labor had long employed PACs, of course. Ever since the creation of the CIO-PAC in 1943 unions had used this device to assemble campaign funds and had increasingly dispensed them almost entirely to Democrats. After the 1971–1974 changes in the law unambiguously legitimated PACs for all interests, the rapid expansion of corporate, trade association, and unaffiliated (mostly politically conservative) committees seemed likely for a time to overwhelm labor's efforts, giving most of their money to Republicans. Especially in 1978 and 1980 Republican candidates, including challengers as well as incumbents, benefited enormously from PAC assistance. Great dangers to balanced electoral competition were prophesied, and proposals for public funding of congressional elections, usually advanced by Democrats, were accordingly dismissed out of hand by Republicans. Since then, however, the balance has shifted. Unaffiliated PACs continue to back conservative candidates, but their funding has not kept pace, and their influence has therefore provoked fewer anxieties. Business PACs meanwhile have redirected their contributions quite sharply in favor of incumbents. Inasmuch as a solid majority of the House and, since 1986, of the Senate are Democrats, they have been the beneficiaries. The pragmatism that has guided PAC contributions by business interests to congressional candidates is in sharp contrast to the ideological fervor displayed by interests active in presidential campaigns. PAC pragmatism is an important indicator of the power of incumbent congressmen—interest groups that depend on them for help on narrow but vital issues give them campaign support, regardless of the broader policy orientation that the incumbent members display.

Away from the electoral process, a broad array of activities may be undertaken by Washington-based lobbyists. The usual characterization of lobbying has emphasized the tasks of making formal and informal contacts with officials and presenting them with information and argument. Schlozman and Tierney found that virtually every group did these things and did them more now than before. Other research shows, however, that this direct lobbying is not the most time-consuming or often the most important concern. Thirty years ago Lester Milbrath found that lobbyists spent a large part of their working time in their own offices, not on Capitol Hill or elsewhere, making contact with officials.[34] This remains true today. The tasks that are both the most time consuming and the most important are concerned not so much with persuading government officials to act one way or another as with keeping track of what is happening in the policy process, alerting the client organizations to developments relevant to their interests, and developing appropriate strategies of response or adaptation. Advocacy of one's cause continues to require attention, of course, and the ways and means of gaining influence over outcomes are in no sense ignored. Schlozman and Tierney are quite right in saying that groups do more of everything than they did two or three decades ago. Even litigation, one of the less highly valued modes of action, is reported to have been undertaken by nearly two-thirds of the interest organizations surveyed by Heinz and others. Nevertheless, there appears to have been a significant shift in the balance among the lobbyists' tasks, and that shift is closely related to the broad movement of groups toward a full-time presence in Washington.

Recall a "classic" model of lobbying. A group sends a representative to Washington to press its case for or against some policy option, or it hires one of the many would-be agents already located in the nation's capital, waiting like defense lawyers in the courthouse corridors for a paying client to come into view. The presumption in this model is that the group knows what its policy interest is. If the group is big enough to have great voting strength, it may expect to gain its ends through the electoral process. If it is small and its needs are limited, it may need only to add lobbying expertise to secure the desired result. Many of these group concerns, richly illustrated in the case study literature, have been ad hoc and discontinuous, adequately served by a single lobbying campaign. Others require continuing attention but may still be very stable with respect to the policy interests sought. Thus for many years the big oil companies maintained a firm lobbying commitment to the depletion allowance, home builders have never wavered in their defense of deducting interest on home mortgages, and veterans' groups have kept up the pressure to maintain Veterans Administration hospitals.

The great expansion in the scope of federal programs since World War II, however, has meant that many more elements of the society are far more extensively affected by what the government does and must, in their own interests, become more involved in trying to optimize those effects. This sea change has been accompanied by two other changes of great importance. One is essentially intellectual: we acknowledge far more fully than we once did that there are profound interdependencies and interaction effects such that any policy decision is likely to be seen as having a major effect not just on its primary target population but on diverse other areas of life. The second is that these external concerns have been the basis of substantial group formation and political action. In consequence, a widespread destabilization of many of the old influence relationships has occurred. But there has been another level of destabilization. In today's world of complex, interdependent interests and policies, it is often quite unclear what the "true interests" of a group or an institution may be. The policy that will be maximally advantageous to an association often cannot even be framed without prolonged and searching analysis involving extensive discussion among those who are knowledgeable about both the technical substance of the issue and the feasibilities of the relevant political situation.

Uncertainty concerning the substance of group interests, as well as about how best to achieve them, forces those we call lobbyists to shift much of their energy away from lobbying, that is, away from advocating policies and influencing government officials. Before they can advocate a policy, they must determine what position they wish to embrace. Before they do this, they must find out not only what technical policy analysis can tell them but what relevant others, inside government and outside, are thinking and planning. Often, indeed, a group may not even know that it has a policy interest requiring attention until it discovers the plans of an agency to propose new regulations or of a congressional subcommittee to hold hearings on a subject. Information, timely and accurate, is absolutely vital to the lobbyist.

This point is nicely captured in the opening paragraph of Edward Laumann and David Knoke's analysis of the organizational networks involved in energy and health policies:

> The executive director of a major petroleum-industry trade association was leafing through the Federal Register, his daily ritual of scanning the Washington scene. Buried in the fine print was an apparently innocuous announcement by the Federal Aviation Administration of its intent to promulgate new regulations that would require detailed flight plans to be filed by pilots of noncommercial aircraft. Recently, several planes had gone down, and search and rescue efforts had been hampered by lack of information on the pilots' intended routes. The trade association director muttered, "We've got a problem," and spent a frantic morning on the phone alerting his group's membership to apply pressure on the FAA to set aside the regulation. The executive realized that once detailed flight plans were on record with the FAA, the open-disclosure provisions of the Freedom of Information Act would allow anyone to learn where his member companies' planes were flying on their aerial explorations for oil, gas, and minerals. The alert director's quick mobilization of collective response saved the corporations potentially millions of dollars worth of secret data that might have fallen into the laps of their competitors.[35]

Laumann and Knoke treat information as a resource of central importance in the policy process and, as I do, see policy interests as "continuously constructed" social phenomena.[36] Their emphasis is on the conversion of information resources into influence over policy outcomes, however, and while it would be extremely foolish to ignore this element, it is important also to recognize that information may often be necessary to adjust one's own behavior sensibly. A corporation that knows the intentions of the Federal Aviation Administration may decide to change its own policies rather than try to persuade the agency to change.

The point of my argument is that the descent on Washington of so many hundreds of associations, institutions, and their agents does not mean that these private interests have acquired greater sway or even a more articulate voice in the shaping of national policy. In many ways the opposite is true. Washington is, after all, the main source of information about what government officials are doing or planning to do. To get that information in a timely way, a continuous and alert presence in the capital is vital. Moreover, in this quest for information the interest representatives are very often in a position of profound dependence. They need access to officials not so much to apply pressure or even to advocate policy as to be told when something important to them is about to happen.

Specialized newsletters are often helpful in this situation, and these expensive aids have multiplied in recent years. Coalitions and trade associations are, among other things, means of enhancing the exchange of information, although trade associations must be careful not to circulate more data about members' intentions than the antitrust laws permit. Withal, the centrality of the need for information and its use by interest groups to help define interests and policy preferences, structure the workday, and adapt organizational behavior to emerging political conditions are clearly reflected in the findings of Heinz and others regarding how lobbyists spend their time. Table 7–2 reports the relative frequency with which 776 interest representatives in the policy domains of agriculture, energy, health, and labor engage in the diverse tasks involved in their jobs. Formal interaction with government ranks well below more informal contacts. Information exchanges claim a higher priority than position taking, and intraorganizational efforts along with monitoring of the political environment are of central importance.

One further consequence of the lobbyists' overriding need to know is that in their contacts with government officials they display considerably less specialization than

TABLE 7–2
FREQUENCY OF LOBBYISTS' TASK PERFORMANCE
(1 = never; 5 = regularly)

Alerting client about issues	4.3
Developing policy or strategy	4.3
Maintaining relations with government	3.8
Making informal contacts with officials	3.7
Monitoring proposed changes in rules and laws	3.7
Providing information to officials	3.5
Preparing testimony or official comments	3.4
Commentary for press, public speaking	3.2
Mobilizing grass-roots support	3.0
Monitoring interest groups	2.8
Testifying	2.7
Drafting proposed legislation or regulations	2.7
Making contacts with opposition	2.6
Making contacts with allies	2.5
Resolving internal organizational disputes	2.5
Litigation	2.1
Arranging for political contributions	2.0
Working for amicus briefs	1.6

SOURCE: Salisbury et al., *Iron Triangles: Similarities and Differences among the Legs,"* American Political Science Association Conference, September 1988.

might have been expected. Rather than focusing on a particular committee or administrative agency, interest representatives report making regular contacts with an average of four or five government units. More often than not these contacts are in both the executive and the legislative branches and include both Republicans and Democrats. Their dependence on information requires the interest representatives to go wherever they can learn something useful. This may well mean that watchful attendance at hearings and markup sessions is more the modal lobbying task than position taking or policy advocacy in any form.

Conclusion

I come back to the apparent paradox with which I began, to the Tax Reform Act of 1986 in which the members of Congress made the choices, excluding the scores of interest group representatives from the process and forcing them to wait outside until it was over. The interpretation I have offered suggests that, rather than being a paradox, this situation simply registered important changes that have been taking place. Many of the old symbioses have given way, destabilized as a result of expanded group participation, of greater electoral security, increased staff, and lessened need or inclination to specialize on the part of Congress, and of more centralized control of the executive branch, which leaves the specialized agencies less able to create their own triangular policy deals.

The uncertainty generated by this political destabilization is compounded by the problematic nature of policy interests. Organizations are often unsure which among the live policy options might be most to their advantage; indeed, they are often in doubt about what the options are. They are engaged in a never-ending process of learning, assessment, and calculation; and timely information, much of it available only from government, is the sine qua non of this process. It would be too much to claim that interest group lobbyists have been wholly subordinated to public officials, but we would surely misread the American political process if we ignored the extent to which these groups have come to Washington out of need and dependence rather than because they have influence.

8
Federalism—
The Great "Composition"

Richard P. Nathan

Federalism as we know it today was invented two hundred years ago in Philadelphia. In *Federalist* No. 39 the brilliant James Madison described the new American political system as "neither wholly *national* or wholly *federal*" but "a composition of both."[1] Before the U.S. Constitution was written in 1787, federalism had been understood as a league or club, with the states voting and acting as member states. In the new American system the citizen, as the British political scientist K. C. Wheare emphasized, was and is a citizen of both the nation and the state: "each citizen is subject to *two governments*."[2] In *Federalist* No. 15 Alexander Hamilton described the "great and radical vice" of the Articles of Confederation as being "in the principle of LEGISLATION for STATES or GOVERNMENTS, in their CORPORATE or COLLECTIVE CAPACITIES as contradistinguished from the INDIVIDUALS of whom they consist."[3]

Today federalism is highly topical around the world. Brazil has just adopted a new constitution that reinstates federal features. Federalism is at the root of the debilitating problems of Yugoslavia, where centrifugal political forces are stronger today than in any other country. The Soviets are experimenting with the federal idea and finding that the forces that underlie it are extraordinarily hard to contain. France and Spain are setting up new regional entities. Feder-

Appreciation is expressed to Martha Derthick, John Lago, and Michael Schill, who provided valuable assistance in the preparation of this chapter.

alism is being strengthened in many ways in the United States. Indeed, in many places in the world—India, Nigeria, Indonesia, Mexico—the ideas of federalism are under close scrutiny and in some cases the subject of constitutional and legal reforms. In this heady environment it is appropriate for Americans to play a leading role in examining federalism as a political form. What is it? What makes it tick? Is it a good idea or a bad one?

Wheare's answer to the first question was legalistic and restrictive. For him the club of modern federal nations was small—four or five countries, maybe eight, but no more than ten. Since his seminal book was published in 1946, however, the dominant view in the academic literature on federalism has shifted. A recent book by Daniel J. Elazar claims that as high a proportion as 70 percent of the people in the world live in countries that are federal or "apply federal arrangements in some way."[4] This expansive view of our subject makes it hard to pin down. A second complicating factor is the position taken by many scholars that federalism is so broad and inchoate a governmental arrangement that it defies close specification. Maurice Vile, for example, believes that definitions of federalism "are almost totally vacuous."[5] In a similar vein, Michael Reagan and John Sanzone contend that we face a situation in which federalism is bankrupt as an operational concept.[6] This situation is unfortunate, not just for scholars but for political leaders as well because of the importance that knowledge of federalism has for modern governance.

I propose a definition of federalism that focuses on the role of regional governments.[7] (Such governments are most commonly called states; but they may also be called provinces, republics, or, as in the Federal Republic of Germany, *Länder*.) The crucial test of federalism is whether a political system has regional governments that have consequential powers. The key to this definition, of course, is the meaning of "consequential." Six criteria are presented here as the framework for constructing a continuum of federalism in terms of the strength of the powers of regional governments:

- *legal powers*—the extent to which regional governments have the power in a written constitution or on some other basis to establish and revise their own political structures and processes and to select their own leaders and officials

• *revenue powers*—the degree to which regional governments are able to determine the kind and amounts of revenue they raise and their power to influence the basis on which revenue sources are shared by the central and regional governments

• *functional-area authority and responsibilities*—the authority of regional governments to control activities and programs in major functional areas of government

• *historical, social, and cultural identification*—the extent to which regional governments have their own historical, ethnic, linguistic, and cultural identification for their citizens

• *role in the affairs of the central government*—the ways in which regional governments through special institutional means influence the actions or activities of the central government

• *power over local units*—the authority of regional governments over local governments within their borders in determining boundaries, functions, finances, and land-use plans

Under this analytical framework Yugoslavia, Canada, the United States, Switzerland, the Federal Republic of Germany, and Austria appear to be the most thoroughly federal countries in the world today.[8]

The Importance of the State Role

The great strength of federalism is its ability to reconcile unity and diversity in a way that adapts to new social, economic, and technological conditions by means of changes in the roles of the different levels and kinds of governments. The middleman role of state governments is the key and swing variable in this adjustment process. In the 1980s the presidency of Ronald Reagan again demonstrated the centrality of the federal-state relationship in American government. In a way that I believe was unintended, the Reagan administration's efforts to advance conventional Republican ideas about devolving functions from the national government to the states led to a "paradox of devolution." The phrase refers to the tendency for the success of the administration's devolutionary policy signals and actions to activate and strengthen state governments in a way that partly negated the administration's parallel and more important efforts (that is, more important to it) to scale down the size and scope of governmental activities in the domestic sector. A major strategy used to pursue the administration's retrenchment objectives was to reduce federal grants-in-aid to state and local governments. These have increasingly become the main instrument—the glue—of intergovernmental relations in American federalism. Kenneth N. Vines observes that grants-in-aid are "a vital way in which the nation and the states relate to each other."[9]

Since 1981 a group of scholars based at Princeton University have been conducting research on the effects of the cuts and the changes in federal grant-in-aid programs under Reagan. His biggest cuts came, not surprisingly, at the beginning of his administration, in 1981. The 1981 budget act reduced federal aid payments to states and localities by 7 percent (13 percent in real terms), the first such cut in actual dollars in twenty-five years. In this research we have been impressed by the impact of these cuts and changes on the structure of American federalism—in particular, by the tendency of state governments to take on a larger role in areas in which the federal government was cutting aid or threatening to do so. The sample for the study consisted of fourteen states chosen to be representative in size, location, and economic and social characteristics and forty local governments within those states.

Five of the sample states were classified as having made the most pronounced response to the Reagan cuts and changes (table 8–1). These states (Florida, Massachusetts, New Jersey, New York, and Oklahoma) took important steps to replace actual or threatened federal aid cuts out of their own funds (fiscal replacement). They also took steps to play a stronger policy-making and administrative role in the functional areas of the Reagan cuts and changes (institutional replacement).

Eight states in the sample were classified in three intermediate-response subgroups. Three of them (Mississippi, Ohio, and Texas) replaced some federal aid cuts out of their

TABLE 8–1
SAMPLE STATES GROUPED BY DEGREE OF STATE RESPONSE
TO FEDERAL CUTS

Great	Moderate/Great[a]	Moderate/Low[b]	Low
Florida	Mississippi	Arizona	California
Massachusetts	Ohio	Illinois	
New Jersey	Texas	Missouri	
New York	Washington[c]	South Dakota	
Oklahoma			

a. Some fiscal replacement; stronger policy and administrative role.
b. No fiscal replacement; stronger policy and administrative role.
c. Rescinded fiscal replacement; stronger policy and administrative role.
SOURCE: Richard P. Nathan, Fred C. Doolittle, and Associates, *Reagan and the States* (Princeton, N.J.: Princeton University Press, 1987), p. 109.

own funds and also took on a stronger policy-making and administrative role in the functional areas affected. One state (Washington) voted to replace federal aid cuts but then was hard hit by the 1981–1982 recession and rescinded its action. It did, however, take substantial advantage of the devolutionary policy changes made by the Reagan administration to allow greater state policy discretion in major federally aided functional areas. The remaining four states in this group (Arizona, Illinois, Missouri, and South Dakota) did not replace federal aid out of their own funds but took steps to exercise a stronger policy-making and administrative role in the areas in which the administration's devolutionary policies were most pronounced. One state in the sample (California) was classified as having made a minimal response to the Reagan changes because, according to our field researchers, the enactment of referendums affecting state finances and debates about others overwhelmed the effects induced by the federal administration.[10]

Past research suggests that innovative policies tend to be adopted by the larger, generally more liberal or progressive state governments. The Princeton University research supports these findings in that the most pronounced response to the Reagan changes usually, but not always, came in states that fit this definition. This is particularly true of the states that from the outset were most willing to commit new or additional revenues from their own sources to replace actual or anticipated federal aid cuts. But there is also evidence of a broader response, in some cases involving traditionally less progressive states, where the state's political ideology was shifting during the period of the study.

One can only speculate about the future: I expect that as state governments take on a larger role they will commit additional resources to the affected programs and services. This is likely to be reflected in increased state spending as program advocates in the areas in which the federal government is pulling back turn increasingly to the state governments as their new arenas for action. Such developments will undoubtedly disappoint conservatives to the extent that they had hoped that shifting responsibilities from the national government to the states would bring about a general decline in governmental activity. According to a 1985 article in the *National Journal*, "Conservatives who gleefully assumed that shifting the responsibility for social programs to the states would mean the end of the programs have discovered that state governments were not as conservative as they thought."[11]

There is already evidence that Reagan's policies have bolstered the states' role both fiscally and programmatically. Thirty-eight states raised taxes in 1983. According to the U.S. Bureau of the Census, the tax revenues of state governments showed a dramatic 14.8 percent increase in 1984. The state fiscal analyst Steven D. Gold noted that "real state general fund spending rose at a significant rate in 1984, 1985, and 1986."[12] Focusing on the condition of state finances in 1984, Gold and Corina L. Eckl note a marked improvement: "State finances are in much better shape today than they have been in the past several years. . . . The upturn is the result of the unexpectedly vigorous economic recovery, large tax increases in 1983, and restraint in spending."[13]

Federal Aid Trends, Nixon to Reagan

Longer-term data on public expenditures from the Census Bureau show the relative decline in the federal role and the rising role of the states under Reagan. Figure 8–1 compares

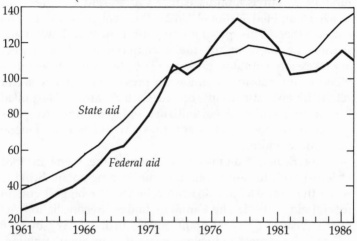

FIGURE 8–1
FEDERAL AND STATE AID
OUTLAYS TO LOCAL GOVERNMENTS, 1961–1987
(in billions of constant 1986 dollars)

NOTE: State aid is shown for state fiscal year, which for most states begins July 1 and ends June 30. Federal aid is shown for the federal fiscal year, which until 1976 also began July 1 and ended June 30. Federal aid outlays after 1976 are for the federal budget period beginning October 1 and ending September 30. Inflation adjustments based on the consumer price index.

SOURCES: Office of Mangement and Budget, *Historical Tables, Budget of the United States Government, Fiscal Year 1989*, table 12.1; and U.S. Census, *Governmental Finances*, various years.

federal aid to states and localities with state aid to local governments in constant dollars from 1961 to 1987. In the early part of this period, which included Lyndon B. Johnson's Great Society and the Richard Nixon years, federal aid rose rapidly but remained below state aid to localities. This relationship shifted toward the end of the Gerald Ford administration, when Congress enacted stimulus spending programs in response to the 1973–1975 recession and also because of the rise in that period of unemployment compensation.

Federal spending reached its peak in 1978 under Jimmy Carter. Carter added to and expanded the stimulus grant programs started under Ford, but after the initial stimulus the picture changed markedly. Federal aid began to fall off at the end of the Carter administration, an event attributable to the shift in the country toward a more conservative mood, signaled by the adoption of Proposition 13 in California in June 1978. Three months earlier Carter sent Congress his much trumpeted National Urban Program to target federal aid to cities. This program, in effect, would have made permanent many of the major components of his earlier antirecession stimulus package. But the new conservative mood of the country, manifest in pressure for public sector retrenchment, apparently cooled Carter's ardor. He pulled back from his urban policy initiative and in the final two years of his presidency took steps to stem the rise in federal domestic spending.

The Reagan administration entered the scene in 1981 well disposed toward continuing this retrenchment. Striking while the iron was hot, Reagan achieved the biggest cuts in federal aid in 1981. The Omnibus Budget Reconciliation Act of that year cut federal grant outlays in fiscal 1982 by $6.6 billion. The largest reductions came in education, training, employment, and social services, where outlays were cut by $4.9 billion, a 23 percent reduction from fiscal 1981. In 1981, however, a sharp recession occurred. Congress shifted its position, responding to the recession by enacting two stimulus measures. Federal aid outlays began to rise again, ultimately achieving nominal levels above those in the Carter years. Although federal aid spending increased in real terms after 1982, it remained below the funding for the last years of the Carter administration, as shown in table 8–2.

Figure 8–1 shows that not only did federal aid rise after 1982 but state aid rose proportionately more. In part, the increase in state aid appears to have been a response to the Reagan administration's decentralization policies: Reagan said the states should do more, and they did. State aid to local governments, which had been relatively flat in real terms in the latter part of the 1970s and the early 1980s, rose at a fast pace from 1983 to 1987—at a real annual rate of 5.2 percent. Note that after 1981 state aid again exceeded federal aid. A lot has happened in this twenty-five-year period. Note also that table 8–2 shows another decline in federal aid outlays in both real and nominal terms under Reagan in 1987.

238

TABLE 8–2
FEDERAL GRANT OUTLAYS IN CURRENT AND CONSTANT (1986) DOLLARS, 1960–1988

	Current Dollars (millions)	Constant Dollars (billions)
1960	7,019.4	26.2
1965	10,910.0	38.2
1970	24,065.2	69.9
1975	49,791.3	105.9
1976	59,093.8	117.0
1977	68,415.0	127.7
1978	77,889.4	133.3
1979	82,858.4	128.4
1980	91,451.0	125.4
1981	94,761.9	117.0
1982	88,194.9	101.7
1983	92,495.3	102.6
1984	97,577.3	104.1
1985	105,897.0	108.9
1986	112,357.4	112.4
1987	108,392.0	105.5
1988[a]	116,665.9	109.2
Change		
1960–70	17,045.8	43.7
Percent	242.8	166.8
1970–80	67,385.8	55.5
Percent	280.0	79.4
1980–88	25,214.9	−16.2
Percent	27.6	−12.9

NOTE: Inflation adjustments based on consumer price index.
a. Estimated.
SOURCE: Office of Management and Budget, *Historical Tables, Budget of the United States Government, Fiscal Year 1989*, table 12.1.

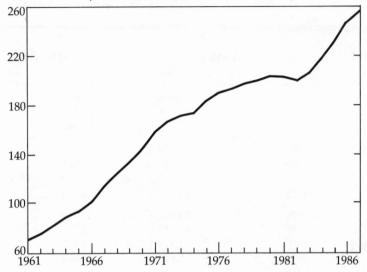

FIGURE 8–2
STATE DIRECT GENERAL EXPENDITURE, 1961–1987
(in billions of constant 1986 dollars)

NOTE: Inflation adjustments based on consumer price index.
SOURCE: U.S. Census, *Governmental Finances*, various years.

This is attributable mainly to the demise of the local share of the revenue-sharing program.

In sum, the states in the Reagan period took the president's rhetoric, or at least part of it, seriously. The resulting state initiatives underlie the rise in total state spending shown in figure 8–2.

Other factors besides Reagan's devolutionary and retrenchment policies underlie the increased involvement of the states in domestic affairs. States on the whole benefited materially from strong recoveries from the 1981–1982 recession; as a result, they had resources to expand their programs in the domestic affairs in which the Reagan administration was cutting federal aid or signaling its intention to do so.

The devolutionary policy initiatives advanced under Reagan, similar to those put forward by conservative politicians in the past as a cover for budget cuts, primarily involved the creation of block grants to consolidate existing categorical grant-in-aid programs in order to assign greater importance and decision-making authority to state governments in the affected policy areas. These block grants under Reagan typically included budget cuts in the consolidated programs (often by as much as 25 percent) on the theory that the greater flexibility allowed would enhance efficiency and thus mitigate the effects of the reduced funding. New block grants were enacted for public health, education, community development, social services, and employment and training. The administration took other steps through both legislation and administrative action (mainly by relaxing regulatory enforcement) to advance the Republican cause of decentralization to the states.

Cycles of Federalism

I now want to advance a cyclical theory to account for the history of the changes that have occurred in the federal-state relationship in the United States. I believe that, if this cyclical pattern had been perceived in advance by the members of Reagan's high command, they might have behaved differently.

The key point is this. Typically the national government has been the source of innovations and policy initiatives in liberal (prospending and expansive) periods of our history; the states (not all states, but many of them) have been the centers of activism and innovation in conservative (retrenchment and contractive) periods. In the 1920s, when the country was keeping "cool with Coolidge," states were the source of major progressive policy initiatives on such matters as unemployment insurance, public assistance, and workmen's compensation. James T. Patterson notes that the states "preceded the federal government in regulating large corporations, establishing minimum labor standards, and stimulating economic development."[14] He adds that "the most remarkable development in state government in the 1920s was the increase in spending."[15] These and other state policy initiatives planted the seeds of Franklin D. Roosevelt's New Deal.

241

This same pattern can be seen further back in time. A spurt of state initiatives in domestic affairs characterized the conservative Republican period in the 1880s. Allan Nevins and Henry Steele Commager wrote that "the first great battles of the reform movement were fought out in the states."[16] Compulsory school attendance laws and the creation of state boards of education, reforms of political processes, a growing role for state boards of charity, child labor laws, and state regulatory policies in licensing and zoning are examples of state innovations in areas of domestic policy at the turn of the century.

In the 1980s, as the pendulum of social policy again swung toward conservatism, we saw another spurt in state activism. A number of factors have contributed to this development. Reagan's domestic policies are one. Another is the modernization of state governments, enhancing the managerial and technical capacity of the states to take on new and expanded functions. In a 1985 report the U.S. Advisory Commission on Intergovernmental Relations noted that "state governments have been transformed in almost every facet of their structure and operations."[17] The states' role has also been enhanced by the effect of the U.S. Supreme Court's decision in *Baker* v. *Carr* in 1962, which helped to reduce the political rural-urban imbalance of many state legislatures.[18] In addition, Martha Derthick stresses the importance of "the end of Southern exceptionalism" as an underlying reason for increased state government activism in domestic affairs in recent years. Integration in the South, she believes, has created a situation in which "the case for the states can at last begin to be discussed on its merits."[19] The economic recovery from the 1981–1982 recession also contributed to the resurgence of the states in the 1980s. State governments tend to overreact to recessions, battening down the fiscal hatches and cutting spending and raising taxes to balance their budgets. The strong economic recovery after the 1981–1982 recession found state coffers filling rapidly late in 1982 and 1983, just as Reagan's retrenchment policies were beginning to be felt. As a result, in the mid-1980s states were in a much better position to move into functional areas in which the federal government under Reagan was either pulling back or signaling that it meant to.

The coming together of these factors has produced the resurgence of the states' role in American federalism. Evidence of this change is seen not only in the response to Reagan's cuts and changes in federal grant-in-aid programs but also in the efforts of many state governments to reform major state programs. Notable shifts have occurred in education, health, and welfare. School initiatives by governors and legislatures, for example, to mandate early education, strengthen instruction in basic disciplines ("back to basics"), and upgrade the performance of teachers through merit pay and other reforms are under way in many states. According to Denis P. Doyle and Terry W. Hartle, writing in 1985, "The last two years have witnessed the greatest and most concentrated surge of educational reform in the nation's history. . . . Indeed, the most surprising aspect of the 'tidal wave of reform' is that it came from state governments."[20] Other programmatic reforms with states in the lead have been undertaken in the health field—for example, to reform existing programs and control the costs of medical care services.

In the field of public welfare, important policy shifts are under way, again with state governments in the lead. The states are experimenting with new-style workfare, obligating welfare family heads to participate in job search, remedial education, training, and jobs. This is an institutional effort to convert welfare programs for able-bodied, working-age recipients from essentially payment systems to systems with a strong emphasis on employment and job preparation. State governments have also taken a leadership role in planning, growth management, and the provision of new infrastructure to enhance economic development. There is considerable variation in all these areas, reflecting Justice Louis Brandeis's likening of state governments to laboratories that can "try novel social and economic experiments without risk to the rest of the country."[21]

The current activism of state governments is not easily gauged. There are no ready calipers for such measurements. Past studies by the political scientists Jack L. Walker and Virginia Gray suggest that the larger, older, and ideologically most liberal (progovernment) states have tended to be most innovative.[22] The Princeton University research, however, suggests a broader distribution whereby younger states and those that are changing ideologically toward a more liberal stance on the role of government are also among the leaders in enhancing the role of the state governments.

This cyclical pattern of federal-state relations in American federalism reflects what I believe is the normal equilibrating tendency of the political system for states to move into areas of public policy when the national government is moving out of them or at least not taking any initiatives. An almost mathematical logic underlies this alternating pattern of national and state governmental initiatives in domestic affairs. When the society as a whole favors governmental action of a new kind or in a new field, proponents of this course are likely to find it easier and more efficient to concentrate their energy for achieving policy change at one point in the political system—namely, at the center. But the reverse side of this proposition is that in periods of conservatism, when there is diminishing support for governmental action in the society, proponents of such action are likely to be most successful in those states and communities in which, for whatever reason, there is support for governmental action. The United States has always been a country in a hurry, one that lives in the present. It is not surprising that in the four decades of growth in the government's role—from the New Deal through the late 1970s—we tended to forget that, in past contractive periods, the states were the engines of innovation in domestic affairs.

According to Woodrow Wilson, the federal-state relationship is "the cardinal question of our constitutional system." Said Wilson: "It cannot be settled by the opinion of any one generation, because it is a question of growth, and every new successive state of our political and economic development gives it a new aspect, makes it a new question."[23] The artful blending of two plans put forward by nationalists and half-hearted federalists at the Philadelphia convention produced the American brand of federalism.[24] Referring to this new form, Tocqueville said: "Evidently this is no longer a federal government, but an incomplete national government, which is neither exactly national nor exactly federal; but the new word which ought to express this novel thing does not yet exist."[25]

Despite Tocqueville's desire for a new word to describe Madison's idea of a "composition," none was ever coined. Martin Diamond's interpretation of the theoretical contribution made by the Constitutional Convention focuses on Madison. The key to the new system was Madison's "great and novel idea."[26] Madison turned Montesquieu's principle that only small countries could enjoy republican government on its head. He argued that "*smallness* was fatal to republicanism" and that "only a country as large as the whole thirteen states and more could provide a safe dwelling-place for republican liberty."[27]

To sum up, the aim of Madison's great composition was to assign governmental responsibilities to two kinds of government on a basis that would produce competition between the national government and the states as one among several checks against the concentration of power in the hands of political factions. We can indeed think of the American idea of checks and balances as having two dimensions. One is horizontal, the division of power among the three branches. The other, federalism, is the vertical dimension of this idea. The pluralism of the American political system is its most distinctive feature. The number of players, said Tocqueville, produces "a picture of power, somewhat wild perhaps, but robust, and a life liable to mishaps but full of striving and animation."[28]

Modern Theories of American Federalism

The ratification of the U.S. Constitution did not establish a political form once and for all. Over time two main theories of the American federal-state relationship have competed for attention. Most observers have chosen sides, arguing for one of the theories and rejecting the other. The thesis advanced in this chapter is that both should be accepted. The shifting sands of American federalism can best be interpreted by using not one but both of the two theories that are dominant in the modern literature.

245

The first is the formal or traditional theory—also called "the dual federalism theory"—associated most strongly with the thirty-year leadership of Chief Justice Roger B. Taney of the U.S. Supreme Court from 1835 to 1865. This position dominated the political science literature on federalism through the 1950s. K. C. Wheare is in this camp. He wrote, "The test which I apply for federal government is simply this. Does a system of government embody predominantly a division of powers between general and regional authorities, each of which, in its own sphere, is co-ordinate with the others and independent of them?"[29] Among American political scientists, Arthur W. MacMahon's writing also typifies this view. He described federalism as a political system that "distributes power between a common and constituent governments under an arrangement that cannot be changed by the ordinary process of central legislation."[30] It can be changed only by constitutional amendment. For MacMahon a further defining characteristic of federalism was that "the matters entrusted to the constituent units (whether their powers are residual or delegated) must be substantial and not merely trivial."[31]

A major element of this traditional approach is associated with "Dillon's rule," which highlights the states' role in American federalism. John Forrest Dillon, an Iowa Supreme Court justice in the late nineteenth century and the author of a textbook on municipal government, is credited with the phrase that local governments in American federalism are "creatures of the states." Their boundaries, functions, and finances are set by the states. It is the state legislature, said Dillon, that "breathes into them the breath of life without which they cannot exist."[32] The focus for the traditional and legalistic view of federalism is on this federal-state, as opposed to federal-local, connection. Proponents of this traditional position point out that the U.S. Constitution nowhere mentions local governments.

The second and contrasting modern theory of federalism came to prominence in the late 1960s, although it has deeper roots in the scholarly literature, particularly in the writings of Jane Perry Clark and Edward S. Corwin. This is the dynamic theory of federalism associated with the famous marble cake metaphor devised by the political scientist Morton Grodzins. Contrasting his view with the traditional layer cake (two-layer) theory of American federalism, Grodzins said that a more realistic metaphor is a marble cake:

> Wherever you slice through it you reveal an insepa-rable mixture of different colored ingredients. There is no neat horizontal stratification. Vertical and di-agonal lines almost obliterate the horizontal ones, and in some places there are unexpected whirls and an imperceptible merging of colors, so that it is difficult to tell where one ends and the other be-gins.[33]

Ironically, Grodzins's position came to be well known as a product of the work of a study commission set up by President Dwight Eisenhower, who himself strongly favored and worked to advance the traditional model of federalism. In the 1960s the Grodzins view that functions are and should be shared in American federalism was used to justify an expanded role for the national government in a wide range of domestic affairs. Michael Reagan and John Sanzone have written that since the 1960s the "sharing of functions is most clearly and dramatically seen in the explosive growth of federal grants-in-aid."[34]

Increasingly, the expanded role for the national govern-ment in the post–World War II period involved not just the federal-state relationship but also more extensive direct rela-tionships between the national government and local govern-ments. These relationships, which Roscoe Martin calls "the expanded partnership," are an important tenet of the Grod-zins theory of federalism, in much the same way that the traditional theory highlights the federal-state relationship.[35] Beginning under President Harry Truman and continuing to the late 1970s, federal grants-in-aid involved direct relation-ships between the national government and cities and also between the national government and a variety of special quasi-governmental entities, some of them created as part of President Johnson's War on Poverty.

The Role of the Courts

Although the structure of intergovernmental relations in American federalism has been shaped in substantial measure

247

by federal grants-in-aid and their attendant regulations, grants are not the only important shaping force. The courts have had a long and strong influence on the roles of the different kinds of government in the American system. On the whole, courts in the modern period have reflected the Grodzins conception of federalism. Derthick notes that from the mid-1930s, especially under Chief Justice Earl Warren, the U.S. Supreme Court emerged as an aggressive nationalizing force.[36] In civil rights in particular, the courts, since the *Brown v. Board of Education of Topeka* decision in 1954, have upheld the constitutional rights of individuals against state and local restraints.

Most recently, in *Garcia* v. *San Antonio Metropolitan Transit Authority* (1985), the effect of the Supreme Court's decision was to uphold the centralizing theory that American federalism entails no intrinsic and immutable divisions of power and responsibility. Writing for the majority in *Garcia*, Justice Harry A. Blackmun said that efforts by the courts to impose limits on the Congress's power in relation to the states ultimately fall short because of "the elusiveness of objective criteria for 'fundamental' elements of state sovereignty."[37] The Court did momentarily explore the contrary view, grounded in the idea of "traditional" state functions, in its decision in *National League of Cities* v. *Usery* in 1976; but this decision was overturned by *Garcia*, a decision, according to a dissenting opinion by Justice Lewis F. Powell, Jr., that "reduces the Tenth Amendment to meaningless rhetoric when Congress acts pursuant to the Commerce Clause."[38] In an unusual and very brief dissent, Justice (now Chief Justice) William H. Rehnquist joined with Powell and predicted a reversal of *Garcia:* "I do not think it incumbent on those of us in the dissent to spell out further the fine points of a principle that will, I am confident, in time again command the support of a majority of this Court."[39]

To summarize, although the situation is now changing, the post–World War II story of scholarly writing about American federalism can be seen as one in which the dynamic sharing position represented by the writings of Grodzins has tended to push out the more formal and legalistic theory that used to emphasize the division of functions between the national government and the states. Politically, liberals have favored the former theory, along with its corollary of an expanded federal-state-local partnership (counterposed to the concept expressed by Dillon's rule highlighting the federal-state relationship). In most of this period the federal role in domestic affairs was expanding both in the customary areas of federal-state involvement (for example, welfare, transportation, public health, and social services) and in new areas of federal involvement at both the state and local levels (for example, elementary and secondary education, urban community development, environmental protection, and antipoverty programs).

One interpretation that has been given for the rise in federal aid is that such an increase has always been the norm. Functions have always been shared; in the postwar period there was simply more to share. Elazar, a student of Grodzins who advocates this position, argues that "cooperative federalism" reflects the historic pattern of American intergovernmental relations.[40] The difference over the years, according to Elazar, is not that the degree of sharing has grown but rather that the role of government has increased in a context in which shared functions have always been the norm. "The theory that the federal and state governments had their own spheres of activity in which each operated independently of the other must be altered to show that at any given time in American political history the great majority of governmental activities were shared by all levels of government."[41]

Elazar's interpretation is not accepted universally. Other observers have interpreted American federalism as involving a general and steady rise in the role of the national government in domestic affairs. This evolutionary interpretation depicts American government as undergoing a process of federalizing, which, according to Carl J. Friedrich, reflects the integration of the political community in the modern setting. "Federalism is more fully understood if it is seen as a process, an evolving pattern of changing relationships rather than a static design regulated by firm and unalterable rules."[42] Friedrich defines this process as one in which "a number of separate political communities enter into arrangements for working out solutions, adopting joint policies, and making joint decisions."[43] Vile emphasizes the same point, describing federalism as territorial in origin and changing over time in a manner that leads to its transformation to something different, an integrated state.

As I have already said, I view this historical experience as cyclical. I note a tendency for the role of the national government in the domestic public sector to expand in liberal periods and to contract vis-à-vis the states' role in conservative periods. This interpretation emphasizes the equilibrating tendencies of American federalism, which, according to this view, is resilient and adaptive, shifting to find a new balance in the relative roles of different kinds of governments as conditions change in society.

Another theoretical point needs to be added here about this cyclical pattern. Public choice theorists depict federalism as a governmental system that creates competition among the states, which holds down governmental taxing and spending. The opportunity of citizens to move freely among political jurisdictions produces pressures that hold back increases in public services. Geoffrey Brennan and James M. Buchanan characterize federalism as "an indirect means of imposing constraints on the potential fiscal exploitation of Leviathan," referring to "the monopoly-state model of government."[44]

Another way to interpret the role of states, however, challenges the conservative interpretation of the public choice theorists. Federalism can be seen as a progrowth force, promoting government spending to the extent that the activism of state governments in conservative periods causes a ratcheting-up effect over time. State initiatives undertaken in conservative periods become the basis for national policy actions in liberal periods. This was the case, for example, for many of the initiatives adopted at the national level as part of the New Deal. Although we can never know what the size of the public sector in the United States would have been under a different political system, I believe there are good grounds for arguing that this ratcheting-up effect has had a "liberal" or progovernment effect over time. It has moderated the strong American norm of limited government and caused the public sector to be larger than would otherwise have been the case.

250

The Sorting-out Approach

An important change occurred in the late 1960s in the development of ideas about American federalism—the emergence of what can be called the sorting-out approach to federalism. This was a reaction to the "proliferation" of categorical federal grants-in-aid in the 1960s. It was also a harbinger of the more conservative decentralization mood on domestic affairs that took hold in earnest in the late 1970s. Proponents of this approach criticized the Great Society "explosion" of federal grants as undermining accountability and rationality in domestic affairs and causing political resentment, confusion, and inefficiency in the management of domestic programs. The U.S. Advisory Commission on Intergovernmental Relations played a strong role in dramatizing the problem of system overload and in advocating new approaches to sort out (or, as it was often described, "rationalize") functions and responsibilities in the American system.

President Nixon's New Federalism, which included welfare reform, revenue sharing, and block grants, reflected this sorting-out approach; it was rooted in a sharply critical view of the effects of Johnson's Great Society. Nixon's program was advanced as a way of rationalizing federalism by realigning functional responsibilities, in the process strengthening the role of state and local governments. In a White House memorandum to senior administration officials issued in June 1970, Nixon explained his program in the following terms:

> Under the New Federalism, major aims are to define more clearly functional responsibilities among levels of government and strengthen governmental institutions at all levels. Welfare, for example, is appropriately a national responsibility. . . . In areas which are primarily State-local responsibilities, revenue sharing and other measures which the Administration has advanced will strengthen the capacity of States and localities to make decisions which reflect their own priorities and needs.[45]

Nixon discussed his views in a similar way, with reference to the environment, in a speech to the National Governors' Association. He suggested that his ideas on the need to sort out functions in the American system involved issues that he was closely familiar with.

> On the other hand, when we consider the problem of the environment it is very clear that clean air and water doesn't stop at a State line. And it is also very clear that if one State adopts very stringent regulations, it has the effect of penalizing itself as against another State which has regulations which are not as stringent insofar as attracting the private enterprise that might operate in one State or another or that might make that choice. This is why we have suggested national standards.[46]

Although Nixon had much to say on the subject, he was by no means unique among recent presidents in this connection. Every president in the modern period has taken a stand on federalism.

As the sorting-out approach to federalism gathered steam in the 1970s, economists and their ideas played an increasingly large role. Economic ideas of spillovers and externalities were frequently put forward as the justification for designating some functions (for example, air and water pollution control) as appropriate for national action and other functions (police and fire protection) as areas in which the national government should have a limited and nonintrusive role, if any.

The essence of the sorting-out approach was a movement away from the Grodzins extensive-sharing view of federalism to one that, in the more traditional way, emphasized the different roles and responsibilities of the national government and the states. Reagan's position on these issues made the point even more sharply.

Reagan's Brand of "New Federalism"

Although Reagan did not use the term "new federalism" (precisely, it is said, because Nixon had used it), the press nevertheless described his efforts to rearrange intergovernmental functions and finances as a new federalism. Reagan's position can be seen as moving further toward the traditional dual federalism and away from the marble cake theory.

Throughout his public career one of Reagan's major goals was devolution from the federal government to the states. As governor of California he argued strongly for such a shift. When he was running for the Republican presidential nomination in 1976, he delivered a speech calling for a systematic $90 billion plan to transfer authority and national government resources and programs to the states. His view had not changed four years later when he was elected president. In his inaugural address in 1981 he promised to curb the power of the national government and to "demand recognition of the distinction" between national government powers and "those reserved to the states." (This is the same terminology used in the Tenth Amendment.) Reagan successfully pressed for changes in domestic policy reflecting his theory in his first year in office. He sought and obtained substantial cuts in federal aid programs for states and localities in part as a way of reducing the national government's role in domestic affairs. At the same time he proposed new block grants to reduce federal controls under grant-in-aid programs and to increase the role of state governments in the affected policy areas. Unlike the funds provided by the block grant programs enacted under his most recent Republican predecessors, Nixon and Ford, most of the funds provided under Reagan's block grants were paid not directly to local governments but to the states.

Reagan continued his efforts to devolve federal programs to the states in 1982 when he devoted the bulk of his State of the Union message to an extensive and elaborate "swap and turnback" plan for fundamentally rearranging the responsibilities for $47 billion in federal grant-in-aid funds, roughly half the total. Although he was not successful in achieving a realignment, the way these proposals would have worked has important implications for the discussion in this section.

It is helpful to introduce a conceptual device here for viewing the structure and operation of federal grant-in-aid programs. All activities of government have three main dimensions: policy making, financing, and administration. We can analyze intergovernmental relations in terms of the level of government that has the principal responsibility for one or several of these three dimensions for any given function or program. Grants-in-aid affect these governmental alignments in important ways by altering the arrangement of the three dimensions. A federal grant typically prescribes rules for a program (thus involving an increased policy role for the national government) and also provides funds for the aided function. Under federal aid programs, however, the administration of the benefits or services is carried out by the recipient government. The net result of the growth in federal grants-in-aid is that, even though the national government comes to play a larger policy and financial role in the affected functional areas, state and local governments retain more real control than critics of the intrusiveness of the national government often credit them with. This is because the states and localities, as well as the national government, have a policy and funding role and also because they administer the benefits and services being aided. In sum, it is not always true that he who pays the piper calls the tune. Under federal grants the piper—the recipients of federal aid—can vary the tune a great deal.

If we use these concepts, we can see that Reagan's grand designs for reform of federalism—that is, his 1976 and 1982 comprehensive reform plans—would have realigned functions by assigning some responsibilities fully to the states and others fully to the national government and that these changes would have included realignments on all three dimensions—policy, finances, and administration. Reagan's "swap and turnback" plan of 1982, for example, would have had the national government assume the full three-dimensional responsibility for Medicaid, in exchange for which the states were to assume full responsibility for aid to families with dependent children (AFDC) and food stamps.

Reagan did not succeed (in fact, he did not get very far at all) with these grand designs for reform. Instead, the devolutionary measures that he advanced successfully (particularly block grants) were incremental.

At this point my earlier observation about the paradox of devolution under Reagan reenters the picture. Government policies involve both signals and substance. The signal given by Reagan's devolutionary policies was that the states should do more. The substance was to reduce the role of the national government in both policy making and financing for domestic programs. The net result was that the states actually did more. In this way Reagan's devolutionary policies in many cases undercut the more important retrenchment goal of his administration by activating state governments.

There is a further irony of the Reagan period in relation to federalism. Reagan had long favored full devolution to the states of the controversial AFDC program. Yet his biggest budget cuts in absolute dollar terms in 1981 came as a result of the ability of the national government to control this program. The cuts were achieved by tightening federal regulations under AFDC with the effect that benefits were cut or people were removed from the AFDC rolls and also from the Medicaid rolls.

Taken as a whole, this experience suggests that the conventional conservative position on federalism (favoring decentralization) may not have been the appropriate policy for Reagan. In earlier periods it may have made sense for conservatives like Reagan to favor converting the AFDC program into a block grant, but in the more conservative 1980s Reagan's ability to curb spending in this area turned out to be a direct function of the ability of the national government to set policies in the welfare field.

We can now sum up for all program areas. In a liberal period conservative politicians may be wise to press for devolution and block grants. But in conservative periods one can argue that they should pursue exactly the opposite strategy. In those periods the states are likely to be the sources of new energy and innovation. Hence, retrenchment measures may be easier to advance in program areas over which the federal government has substantial policy control.

A Synthesis

I can now pull together the several strands of my argument. In the postwar period, during which there has been an advance in the role of government at all levels in the society, the pattern has been for liberals (governmental expansionists) to favor centralization and with it Grodzins's marble cake view of federalism. On the other side of the fence politically, conservatives (contractionists) have pressed for devolution and have generally embraced the traditional theory of dual federalism to support their position. For both sides these strategies make sense in a period of governmental growth but can be called into question when the pendulum swings to contraction. Reagan achieved his biggest retrenchment successes in programs where the national government could call the shots. Moreover, some of the standard devolutionary measures he was able to enact (notably block grants) appear to have undermined his paramount retrenchment aims.

The nub of these unanticipated responses—at least unanticipated by politicians—concerns the role of the states. I have argued that the role of the states as the middlemen of federalism changes as conditions change in society and the economy. The states' role diminishes as the federal government's role in domestic affairs increases in liberal periods. The opposite is true in conservative periods, when the American governmental system reflects more strongly the traditional theory of federalism as the states assert themselves. Neither the marble cake model nor the dual federalism model fully serves our needs. American federalism can be thought of as involving a continuum between the two positions, with the movement along this continuum strongly influenced by ideology. The states are now resurgent on a basis that reinforces their role in domestic affairs. I expect this trend to continue, though not indefinitely.

The politics here are not what they may seem on the surface. Liberals do not always gain by being centralists, and conservatives do not always gain by favoring decentralization. Politicians would be well advised to eschew orthodoxy; a doctrine for one era may have very ideological consequences in a different period. This is the beauty of the system—its ability to adapt governmental structures to changing values.

Federalism and the Urban Crisis

Some readers may feel that the discussion of American federalism so far has been too theoretical. Government is about people. What are the implications of the changing nature of federalism for people? I treat this subject under the heading "the urban crisis" because I want to focus on the connection between federalism and social policy.

The term "urban policy" refers to ways of dealing with the social and economic needs of distressed communities, typically older communities with high concentrations of poor people and minorities. The widespread sharing, three-layer theory of federalism that liberals embraced in the 1960s and 1970s (and still support to a considerable degree today) was in large measure a strategy designed to bypass the states so that the national government would deal directly with urban needs. A basic tenet of the proponents of a strong role for the national government in urban policy was that the federal government should act in a way that was more strongly redistributive than would be expected of state governments either on their own or in their role as administrators of federal aid funds.

The idea of directing resources to the local communities with social and economic problems—the term "targeting" has come to be widely used to express this objective—has appeal on the surface. But formidable difficulties lurk below. Two kinds of problems stand out. One is mechanical. The other is substantive, concerning the equity of direct federal-local subventions. Both need to be considered.

More than any other, the characteristic of American political geography that stands out is its diversity. The organization of local government varies widely, indeed tremendously, among and within the states. In addition, local government is highly fragmented. The United States has over 80,000 local governments. In 1980 these included 18,076 municipalities, 3,041 counties, 16,734 townships, 14,851 independent school districts, and 28,588 special districts for a wide variety of purposes. To add to this complexity, local governments are layered in ways that vary greatly among local areas. This layering and the differences in the ways in which the states assign responsibilities for functions and finances produce a multiplicative—one might even say turbulent—picture of American local government, one that begins to convey its true character.

For federal grants-in-aid and their attendant requirements, the question raised here is the way in which the

257

national government relates to local governments. Until the Truman period the conventional wisdom was quite simple: it should not. Proponents of this position held that Dillon's rule that local governments are the creatures of the states should be used to ensure that the national government keep its distance from local government. But gradually this changed. Direct federal-local relationships grew under Truman for urban renewal and housing, under Johnson for a wide array of social programs, and under Nixon and Ford for revenue sharing and block grant programs. The result was a substantial increase in direct federal-local relationships, both fiscal and regulatory. This was reflected in the amount and proportion of direct aid provided by the national government to localities. By 1978, the peak year for direct federal aid to localities, nearly one-half of all federal aid for nonwelfare purposes—that is, omitting AFDC and Medicaid—was in the form of direct grants to local entities. Among the major categories of this aid were community development, environmental protection, mass transit, antipoverty social services, revenue sharing, and employment and training. In sharp contrast to the 1960s and 1970s, federal aid to localities declined under Reagan from 25 percent of all federal aid in 1980 to 15 percent in 1986.[47]

Decisions about the distribution, character, and attendant regulation of direct federal grants to localities are the raw material of urban policy. Carter's short-lived National Urban Program of 1978 was primarily a targeting program. The central idea was that federal grants-in-aid should be concentrated on those communities that had the greatest needs. Carter's program included both the revision of existing formula-grant distribution systems and the establishment of new targeted intergovernmental fiscal flows to localities. Carter's urban program, however, did not come close to achieving its objectives, in large part, as we have seen, because of the sharp change in the national mood toward greater conservatism on social issues in the late 1970s.

The Carter program not only faced substantive problems. Even if it had gone forward, it would also have faced formidable technical problems. The urban crisis in the United States is a function of geography. Old cities, especially those settled in the last century before the automobile, tend to be the most needy, in part because suburban voters have been unwilling to expand their boundaries to share core-city burdens on a broader geographical basis. This produces the classical "doughnut" constellation of urban distress, with the empty core in resource terms surrounded by "doughy" suburbs. Racial differences are often the main reason for the tendency of older cities and suburbs to resist merging with the inner cities or expanding their boundaries. Newer cities, however, particularly those in the South and Southwest (chartered in the automobile age), often cover a much larger territory.

These geographical patterns mean that efforts to equalize fiscal subventions among localities must contend with substantial definitional problems. One problem is that they are likely to penalize a kind of behavior that many people consider desirable—the willingness to expand boundaries and share burdens within a metropolitan area. Another is that such schemes may fail to take into account different state financing arrangements, whereby a state government will pay for services in one city but not in another. Wrestling with all these equity, boundary, functional, and financial considerations has always been difficult in U.S. domestic policy.

On the whole, the rise of direct federal-local grant-in-aid programs has not involved successful efforts at targeting. Federal aid funds provided directly to local governments have been spread rather thin. The politics of these programs are what one might expect. The bigger and more general a direct federal-local grant (for example, revenue sharing and block grants), the more likely are the funds to be allocated on an essentially distributive basis since every local government likes money. The best way for those groups and individuals who favor targeting to deal with this problem is probably to promote federal aid for functions that not all local governments want or need to fulfill. The dilemma here, however, is that such programs—for example, slum clearance, high-crime-area aid, mass transit—are often the least salable in the Washington policy process precisely because their benefits are geographically concentrated.

There are basically three ways of dealing with the special

needs of distressed communities. One is to provide aid directly to local governments or organizations, an approach that involves substantial tactical and intellectual problems. A second is to focus on aid to poor people, in the form of transfer payments.[48] Still a third, not inconsistent with the second, is to rely on the states for fiscal relationships with local governmental entities.

This third approach to intergovernmental fiscal relations has the advantage of letting the states work out distributional problems that are a function of state political and financial structures and the fragmentation of local units and that are therefore more likely to be amenable to state than to federal solutions. The evidence, however, is mixed on the targeting commitment and capability of state governments relative to those of the federal government. Some studies conclude that state governments on the whole are more prone to redistributive intergovernmental fiscal policies than the national government; other studies draw the opposite conclusion.[49]

Although it is hard to generalize, the sad truth for those who favor redistributive social policies—whether for people, for places, or for both—is that in conservative periods many governments, including the national government, turn away from social issues and the poor. We are back to our cyclical theme. The old argument of liberals that the national government cares more than the states about social needs does not appear to hold up in conservative periods. In these periods states that care about social needs are likely to outperform the government in Washington.

Final Thoughts

Not everyone will agree with the conclusions reached in this chapter about the cyclical nature of federal-state relations and its implications for domestic and social policy. In short, my view is that no approach to assigning functions in the American federal system is intrinsically right for all times for liberals and conservatives. Although this may be a good thing for American society (I think it is), it makes life harder for experts and analysts who like to deal with nice neat systems and strong generalizations that hold up over time.

What about the future? Will a cyclical pattern of alternating state and national government activism recur? Will the national government expand domestic policy initiatives in the 1990s, and will the states become relatively more quiescent?

My inclination is to think that the near future, including the next decade, is not likely to be a period of dramatic federal government innovations in domestic affairs on anything like the scale of the New Deal or the Great Society or the Nixon New Federalism. One obvious reason for this is the serious budget pressure in Washington. Another is less obvious. The social agenda involves fewer big-spending issues on which there is a broad consensus for national action such as spurred past periods of substantial domestic program innovation by the national government.

The essential point is that the development of American federalism has not been a one-way street toward greater centralized control over public spending and public policy in the way some earlier scholars claimed. The vertical or federalism dimension of the distinctively American pluralist model has changed as our values and goals have changed, sometimes with central authority increasing and at others with the states' role increasing. This, I believe, is the right way to understand federal-state relations in American federalism. Others may put a different interpretation on the changing roles of the national and state governments. My aim is not to convince readers of all the details of a particular interpretation but rather to urge that the states' role in American federalism—which Woodrow Wilson called "the cardinal question of our constitutional system"—be seen in a way that highlights its ebb and flow as the key to understanding the great "composition" invented by the framers.

9
A World of Difference—
The Public Philosophies
and Political Behaviors
of Rival American Cultures

Aaron Wildavsky

In his luminous essay "In Search of a New Public Philosophy," which opened the first version of *The New American Political System*,[1] Samuel Beer asked what had replaced the New Deal as a broadly acceptable doctrine that both guided the definition of problems of economic inequality and indicated where through action by the federal government a solution might be found. Turning to the Port Huron statement of the Students for a Democratic Society, Beer noted the advocacy of "self-cultivation, self-direction" in "a participatory democracy" designed to bring people "out of isolation into community."[2] Here, in the 1960s, the combination of individualism (the self that was to do its own directing and cultivating) and collectivism (the bringing out of individuals from isolation into community) was made manifest. How, if this bid for a public philosophy were accepted, we may ask, could self-direction (the isolated individual) be joined together with group direction (the participatory community)? This chapter traces the influence on the broader political system of the egalitarian political culture that attempts this very task.

Beer identified the "sharp new twist . . . to any future public philosophy"[3] as "the new egalitarianism"—an "equality of results for each cultural group."[4] His essay recounts the successes, failures, and mixed results of this doctrine with its vision of desired social relations. Along the way he observes a conservative strain in the variety of federal programs that, in one way or another, also sought to reduce inequalities. For, as he says, "Without an appreciation of this conservative activism—mesoconservative, since it was formulated mainly during the Great Society period—it is hard to understand the prodigious growth in the public sector which, beginning under Lyndon Johnson, continued unchecked for eight years under Republican Presidents."[5] There must have been a belief that the central government, acting as the collective agent of the society, had some sort of obligation to help citizens in need of aid. This is the idea that the parts should sacrifice for the whole, which is part of a hierarchical way of life. It not only is a product of our times but also was a staple of the two predominantly hierarchical parties of early American history, the Federalists and the Whigs, with their penchant for "internal improvements." Since Americans are also egalitarian and hierarchical, competitive individualism cannot be the only American way.

Competitive Individualism versus Egalitarian Collectivism

The single worst misunderstanding about American politics, in my opinion, is the joining together of two separate and distinct political cultures with opposing preferences for policies and institutions—competitive individualism and egalitarian collectivism—as a single entity. Between equality of opportunity, so that individuals can accentuate their differences, and equality of results, so that individuals can diminish their differences, there is a vast gulf.

Individualistic cultures seek self-regulation as a substitute for authority. They prefer minimum authority, just enough to maintain rules for transaction, but they do not reject all authority. If it leaves them alone, they will leave it alone. These competitors are individualistic in two senses: they transact for themselves rather than being bound by group decisions, and they prefer as few prescriptions as possible, other than the absence of physical coercion, binding their behavior.

Egalitarians are collectivists. While they also like to live a life of minimal prescription, they are part and parcel of collectives in which, so long as they remain members, individuals are bound by group decisions. This critical distinction in group boundedness—the freedom to transact for themselves with any consenting adults, as against the requirement of agreement with group decisions—makes for a radical difference in the formation of political preferences. The two cultures, individualism versus egalitarianism, differ in regard to economic growth, technological danger, taxing and spending, defense and foreign policy, the legitimacy of institutions, and on and on. Yet each, because of its dependence on personal consent, is called individualist, totally ignoring the consideration that egalitarian cultures form collectives while individualistic cultures do not.

The left-right distinction that is used to classify beliefs is beset with contradictions. Hierarchical cultures favor social conservatism, giving government the right to intervene in matters of personal morality. Hence egalitarians may support hierarchical intervention in the economy to increase equality but not in social life to maintain inequality. Competitive individualists protest both social and economic intervention. Triangular we stand, says cultural theory, invoking egalitarianism as well as individualism and hierarchy, but dichotomous—left or right, liberal or conservative—we fall because these categories contain an insufficient variety to account for what we know.[6]

A division of the world into left and right that is equally inapplicable to the past and the present deserves to be discarded. Efforts to read back the left-right distinction into American history, for instance, succeed only in making a hash of it. In the early days of the republic, egalitarians pursued their objectives through severe restrictions on central government because they regarded the center as inegalitarian. Nowadays, egalitarians view the central government as a potential source of equality, thereby supporting its efforts to diminish power differences in society. How, then, can one make sense of the Republican alliance of economic free markets and social conservatism or the Democratic combination of statism with distrust of authority? Is it the "left" that supports the authority of central government and the "right"

265

that opposes it, or is it the "right" that respects authority and the "left" that denigrates it, or what? The confusion over liberal versus conservative is magnified by the prevailing conception of a single American political culture united in its distrust of political authority.

Individualists Are Not Egalitarians

In his powerfully argued *American Politics: The Promise of Disharmony*, Samuel Huntington sees the United States hung up between the opposition to authority of the political culture and the necessity of supporting institutions if its ideals of liberty and equality are to be realized:

> This gap between political ideal and political reality is a continuing central phenomenon of American politics in a way that is not true of any other major state. The importance of the gap stems from three distinctive characteristics of American political ideals. First is the *scope* of the agreement on these ideals. In contrast to most European societies, a broad consensus exists and has existed in the United States on basic political values and beliefs. These values and beliefs, which constitute what is often referred to as "the American Creed," have historically served as a distinctive source of American national identity. Second is the *substance* of those ideals. In contrast to the values of most other societies, the values of this Creed are liberal, individualistic, democratic, egalitarian, and hence basically antigovernment and antiauthority in character. Whereas other ideologies legitimate established authority and institutions, the American Creed serves to delegitimate any hierarchical, coercive, authoritarian structures, including American ones. Third is the changing *intensity* with which Americans believe in these basic ideals, an intensity that varies from time to time and from group to group.[7]

Americans do not, I contend, agree to these ideals or to the social practices they support. Although none but the hierarchical culture supports authority, holders of these values and supporters of these practices are not in fact antigovernment per se.

266

The individualistic culture that wishes to minimize authority is not in agreement with the egalitarian culture that wishes to reject it. I emphasize this difference in motives not merely because the reasons people give may matter but also because these rationales are integral parts of different ways of life. Hence the behavior that follows varies considerably. The individualist is content to let government do less, for instance, without challenging its right to rule; the egalitarian wishes government to reduce inequalities while rejecting its authority as constituting prima facie inequality, which is something else again. Dispositions toward government, moreover, may well be instrumental, as the egalitarian abolitionists (previously pacifistic) showed during the Civil War. Action to increase equality led egalitarians to support coercion by the central government.[8] While what the competing cultures want may stay the same (say, greater or lesser equality), the means (central government as a source of equality or inequality) vary with their historical experience.

Intensity of belief does differ over time. But this need not mean that the political dispositions of all cultures become more intense or move in the same direction. Given their varied internal organizational structures, these cultures differ markedly in their proclivities toward political passion. Is it pure happenstance that the hierarchical Federalists and Whigs stressed cool consideration, self-control being a cardinal virtue, while the egalitarian abolitionists, the Student Non-Violent Coordinating Committee, and Friends of the Earth are known for their passion? Do the periods of creedal passion that Huntington stresses—the revolutionary period, the period before the Civil War, and the civil rights movement—just happen to coincide with the rise of radical egalitarianism?

Huntington asserts, however, that the gap between institutions and ideals is responsible for recurrent convulsions in American politics: "No government can exist without some measure of hierarchy, inequality, arbitrary power, secrecy, deception, and established patterns of superordination and subordination. The American Creed, however, challenges the legitimacy of all these characteristics of government."[9] So far as it goes, this statement is true, but it does not go far enough. For if there were no support for hierarchical institutions, the qualities complained about would not exist at all. Without a hierarchical political culture, albeit weaker than elsewhere, there would be no established authority to be against. No orthodoxy, no heterodoxy.

"The essence of the [American] Creed," Huntington informs us, "is opposition to power and to concentrated authority."[10] How, then, is it possible to explain why the very same people who urge American national government to undertake ever-larger measures to reduce inequalities also oppose large defense budgets? Why do those who favor ever-larger preparedness in defense urge ever-smaller intervention in the economy? To go back into American history, why did those who opposed economic development by the national government favor the same thing by state governments if it was governmental authority per se they opposed? Once we understand that the Jeffersonians and the Jacksonians were coalitions of egalitarians and individualists, and that in those days both cultures identified the central government with hierarchy, the answer becomes evident.

It is true that from the beginning hierarchical cultures have been weak in America compared with Europe. It is also true that the often dominant individualist culture and the sometimes influential egalitarian culture are not exactly enamored of authority. But that is not the whole truth.

The different attitudes toward authority in individualistic and egalitarian cultures make a world of difference in the policies they pursue and, hence, in the problems they pose for government. An egalitarian culture, whose adherents believe that people are born good but are corrupted by evil institutions (being basically anti-institutional), offers a far more severe challenge for the conduct of foreign policy (America pure or polluted, with nothing in between) than one whose adherents are reluctant to pay for defense but basically believe that the American political system is benign. An individualist culture that is willing to compromise offers quite different prospects for domestic reconciliation than would an egalitarian culture that is opposed, in principle, to compromise. Insofar as the undermining of authority in the midst of expanding government is concerned (a major anomaly of our time), it is the challenge of egalitarianism, not individualism, that should occupy our attention.

There is more involved in dispositions toward authority than mere acceptance or rejection. People may also feel that, while they accept the need for authority under some circumstances and within stipulated conditions, this authority is too large and strong or too small and weak. Authority may be deemed to have too broad or too narrow a scope or to be applied with too much or too little rigor.

The utility of these distinctions lies in their ability to make sense out of variations in the behavior of different cultures toward authority. Advocates of hierarchy support authority as legitimate—moral, right, and appropriate. Egalitarians reject authority as illegitimate—immoral, wrong, and improper—unless it promotes equality. But there is more to be said about those who accept authority but differ as to its scope and rigor. Fatalists accept authority as inevitable and uncontrollable. They can do nothing about it. Individualists accept authority in narrow and circumscribed areas, generally thinking it too broad and rigorous.

To the detriment of our understanding, adherents of exclusive hierarchies are generally excluded from analytic consideration, being lumped in with adherents of inclusive hierarchies. Inclusive hierarchies are large, integrative organizations that seek to accommodate diverse desires, while exclusive hierarchies are smaller, more cohesive, and rigid, demanding adherence to a narrow program. While accepting, even demanding, authority, exclusivists do not necessarily support existing institutions. These social conservatives want larger and rigorously enforced moral and social differences. Their complaint about American society and government is not that government is too strong but that, in regard to individual behavior, it is too weak. To them, differences between what they deem right and wrong are not enunciated clearly enough and not enforced vigorously enough by governmental authority.

Even if a substantial majority of citizens and elites actually do approve of authority in some way, therefore, the officials in power may not gain the benefits of this support since they are besieged by individualists who tell them they

269

have exceeded their warrant, social conservatives who condemn them for moral confusion and cowardice, and egalitarians who believe that authority is necessarily inegalitarian and hence illegitimate. The attack on authority is thus multifaceted; it comes not only from egalitarians but also from adherents of exclusive hierarchy. This three-pronged attack on authority (simultaneously too strong and too weak, too broad and too narrow) is important in understanding American political history, and never more so than now.

Instead of considering a single American culture, I propose that analyzing American political life in terms of conflicts among at least three political cultures—hierarchical, individualist, and egalitarian—will prove more satisfactory. This approach will generate fewer surprises and provide explanations that better fit the phenomena.

Egalitarian Domestic Institutions and Policies

In the United States, every major institution that tries to accommodate diverse interests—political parties, trade unions, mainline churches, the bureaucracy—is undergoing severe attack and decline.[11] By contrast, disintegrative movements—single-issue special interest groups, charismatic religions, candidate-centered political movements, a critical press—are flourishing. Accompanying the weakening of integrative institutions is the diminution of distinctions that once separated authority from disorder. Even a short list of eroded distinctions is impressive: those between black and white, male and female, young and old, gay and straight, parents and children, teachers and students, even animals and people. As old boundaries are breached, new ones begin to take their place. Smokers are separated from nonsmokers, polluted areas from unspoiled nature, pure wilderness preservation from impure money making, affirmative from negative discrimination. Egalitarianism is at the root of this social revolution.

The rise of egalitarianism is responsible for other anomalies that puzzle us in our public life. When we ask why the growth of the welfare state is severely criticized by those who demand it, why permissiveness in personal life goes hand in hand with regulation of public activity, why, in the end, there is condemnation of established authority without anything to replace it, I offer the egalitarian hypothesis.

The political consequences of an egalitarian culture are nowhere more apparent than in the changing fortunes of our institutions. Why have American political parties, for instance, declined in membership, in allegiance among the citizenry, and in support by politicians? Why are they no longer able to keep divisive issues, like abortion and busing, out of national life? Why have parties become less popular even while they reform their procedures to make themselves more participatory?

The textbook definition of a political party is an organization that nominates candidates for office. If this vital function is transferred to primaries, where voters cannot know the candidates and where no deliberation about their qualifications can take place among knowledgeable politicians, parties can no longer integrate various political viewpoints. Coalitions that will help candidates govern cannot be formed before the election.

The more Congress reforms itself by encouraging individual members to express themselves and show their moral sincerity, the worse its collective performance becomes. Thus egalitarians will agree that there ought to be confrontation over issues such as budget and taxation resolutions, but they cannot, of course, agree with others over what these levels should be. Hence the stultification of Congress over the budget. Congressmen spend more time catering to their constituents today, and this affection is mutual. Voters love their members of Congress; it is only Congress they hate. As each member becomes more practiced at self-expression— through less emphasis on seniority, better committee assignments, more staff, and other such equalizing devices—Congress as a collectivity becomes less cohesive.

Studies of media elites reveal that they are disproportionately egalitarian. Aside from equalizing income, which would hurt their pocketbooks, they are far more in favor of equalizing differences among the general population than are most Americans. It is not so much party partisanship but opposi-

271

tion to authority as a form of inequality that characterizes media elites.[12]

Matching the failure in integrative institutions is the apparent success of disintegrative institutions. Single-issue special interest groups (the term now rolls off the tongue as if it were a single word) are known for what they do *not* do—taking positions on a wide range of issues and attempting to reconcile preferences and establish priorities among them.

They are altruists for especially deserving interests, of course, while "private-interest" groups are in it only for themselves. The purity of special interest groups lies in their motives, just as the impurity of the opposition (labor unions or corporations) lies in their devotion to material gain. These interest groups are no novelty in American life. But today integrative institutions, like political parties, Congress, and the presidency, are weak in resisting their claims. Demand making is on the rise in American politics, while demand shaping and demand resisting are on the decline.

Declining political institutions in America share three characteristics: they are organized on a hierarchical basis; they reconcile the preferences of their members or constituents on a wide variety of issues; and they attempt to integrate their views with those held by others of somewhat different persuasions. The ascendant organizations are just the opposite: they accept no authority unless it be the occasional charismatic leader (for instance, a Ralph Nader) who provides a substitute for that otherwise missing authority; they are single, not multiple, issue groups; and they reject rather than reconcile themselves with groups that differ from them. This accounts for anomalies that have hitherto proved puzzling.

Why, for example, as government grows bigger is it subject to a corresponding crescendo of criticism? We understand the critique of individualists who were always opposed to a large public sector, but how do we explain the hostility of those who were and still are its strongest supporters? The egalitarian hypothesis explains that both a preference for programs to redistribute income and an opposition to government authority make sense to people in a political culture that favors the equality of result but not the exercise of hierarchical authority. If government is told simultaneously that its welfare programs are woefully insufficient and that they lead to abject dependence and coercion, that is all to the good as far as egalitarians are concerned. Caught between coercion and inequality, established authority is in conflict.

There is a torrent of criticism of these established institutions. We all see that. But why is it so unrelievedly negative? Despite the disarray of democratic institutions induced by the Vietnam War and the Watergate scandal, no rival program, party, or leader profited from the situation. Why not? In a country characterized by the lack of hereditary hierarchy and the presence of strong individualism, socialism is not a real option. A culture of communes, moreover, each interacting on an equal basis under agreed rules, comes uncomfortably close to the individualism that egalitarians avoid. Far better for the egalitarians, who abhor compromise as insincerity, to remain faithful to the principle of pure criticism. Hence the search for a single issue—an unspoiled environment, for example, or complete safety—on which they can maintain a consistent stand.

While egalitarian culture, described as "the permissive society," sets aside many rules formerly acknowledged to guide personal conduct, its opposition to authority forces it to set out even stricter rules governing the behavior of public officials. Officials must divest themselves of assets connected with the interests they are supposed to regulate, thus converting what was formerly the advantage of expertise into the disability of contamination by selfish interests. "Getting things out in the open," sunshine laws, open meetings, and freedom of information acts all serve to reveal hidden hierarchy. Along with Lady Macbeth, we observe that the more government cleanses itself, the dirtier it gets; the ineradicable stain lies in the authority that constitutes hierarchy and in the inequality of result embodied in individualism.

Bureaucracy without Authority

For us to see how egalitarianism affects government policy today, it is useful to distinguish the European and the American welfare states along three lines: social insurance, subsidies, and regulation. Europe does much more than the

United States to provide social welfare programs because hierarchical collectivism is much stronger there and competitive individualism much weaker.

The important difference between the American and the European welfare states, so far as egalitarianism is concerned, is in regulation. Why is there so much more regulation in the United States, especially in health, safety, and professional behavior, than in Europe, where the tradition of government intervention is so much stronger? Ordinarily, individualism rejects regulation and hierarchy favors it. But hierarchies also favor specialization because it confers expertise; a major rationale for the acceptance of inequality is that people who have the appropriate credentials for their positions really do know best. Hence, hierarchies are not disposed to place fetters on professionals, making it difficult to do such things as filing or winning medical malpractice suits. Only in America are governmental bureaucracies supposed to have hostile, standoffish relations with industry.[13]

The dramatic turn America has taken from the welfare to the regulatory state is attributable to the egalitarian desire to punish departures from purity that are conceived of as implying inequality. Damage to nature, in the eyes of egalitarians, is a mirror of our damaged social relations. Endangered species are deprived people. Thus egalitarians impose regulations on their enemies and affirm the connection between bad business ethics and poor health.[14]

An egalitarian political culture demands both an increase in bureaucracy and a decrease in authority. This explains why, as scientists are increasingly involved in public policy debates, they are respected less and less. On the one hand, those who wish to show that the cultures they criticize cause contamination must invoke scientists and scientific knowledge on their side. On the other hand, their egalitarian social order has a congenital distrust of expertise because it is suggestive of inequality.

There is a catch. Society, as Frederic William Maitland told us, is a seamless web. The denigration of scientific expertise can hurt people with whom egalitarians identify. Malpractice suits are acceptable if they damage doctors who already have too much, in the egalitarians' view, but not midwives who have too little. Similarly, egalitarians identify with gays as an antiestablishment group in that they diminish differences among people. Hence they wish to dampen alarm about AIDS. But it may not prove so easy to urge people to follow mainstream scientific opinion on AIDS while denigrating such established authority in regard to technological dangers, especially when it is alleged that scientific experts do not sufficiently warn the public.

To expand on the contradictions we are considering, why do the same people who support populist democracy (one person, one vote) also support judicial activism, which appears to negate this principle? Judicial activism is encouraged on behalf of causes that blame the system rather than the person, such as abolition of the death penalty, due process for prisoners, the rights of the accused, and damage from defective products. "Blaming the victim," as egalitarians see it, or "personal responsibility," as the establishment calls it, justifies existing social relations. Blaming the system, requiring it to clean up its messes, and holding it responsible for untoward events are peculiarly useful to egalitarians who see themselves as judges of a corrupt society. The sea change in judicial interpretation from special protection of property to the preferred position currently accorded to civil rights and the corresponding secular movement of the law of personal injury (torts) from individual blame to system blame are but two indicators of egalitarian influence.[15]

The anomalies in American politics attributable to a rise in egalitarianism may be summarized by the observation that egalitarians impose contradictory demands on government and society. They insist that equality increase, while demanding that government stay small. They insist on bureaucratic regulation to show that government is ridding itself of moral impurities, while at the same time challenging governmental authority. The very government that egalitarians call into action to enlighten the people is the same one that is always acting underhandedly to deceive the people.

The phenomenon of ungovernability, which has been said to afflict Western democracies in the era of the welfare state, undoubtedly has many causes. It may be, as both conservatives and Marxists contend,[16] that buying votes leads to ever-greater demands (the electoral spending cycle) until there is a "fiscal crisis of capitalism." Quite possibly, government has taken on tasks it cannot perform or that its people will not support. Were this the whole matter, however, a sense of crisis would not be in the air. Rather, one would hear of modest retrenchment, of a pause in the growth of the welfare state until the costs of oil or pensions could be better accommodated. There is nothing surprising about outrunning one's resources or spectacular about the difficulties of accommodating a modest decline in standards of living. Why not just produce more and distribute more? But when those who demand redistribution also oppose economic growth and when those who expand government also condemn it for being too big, government is programmed for failure. Egalitarians make inconsistent demands because the rejection of authority and the redistribution of resources cannot be reconciled. Nor can one easily reconcile support for national defense with the belief that the system being defended is unworthy, that is, inegalitarian.

Egalitarian Opposition to Defense Policy

A significant part of the opposition to the main lines of American defense policy is, I claim, based on deep-seated objections to America's political and economic systems. This is not to say that existing defense policy is necessarily wise or that there may not be good or sufficient reasons for wishing to change it. Indeed, at any time and place, the United States might well be overestimating the threat from the Soviet Union or using too much force. What I wish to suggest is that the across-the-board criticism of American policy as inherently aggressive and repressive, regardless of circumstance—a litany of criticism so constant that it does not alert us to the need for explanation—has its structural basis in the rise of a political culture opposed to existing authority.

To the extent that this criticism is structural—that is, inherent in domestic politics—the problem of fashioning foreign policies that can obtain widespread support is much more difficult than is commonly conceived. For if the objection is to American ways of life (and therefore to the govern-

AARON WILDAVSKY

ment "for which it stands"), only a transformation in the
power relationships at home, together with a redistribution
of economic resources, would satisfy these critics. Looking to
changes in foreign policy to shore up domestic support
radically confuses the causal connections and therefore the
order of priorities. Unless or until people face an overwhelming external threat, how they wish to live with one another
takes precedence over how they relate to foreigners. Foreign
policy is fought at home.

One way to describe what has happened is that, while
mass opinion is slightly more skeptical, elite opinion has
turned against those authorities who formally determine
foreign policy. Whereas before, the formal decision makers
had the benefit of the doubt, now they are guilty until proved
innocent. The accusations against them, moreover, are of a
single kind: they are too warlike. They overestimate the
danger of communism; they use too much force; they spend
too much on defense. It is America as well as the Soviet
Union that poses a major threat to peace.

A difference between the 1950s and the 1970s and 1980s
lies in what is missing. In earlier times, a politician could be
for both welfare and warfare. Henry Jackson and Hubert
Humphrey exemplified the dual commitment to a strong
defense and to provision for those in need. No longer. There
must be prominent politicians today who publicly espouse
this dualism, but aside possibly from Senator Bill Bradley, I
cannot think of any (Senator Sam Nunn is too conservative
on social welfare). Indeed, the six major candidates for the
Democratic party presidential nomination in 1988 all specified
conditions—completely containable consequences, impecca-
ble moral character, Soviet acquiescence, and the like—for
armed intervention that could never be met. What is more,
Republican Secretary of Defense Caspar Weinberger's specification of the conditions required to justify military intervention was, in a different way, just as stringent. This open-
ended commitment—whatever it takes to prevail no matter
what, for which Weinberger asked—is impossibly stringent
in practice because it can almost never be given. The military

277

does not want to fight without the full support that the politicians and the populace are now unwilling to give them.

In an article in *Commentary*, Owen Harries traces the "deeper roots" of such ("best-case") thinking to the universalist liberal tradition that denies "the reality of conflict in the name of a fundamental harmony of interest." Since "there are no real intractable conflicts of interest," it follows that enmity among nations "is illusory and unnecessary."[17]

But explaining one set of ideas by another separates them from their social context, as if they existed apart from the people who believe in them. If we ask a different kind of question—what sort of people, sharing which values and justifying what kind of practices, would act on these beliefs to shore up their way of life and tear down their opponents'?—the tenacity with which these ideas are held and the immense challenge they pose to American foreign policy will become apparent.

Does anybody actually believe in the universal harmony of interests? I think not. The idea is recognizably wrongheaded. In fact, the very people who argue the best-case thesis in foreign policy also argue the worst-case thesis in domestic policy. Harmony in domestic policy, they claim, is the ideology of the oppressor. There are irreconcilable conflicts between the haves and have-nots, conflicts that cannot be compromised but overcome only by struggle. Foreign policy, apparently, is different. Why?

No reasonable person believes in a worst case or a best case all the time in regard to everything. In fact, many of the people who hold a best-case belief about the Soviet Union hold a worst-case belief about capitalism. Is there a single committed environmentalist who is also a proponent of a strong national defense or vice versa? There must be some, but they are few and far between.

We now have a more varied and more interesting question to ask: Who sees harmony in international affairs and hostility in domestic politics? What else do the people who claim that the U.S. government is perforce the aggressor in world affairs believe? They believe in equality of condition. They are part and parcel of many other movements dedicated to the diminution of distinctions among people.

When I grew up, children could never do enough for their parents; now all we hear about is child abuse, state intervention obviously being required to prevent parents from doing terrible things to their young. Harmony of interests, indeed!

How can harmony abroad be reconciled with hostility at home? Take the critics at their word: the intolerable, unconscionable, unbearable inequalities at home, they believe, are justified by paranoia about threats from faraway places. It is not that they think the Soviet system is benevolent or that it provides a better way of life. They are neither dumb nor, for the most part, Marxist. It is rather that they care about how people live with each other in the United States, not in the U.S.S.R. It is their passion for equality of condition and their anger at inequality that leads them to portray an international heaven spoiled by people bent on maintaining a domestic hell. Acknowledging a Soviet threat would mean agreeing: (1) that the social system of the United States is worth defending; (2) that other systems are worse; and (3) that a morally legitimate government has the right to divert resources from domestic (that is, egalitarian) to military (that is, inegalitarian) purposes.

Current differences over whether the deficit should be reduced by cutting defense or by cutting domestic programs are instructive. To the extent that sacrifices are imposed, sharing them among beneficiaries, of course, makes sense. When civilian pensions are reduced, for instance, military pensions may follow suit. But there is more to it. Not only is defense being treated as just another domestic interest (the military-industrial complex, say, as opposed to what used to be called the common defense), but also it is being placed in a zero-sum relationship to welfare programs (canes versus guns, I suppose).

Precisely because those who adopt the best-case thesis abroad do so to support a vision of the worst case at home, we should not be surprised at the tenacity with which they hold on to optimistic views of Soviet behavior. People who see themselves threatened by mobilization for war, under the aegis of military hierarchy and capitalist competition, are not likely to accept the hypothesis of threat if some other mode of explanation will leave their dreams of the good, that is, egalitarian, life intact.

Imagine that the United States government is deemed immoral or even perhaps illegitimate because it fails to provide social justice, understood as much greater equality of condition (a current codeword is "fairness"). What follows from this assumption?

Unfairness at home becomes transmuted into exploitation abroad. The third world serves as a surrogate proletariat, its poverty a result of U.S.-led domination by multinational capital. Inequalities within the United States thus spread their tentacles to the rest of the world. It follows that the United States owes redress to the poorer nations, just as it owes reparation to its own poor. Assuming, further, a fixed limit to the world's goods since egalitarians are also anticapitalist, more for arms means less for welfare. In brief, the industrial north exploits the third world south; the United States rules the north; and capitalists rule the United States. Hence an end to inequality in the United States is necessary for social justice in the world.

Immoral does as immoral is. Any use of force by the United States is illegitimate. This point of view accounts for the exclusive emphasis on negotiations as a way to handle conflict. It also contains the answer to former Secretary of State George Shultz's perplexity:

> From one side, we hear that negotiations alone are the answer. If we will only talk (the argument runs), we can have peace. If we will only talk, our differences will easily be resolved. It is as if negotiations were an end in themselves, as if the goal of American foreign policy were not primarily to protect the peace, or defend our values, or our people, or our allies, but to negotiate for its own sake.[18]

Negotiation is an end in itself if one side is morally tainted. Force corrupts because it is coercive; and coercion is wrong because those who coerce are morally unworthy.

In the absence of definitive information (an attack itself, for instance), external threats must be problematic. Since motives can be known only by those who have them and even they may engage in self-deception, residual uncertainty about foreign danger cannot be resolved by anything short of experience. When we say the external threat is real and apparent, therefore, we mean that there is widespread social agreement on its existence. Lacking such a consensus, citizens use whatever preconceptions they have—call it theory or ideology—to connect how they would like to live (their values) with how they think the world works (the facts). The most general theories held by citizens are their political cultures. The more citizens support an existing regime, the more they will accept the desires of its leaders and be ready to pay for preparedness. On the contrary, if they see their regime as unworthy, they are more likely to believe that the regime produces rather than alleviates danger to national security. Hence, they will not favor military spending (or action) in advance of certain evidence.

Among our several political cultures, we may ask, which would interpret events to support more defense spending or which less? Hierarchies believe in defending the collective. Doubts about military spending would suggest that military experts and the civilian leadership cannot be trusted to appraise the situation and are incompetent to know what to do about foreign dangers.

There is not much place for competitive individualism in war except, perhaps, for prima donna generals. Individualist forces fear war for its disruption of trade and its subordination of economic motives. During wars of mass mobilization, they give up their individualism in return for being sheltered from competition. During peacetime, they are reluctant to pay higher taxes. Individualist cultures make reluctant warriors, especially when there is no booty.

The antimilitary culture is egalitarian. Opposing authority, blaming society for immoral differences, fearing subjugation by established institutions, egalitarians favor, at most, a small volunteer army. Only by sustaining the belief that their cause is entirely just, and their opponent's entirely evil, can they accept even minimal subordination to authority. Hence they respond to such unifying slogans as "The war to end all wars" or "The war to make the world safe for democracy" or "Unconditional surrender!"

The foreign policy of egalitarianism flows naturally from its commitment to redistribution. First is redistribution from rich to poor countries. Second is redistribution from defense to domestic welfare expenditure. Third is redistribution of authority from government officials to mass movements, from those now in power to those (to use their favorite phrase) left out of power. Aside from its effects on the government's ability to conduct consistent defense and foreign policies, this fundamental challenge to authority hits hardest the commander in chief and chief executive of the federal government, the president of the United States.

Leadership is a prime instance of power asymmetry. Followership, to egalitarians, is subordination. Thus the series of failed presidencies in recent times—Johnson, Nixon, Carter, Reagan (almost)—testifies not only to their incapacities but also to the animus against them. Or are we to assume that American citizens are so wonderful that it is simply bad luck that they continue to choose poor presidents?

Alternative Futures

In the last paragraph of his Tocquevillian essay, Samuel Beer urged:

> One should not exaggerate. We do not enjoy a public philosophy. But there is such a thing as equilibrium without purpose. The balance of social forces today tends toward a kind of peace. Moreover, a great hinterland of common belief, the American political tradition, helps to hold conflicts within manageable limits and to enable exchange, economic and political, to flourish. The question is whether the nation will be able to elicit from this body of belief the forces of renewal constituting a new public philosophy.[19]

There may be a point in what Beer calls "equilibrium without purpose," a period of political latency in which the surface calm belies the underlying flux. For there is, I think, a public philosophy available for Democratic party activists. It is called European or perhaps Scandinavian social democracy—a hybrid, in cultural terms, of hierarchy and egalitarianism. It would pursue egalitarian policies, such as national health insurance, redistributive taxation, affirmative action, and a cushioning of the impact of industrial change at home. Abroad, it would be internationalist, seek arms control, reduce nuclear arms, and pursue human rights. The question here is not whether social democratic policies would be effective in practice but whether the party could be persuaded to attempt them—building up government *and* supporting its authority—while keeping its supporters together.

The Republicans could also fashion a public philosophy by expanding individualism into social self-reliance. Here, too, the hierarchical emphasis on self-control would be linked to the encouragement of individual self-help. Policy issues would include the balanced budget-revenue and spending limit amendment, less government regulation, lower taxes, obligations of recipients of government funds to act according to acceptable social norms, and the encouragement of institutions that mediate between citizen and government at the local level.[20] Foreign policy would be internationalist but with a much greater emphasis on self-help and burden sharing. The key question, as with the Democrats, would be whether this cultural hybrid—strengthening social hierarchy while retaining economic individualism—could cohere.

If there is something in the egalitarian influence as I have described it and if there are parallel individualist and hierarchical political cultures alongside it, compromise within the existing Democratic and Republican parties will not be easy. Whether they split off because they are unable to obtain political office or because dissatisfactions increase when they do, egalitarian demands for equal results will be difficult to contain within such a diverse party. Absent Ronald Reagan, Republicans will be hard put to retain their libertarians while meeting the demands of their exclusivists.

If there is not now a public philosophy in the United States, there remains a public ideal. One part is well known: opposition to authority, though this hides differences between rejection, minimization, and maximization. But an ideal cannot be defined entirely by what it is against. It is American individualism, the belief that under American conditions equality of opportunity will lead to an approximation of equality of condition, that makes America's striving truly exceptional.[21] Within the micro-conflict that is seen as a healthy manifestation of a free society, there lie two extraordinary expectations: interests among Americans can be made compatible, and the order regulating this competition can be spontaneous, welling up from below rather than imposed from above. Provided only that the competition be natural—that is, be based on human differences rather than on those artificially imposed by institutions—the ensuing social order will prevent the cumulation of inequalities.

Just as supporters of hierarchy understand that their social organizations are likely to be rigid and egalitarians recognize that perfect equality is unattainable, so adherents of American individualism understand that liberty can conflict with equality and vice versa. What they deny is that this conflict is immutable, and what they affirm is that their two cherished passions, liberty and equality, can reinforce one another. No wonder individualists would not legitimate class conflict!

Needless to say, this ideal has not been realized, although one might argue about its approximation. What matters is that American individualism—the fundamental reinforcement of opportunity and equality—remains an ideal against which to judge departure. Is it now being abandoned?

In assessing what is likely to happen next, I have argued that two may be company but American politics is, in fact, more like a crowd. We need at least three doctrines, or public philosophies, held up by the distinctive ways of life (the political cultures that sustain them) to make sense out of American politics—past, present, or future.

The alliance of egalitarianism and individualism that has given Americans their special character (association without nationalization) was rooted in specific historical circumstances: a revolution against a hierarchical system. At that time, egalitarians believed the national government to be a source of artificial inequality. After the industrial revolution, the rise of corporate capitalism, the Great Depression, and the growth of egalitarian movements, egalitarians came to believe that the national government could be a force for greater equality. Anyone who listens to egalitarians can see that they identify individualism with capitalism and hence with greed, exploitation, deprivation, pollution, war, and worse. Despite their distrust of authority, the natural ally of egalitarians at the present time would be hierarchists. But not in America. Here the adherents of hierarchical social relations, awakened to political action by judicial attacks on school prayer and support for abortion, are now firmly allied with individualists. The Federalist and Whig parties that preceded the Republicans were not able to mobilize popular majorities. But they were hierarchical with an individualist overlay. Lincoln's achievement was to shape a party that was individualist with an overlay of hierarchy. If the social conservatives become the mainstream of the Republican party, they too could suffer the fate of their predecessors. If Republicans gain no support from the fastest-growing segments of the population, especially from Mexican-Americans, they may also decline.

It is not easy for egalitarians to govern; that is why the historical record offers so few examples. Nor is it likely that a unicultural party will gain office or keep it for long, precisely because of its adherents' objections to compromise and coalition, both of which to them signify selling out.

Democrats do too much to satisfy individualists and too little to satisfy egalitarians, as it is not easy to diminish differences among people. Their egalitarianism leads them toward nationwide hierarchical solutions, but these discomfort their individualists. Whether it is Mondale's embrace of "special interests" or Dukakis's avoidance of them, Democrats do not satisfy either the individualists or the egalitarians. Republicans, aside from their uneasy alliance of individualism and hierarchy, lack sufficient egalitarianism to attract the largest and most rapidly growing minorities. They can take advantage of Democratic egalitarianism, which has alienated many white Christian males, but they cannot extend their reach into Congress so as to govern by themselves. Perhaps now we understand why everyone in office seems to do so poorly but no one can take advantage of the fact.

The extraordinary events of 1990 in the Soviet Union and Eastern Europe, which amount to a massive loss of legitimacy, alter everyone's expectations. The regime values of the

West—democracy and capitalism—have been given a remarkable vote of confidence by those who have been denied them.
It remains to be seen whether those who already have what
others desperately seek will reinforce those convictions or
turn against these regime values on the grounds of unconscionable inequality.

10
The American Polity
in the 1990s
Anthony King

There have been many changes in the American political
system since the era of Eisenhower and Kennedy, but before
we assess their significance, perhaps we should remind our-
selves how much has *not* changed.

Americans pride themselves on their technical inventiveness, but other people are technically inventive too. British
engineers developed the steam engine; German engineers,
the internal combustion engine and hence the automobile. A
Frenchman invented photography; an Englishman, television; another Englishman, the jet engine. It was Germans
who developed the liquid-fuel-propelled rocket. Given that
technical inventiveness is so widespread in the world and
that technical innovation so frequently takes place in different
laboratories and countries at the same time, Americans ought
to take an equal pride in their social inventiveness. Americans
have succeeded in inventing the supermarket, the Marshall
Plan, and, above all, the American political system.

When the United States celebrated the bicentennial of its
independence as a sovereign state in 1976, many parades
were held, medals struck, speeches made, and fireworks let
off. But in fact achieving national independence is no great
trick, especially when the colonial power is half-hearted,
internally divided, and 3,000 miles away. At least eighty-
seven nations have achieved national independence since
1945. What is impressive, rather, is to establish a set of
political institutions that are liberal and not repressive, that
are highly adaptable, and that are capable of enduring for

more than two hundred years. American stability, despite the 1861–1865 Civil War, is every bit as impressive as American liberty and American democracy.

Foreigners often wonder how it was done. Part of the answer—though an answer that in itself begs a lot of questions—is that in the last quarter of the eighteenth century America was blessed with an extraordinarily large number of men of creative political genius: James Madison, Alexander Hamilton, Thomas Jefferson, George Washington, John Jay, and John Adams; their names are familiar. It is a curious coincidence that German-speaking Europe was blessed, at exactly the same time, with an extraordinarily large number of men of musical genius. There is something pleasing in the idea that the American Constitution was produced in the same year, 1787, as both *The Marriage of Figaro* and *Don Giovanni*. That was also the year in which Mozart said of the young Beethoven: "Keep an eye on him: some day he will give the world something to talk about." Mozart might have said the same thing about the United States.

Two other factors are worth mentioning. "Westward," Bishop Berkeley wrote in the eighteenth century, "the course of empire takes its way." There was one tremendous difference, however, between America's empire and the British and Russian empires that were being established at about the same time. When the British arrived in India, Africa, and elsewhere, there was almost invariably an indigenous population already in residence, a population that had to be subdued before it could be incorporated into the empire. The same was true of the Russians, not perhaps in Siberia, but in all of the other countries that Russia conquered and absorbed in eastern Europe and Asia. The Poles, Ukrainians, Moldavians, Georgians, Armenians, Azerbaijani, Uzbeks, Kazakhs, Tadzhiks, and Tatars were hard facts that Russia's leaders had to deal with—and still have to deal with today.

But of course the North American continent, by contrast, was empty except for a few million widely dispersed "Indians" (the English and Americans could not even get their name right), who either died from disease or else, in line with the tenets of a very rough nineteenth-century morality, were killed off as "savages" without anybody (except them) worrying much. In any explanation of America's political success, as well as its geographical expansion, it is easy to overlook, because it is so obvious, the central fact of North America's emptiness. A nation in North America could build itself; it did not have to be built out of other nations. Newcomers could be absorbed on the new nation's own terms as they arrived in their successive waves.

The other factor worth mentioning is also one that almost everyone, not only in the United States, takes completely for granted.

In the years leading up to the bicentennial of the drafting and ratification of the present American Constitution, a commemorative magazine was published under the title *This Constitution*. It contained numerous scholarly articles on the constitutional debates in Philadelphia and their aftermath; but nowhere in the index to the magazine is there any reference to an article on that quintessentially American political principle, the "principle of periodicity." This principle embodies an idea that is contained in very few other constitutions (and most of those derived from the American): the idea that, come what may, almost the whole of America's governing elite should be renewed every two or four years— that is, at regular and fixed intervals. It is not, but ought to be, a source of wonder and amazement to Americans and foreigners alike that congressional elections were held on schedule at the height of the American Civil War in 1862, that congressional and presidential elections were likewise held in 1864, and that regular elections also took place during both World War I and World War II.

This book is being published in 1990, a year of midterm congressional elections. A presidential election will be held two years hence, in 1992. It is reassuring to know that if the human race survives, and if the authors and readers of this book were still alive in a hundred years' time, they would confidently be looking forward to the election of a president, the whole of the House of Representatives, and one-third of the Senate on the first Tuesday after the first Monday of November—in 2092. Of how many countries in the world can one say that? Americans did celebrate the bicentennial of their constitution in 1987, but the celebrations should have been more exuberant. The staying power of America's political institutions, rather than the mere fact of American independence, is the truly remarkable political phenomenon.

The New System

When the first version of *The New American Political System* appeared in 1978, it drew attention to a number of changes that had taken place over roughly the previous twenty years and that seemed to justify, at least to the authors, the book's title.

Chief among these in the realm of ideas were a decline of the themes of Franklin Roosevelt's New Deal as the organizing principle of American political life and a new emphasis on the value of active political participation by citizens. During the 1960s and 1970s the political trench warfare of the New Deal and post-New Deal periods—with politicians and (to a lesser extent) voters arrayed in two opposing camps over a wide range of seemingly disparate political issues—gave way to a much more complicated and unpredictable war of maneuver. Cross-cutting issues (the environment, women's rights, abortion, many aspects of foreign policy, and the like) became the norm rather than the exception, and predicting a politician's stand on one issue from his stand on another became more and more difficult. The New Deal disappeared as an ideological ordering device, but nothing took its place. At the same time, it came to be thought good for both the participating individuals and the polity as a whole that ordinary men and women should have a direct say not merely in the selection of public office holders but in the making and implementation of public policy.[1] The good citizen was also an active citizen.

These changes in ideas were accompanied by changes in institutions, notably in the presidency and in Congress. In 1978 the presidency seemed, and indeed was, an institution under considerable threat. Kennedy had been assassinated, Johnson had been more or less driven from office, Nixon had had to resign, Ford had failed in his attempt at reelection, and Carter was about to fail in his. The time had come when presidents and the people they did business with had to operate on the assumption that the man in the Oval Office might not remain there for very long. Suspicion of presidents and the presidency in the Congress manifested itself in a series of legislative enactments—notably the War Powers Resolution of 1973 and the Impoundment Control Act of 1974—designed specifically to curb presidential power. Meanwhile, power in Congress was also being curbed and dispersed. Committee and subcommittee chairmen lost many of their former prerogatives. Committees and, in particular, subcommittees were far more numerous than in the past. Congressmen and senators surrounded themselves—and their committees and subcommittees—with larger and larger professional staffs. The powerful few in both houses of Congress became the considerably less powerful many. But an increasingly amorphous Congress was not prepared to take a lead from, let alone be given any vertebrate form by, the president. On the contrary, as its president-limiting resolutions and acts showed, Congress was anxious to assert itself against the president, to become, in effect, a kind of alternative government.

To these changes in the formal institutions of government were added changes in America's informal institutions: the political parties, the electorate, and the interest groups. America's political parties, never as strong organizationally as most of their counterparts in Europe, were being weakened still further by the growth in the number of primary elections, by new, more candidate-centered forms of campaign finance, and by rule changes in both the Democratic and the Republican parties that undercut the position of party regulars and opened up the parties to a constantly shifting congeries of "issue and candidate enthusiasts."[2] In 1978 it was an open question whether the United States still possessed such things as political parties, at least for the purposes of nominating and electing presidential candidates. The decline in the parties' organizational strength ran in parallel with a decline in their ability, whether as organizations or merely as cue givers, to influence the behavior of ordinary voters. Party identification among the electorate decreased in both amount and intensity; split-ticket voting increased. Large numbers of American voters marched to the beat of new drums—issues, candidates, causes—insofar as they marched at all. With few exceptions, the major interest groups were similarly being displaced as mediating and aggregative institutions in the American system. Interest groups were far more numerous than in the past; a larger proportion of them espoused "concerns" or "causes" rather than mere interests; and more and more of them were enmeshed in highly professionalized "issue networks," which were to some extent impervious to external political influences.[3] In short, the American political system was considerably more fragmented in the late 1970s than it had been a generation before, with power more widely diffused.

A decade later, this picture of the new American political system remains largely true to life. The trends that marked American politics in the late 1960s and the 1970s continued through the 1980s and in some cases were accelerated. A politician who survived from the era of Sam Rayburn and Lyndon Johnson into the era of Jimmy Carter and Ronald Reagan had to learn a lot of new tricks; a politician who arrived in Washington for the first time in, say, 1972 or 1974 had much less to learn. Tip O'Neill in his memoirs describes somewhat ruefully how the Democrats' post-1974 "Watergate Babies" effectively rewrote the rules of Congress by being independent, inexperienced, ignorant, and disrespectful— and by not being ashamed of being any of these things.[4] The Watergate Babies are now grown up, but their modes of political operation have outlasted, and will outlast, those of Speaker O'Neill, because they are adapted to late twentieth-century rather than mid-twentieth–century political realities.

As Austin Ranney shows in chapter 6 of this volume, television has done as much as any other single agency to bring the new American political system into existence. By establishing a direct link between the individual politician and the individual citizen, television has further weakened the political parties, encouraged split-ticket (even "no-ticket") voting, and, not least, made it possible for individual members of Congress to advance their own causes and careers by means other than adherence to (and indeed often in defiance of) traditional House and Senate norms.[5] Television feeds ambition and can be the means whereby the ambition thus fed goes on to be fulfilled.

Two modifications, however, need to be made to the picture originally painted in 1978. One, probably the less important of the two, concerns the political parties. On the strength of the evidence presented by James W. Ceaser in chapter 4, it seems that the decline of America's political parties, both as organizations ("institutions") and as aggregations of individuals holding similar opinions ("associations"), has been halted or, at any rate, slowed down. The Republican party, in particular, is stronger organizationally than it was a generation ago. In addition, in both major parties some, though not many, of the hyperparticipationist rule reforms of the late 1960s have been thrown into reverse. At the same time, the Republicans are a somewhat more like-minded group of people than they were when Robert Taft and Dwight Eisenhower, or Barry Goldwater and Nelson Rockefeller, struggled for the party's soul. The Democrats, although they are finding it hard to define a common post-New Deal political philosophy, have achieved a somewhat greater degree of unity by the simple expedient of shedding the greater part of their Southern conservative wing. As Ceaser cautiously says, "Each party in a certain sense has become less heterogeneous."[6] Even so, despite these changes, it remains true that the parties, especially considered as organizations, are less powerful than they were before the late 1960s and that they have not succeeded in establishing any significantly greater degree of control over the presidential nominating process.

The other modification that needs to be made to the 1978 picture is probably more important—and is also more ambiguous. It concerns the presidency. By the late 1970s, fears of an "imperial presidency"—with the man in the White House seen to be dominating America's national government to the exclusion of others, notably in Congress, who had a legitimate claim to a share in that domination—had given way to worries about a "postimperial presidency," an office whose increasingly unhappy occupants seemed doomed to frustration at the hands of Congress, the Supreme Court, and ultimately the American people. The personal and political histories of Johnson, Nixon, Ford, and Carter were there for all to see; the various pieces of presidency-curbing legislation were on the statute books; Congress was wary of the president, when not downright hostile; and the American public felt increasingly let down.[7]

After eight years of Ronald Reagan, it all feels different. Reagan survived for eight years. He was reelected. He established himself as one of the best-loved presidents in the history of the republic. No one threatened him. No one felt threatened by him. He undoubtedly benefited from the fact that so many of his immediate predecessors had been failures. There was a widespread feeling, almost a yearning, that *this* president—or at least *some* president—should be seen to succeed. Americans did not mind this or that individual president coming unstuck; they did mind the presidency as an institution—one of America's most potent national symbols—appearing weak and discredited.[8]

The presidency feels different in 1990; it has a different aura about it. But how different is it in fact? It is too early to say for sure, but a good interim guess is probably not very. It is arguable that President Reagan had four, and only four, substantial successes during his eight years in office: his budget and tax cuts of 1981, his subsequent creation of a political climate in which increases in tax rates in the United States became virtually unthinkable, the breakthrough on disarmament that he began to negotiate with Mikhail Gorbachev, and, of course, his own personal popularity and successful reelection. Otherwise the Reagan presidency, given the president's own frustrations and setbacks, does not appear so very different from the so-called "failed" presidencies of the 1960s and 1970s. Remove the dignity, the presidential bearing, the broad grin, and the warm handshake, and Reagan, too, seems distinctly "postimperial." His policies failed in Lebanon and Nicaragua. He was actually less successful than President Carter in freeing Americans held hostage in the Middle East. He allowed himself to become embroiled in the Iran-contra scandal. He bequeathed an enormous burden of public debt to his successor. The 1981 budget and tax cuts apart, he succeeded in securing congressional assent to almost none of his domestic program. Such a record would probably have doomed a Jerry Ford or a Jimmy Carter. It was Ronald Reagan's skill to be able to make Americans feel good about themselves—and also to be able to deflect public (and journalistic) attention from his many errors and misjudgments. He succeeded because people thought he succeeded, not for any other discernible reason.[9]

If this judgment is correct, or even partially correct, it has important consequences. It means that, although congressional suspicion of the presidency qua presidency was substantially dissipated during the Reagan years, the position of the president in the American political system has not been changed substantially. On the contrary, as Charles O. Jones points out in chapter 1 of this volume, the past quarter-century has seen the Congress moving increasingly "in the direction of functioning as an entire government, alongside, or in competition with, the executive," a decline in the agenda-setting capacity of presidents, and a virtual institutionalization of the circumstances in which the presidency is in the hands of one political party, the Congress in the hands of the other. As Jones says, the traditional "separated institutions sharing power" appear to have given way to "separated institutions competing for shared power."[10] President Bush's comportment in office during his first year suggested that he recognized this fact and that, knowing he could seldom win any outright competition with a Congress in Democratic hands, he preferred on the whole to play the role of an Eisenhower or even a Ford rather than a Nixon or a Reagan.

Coalition Politics in Decline

The overall picture painted in the first version of *The New American Political System* was one of fragmentation and atomization, with individual politicians and other public officials—not to mention such more peripheral persons as interest group leaders—functioning largely in highly individualistic, utility-maximizing ways, with little regard for either the stability or the long-term effectiveness of the institutions within which—or, increasingly, around which—they worked. American politics in the late 1970s resembled an unstructured market (say, a street bazaar) more than it resembled a "system of government" in any traditional sense of that term. Political parties had largely gone; so had many of the rules and norms that made individual politicians identify themselves and their interests with bodies like the House or the Senate (will any future Speaker of the House entitle his memoirs *Man of the House?*); so also had the institutional integrity of bodies like the pre-1970 Bureau of the Budget and several of the executive branch "line" departments.

The first version of this book called into question, in particular, the idea that American politics is best understood as "coalition politics."[11] If genuine coalitions are to be formed, it was argued there, two antecedent conditions have to be fulfilled. First, there have to exist distinct, identifiable political formations (parties, factions, interest groups, and voting blocs) out of which a coalition or coalitions can be built. Second, those political formations have to have some minimal degree of internal structure, so that, for example, leaders of one group can bargain with leaders of another group to bring a coalition between the two into being. The formation of a coalition also implies a degree, however limited, of stability. A coalition is rather like an alliance. On the one hand, it is not, and is not meant to be, permanent; on the other, it is meant to exist long enough to achieve some reasonably broad political purpose.

In 1978 it seemed that the traditional language of "coalition building" was no longer the most appropriate language in which to describe American political processes. American politics had become too atomized; the structured formations out of which coalitions could be constructed either no longer existed or were far too numerous and amorphous to make stable coalition building possible. In the language of the 1978 version of this book,

> American politicians continue to try to create *majorities;* they have no option. But they are no longer, or at least are not very often, in the business of building *coalitions.* The materials out of which coalitions might be built simply do not exist. Building coalitions in the United States today is like building coalitions in the sand. It cannot be done.[12]

Although little in this regard has changed in the ensuing decade, interestingly, the language of coalition building hangs on. A striking instance of it, and of its inappropriateness, is to be found in Hedrick Smith's rightly acclaimed account of how politics in Washington works, *The Power Game*.[13] In his chapter entitled "The Coalition Game," Smith writes: "The coalition game—building coalitions and making coalitions work—is the heart of our system of government."[14] Yet almost the whole of the evidence actually cited in the ensuing chapter contradicts this description. Smith himself spells out in considerable detail the unusual set of circumstances that enabled Ronald Reagan to construct a budget-cutting, tax-cutting coalition of Republican loyalists and Democratic "Boll Weevils" in 1981 but then goes on to emphasize not only that the 1981 tax-cutting coalition was temporary, indeed ephemeral, but that Reagan was never again able to put together a comparable winning coalition during the whole of his subsequent seven years in office.[15] Smith is led to describe the later Reagan as "floundering": "His governing coalition was gone. . . . His success in 1981 had been a one-shot achievement."[16] Smith largely blames Reagan, but on his own account the president's problems lay in the political material he had to work with (or, rather, did not have to work with) more than in his limitations as a political strategist. Smith even uses as a headnote to the chapter a quotation from Senator Robert Dole that cuts athwart the same chapter's central thrust: "Putting a majority together is like a one-armed man wrapping cranberries: You can't get them all in the wrap."[17] If transient *majorities* are that hard to construct, genuine *coalitions* are well nigh impossible. Old language conceals new realities.

It was hypothesized in the 1978 version of this book that an atomized politics would be likely to have a number of attributes. Leadership, except in a purely symbolic sense, would become more difficult. Politics would become harder to understand and more unpredictable. The links between the act of voting and any probable governmental outcome would become more tenuous (how many of those who voted for the budget-balancing Reagan in 1980 imagined that they were letting themselves in for the largest budget deficits in

American history?). Not least, an atomized politics would be likely to be one in which stalemate was punctuated by bursts of frenetic—and quite possibly productive—activity. Atomized politics is likely to share one characteristic with a large human crowd: a "tendency to move either very sluggishly or with extreme speed."[18]

This last point is worth pausing over, especially since in the 1980s politics in the United States seemed to illustrate it rather well. It is often said that throughout American history periods of radical change, such as the New Deal and the Great Society, have alternated with more numerous and usually longer periods in which the conservative forces in society and government (in the neutral sense of that term) have been in the ascendant. The men who wrote the Constitution in 1787 wanted change to be difficult to bring about, and in that they have largely succeeded. As Nelson W. Polsby points out in chapter 2, "To undertake great public works it helps if everyone speaks the same language"—and large numbers of Americans have seldom simultaneously spoken the language of change.[19]

All this is undoubtedly true; but what is striking about recent American history, and is easily overlooked, is that episodes of change and nonchange, far from alternating in time, are increasingly coinciding, radical change in one field of public policy overlapping with the total or near-total absence of change in another. In the 1970s the sudden and unexpected abolition of the mandatory retirement age—an act capable of bringing about, in time, a veritable social revolution—was undertaken by the Congress during a period when the same institution was finding it virtually impossible to work out policies to contend with the far more pressing (as it then seemed) energy crisis. In the following decade, the same pattern of coincidental action and inaction, of radical change and stasis, was, if anything, even more apparent. The political system that produced the budget and tax cuts of 1981, the social security reform of 1983, and the radical tax reform measures of 1986 was the same political system that was contemporaneously failing to deal effectively, at least in the short term, with the budget deficit, even though the deficit was almost universally regarded among Washington policy makers as being of monumental importance, a potentially grave threat to America's long-term prosperity.

What accounts for this disparity? Or, more precisely, what explains the highly nonincremental lurches forward in public policy in the 1970s and 1980s (since stalemate of the kind that occurred on energy policy and the deficit is supposed to be, and usually is, the American norm)?

Two answers suggest themselves. One is intellectual, or at least quasi-intellectual, and can be related to the crowd metaphor mentioned earlier. The members of a crowd are apt to move all at once, very rapidly, and in the same direction if they come simultaneously to hold the same idea, if as individuals they perceive that it will be safe for them to move in the same direction as the crowd, and if as individuals they also perceive that, on the contrary, it may be unsafe or even positively dangerous for them not to move in the same direction as the crowd. This is the phenomenon, ill understood but universally recognized, to be found under such headings as (at worst) "panic" or "the herd instinct" and (at best) "a change in the climate of opinion" or "the power of an idea whose time has come." There is every reason to suppose that men and women will be moved most by such an idea if, despite being members of a crowd, they feel themselves to be essentially isolated and to lack the support of networks of like-minded colleagues and other protective—the word "protective" is crucial—institutions. It does not matter whether the idea in question is sound, sensible, or well thought through. What matters is that men and women believe in it—and believe that other men and women believe in it. Under such circumstances, and in the absence of competing or countervailing ideas, the potential for very rapid action is enormous.

The dangers of thinking metaphorically are obvious, but this particular metaphor does help to make sense of much policy innovation in the United States in recent decades. Isolated political actors in an atomized political system are more likely than, say, old party war horses or machine politicians to fall prey (for better or worse) to prevailing political fashions. They are also likely to feel that there are more risks to them attendant upon *not* falling prey to such fashions. The loner is very much easier to pick off politically than the member of a majority, especially a large majority.

It is striking how often, in their accounts of such episodes as the 1981 budget and tax cuts, political observers resort to the language of "fashion," "climate," and "mood"—and refer also to the intellectual frames of reference that made Ronald Reagan's version of supply-side economics irresistible, if not entirely plausible. At one level, Hedrick Smith, referring mainly to the triumphant Republicans but not only to them, writes:

> Politics is like sports: There are electric moments which transform group psychology, dramatically altering the dynamics of the game. When the lead suddenly changes hands, emotions swing from one team to another. Elan soars; partisan juices flow; the other side is thrown off balance. A team or a party, once faltering, gains inspiration; it is suddenly energized. Riding a collective high, individual players pick up tempo and confidence. . . . That climate was a boon to Reagan.[20]

At another level, James D. Savage has drawn attention to the extent to which Reagan owed his 1981 success to his claim that his budget- and tax-cutting proposals would ultimately lead to the goal of a balanced budget, a goal that, as Savage says, "has played a central role in American political life."[21] The almost universal feeling that tax cutting was an idea whose time had come completely disarmed the opposition. "I've been a politician," Speaker Tip O'Neill said, "long enough to know when to fight and when not to."[22] This was seen as a time not to.

Ideas and a changed climate of opinion played an equally important, if also more subtle and less overtly spectacular, role in the late 1970s and 1980s in bringing about the deregulation of the airline, trucking, and other industries—another instance of policy change that was at once radical and wholly unexpected. Looking to account for the change, Martha Derthick and Paul J. Quirk point to a concatenation (to some degree fortuitous) of several factors: the convergence of elite opinion in support of reform, the willingness of officeholders in leadership positions to take initiatives, the fact that some of the most important initiatives did not require the approval of Congress, and the inability of the economic interests that were under threat to defend their position effectively. But Derthick and Quirk are also at pains to emphasize the importance of an idea, deregulation, whose time had come. It appealed to a remarkably wide range of ideological constituencies, and it also addressed two major concerns current during the period: inflation on the one hand and "intrusive government" on the other. Long before Jimmy Carter left the White House, the idea of deregulation had come to have a life and a power of its own: "The notion of deregulation itself, as prescription turned fashion, had an influence on events that was to some degree independent of the resources deployed by particular advocates."[23] Deregulation, Derthick and Quirk point out, conformed to traditional values and common sense and "could be rendered in simple symbolic, intuitively appealing terms."[24] In consequence, a line of policy once deemed unthinkable suddenly became unstoppable. The crowd was moving.

Not all sudden and radical policy shifts, however, can be so largely explained in intellectual or quasi-intellectual terms. Policy change sometimes seems to take place very rapidly for a second reason, which might be termed "the collusion of elites." Whether or not the climate of opinion has changed, key policy makers may decide that some specific matter is of such gravity and urgency that they should in effect remove it from the public arena—and then stand together to protect one another from any adverse political consequences. A good deal of foreign policy during the immediate postwar period, notably the Marshall Plan, seems to have been of this character, and in the era of political atomization this style of policy making—"we had better get together to sort this one out"— seems to have revived among responsible public officials.

The 1986 tax reform is a case in point. A change in the climate of opinion, which made the existing federal tax code no longer defensible, coincided with a change in the mode of policy making, which made it possible for members of Congress to stand shoulder to shoulder—rather like the English before Agincourt—against the army of special interest lobby-

301

ists so colorfully arrayed in "Gucci Gulch." It seems doubtful whether the tax reform would have been enacted, despite the new public and congressional mood on the issue, if men like Senator Robert Packwood and Congressman Dan Rostenkowski had not been prepared to work closely together and also to protect one another—and their hesitant allies—in public.[25] On an issue like tax reform, on which everyone agrees that something should be done but on which no one on his own is in a political position to do it, some degree of collusion of elites may well be a necessary condition of innovation.

An even purer instance of this technique is described by Paul Light in *Artful Work*, his detailed account of the social security reform of three years earlier.[26] A crisis of the entire social security system was imminent; yet the political costs to any individual in either the administration or Congress of taking a lead on the issue were exorbitantly high. Everyone wanted reform and knew it was necessary, but no one wanted to pay for it—or to be seen to be making others pay for it. The solution that was finally hit upon, given a degree of goodwill on all sides and a shared sense of the urgency of the problem, was a protracted series of secret negotiations (the secrecy was essential) accompanied by a collective determination to stand together when the time came for the issue to be presented to Congress—and, by standing together, to make it easier for others to do the same.

Light writes of the first set of negotiations, involving the so-called Gang of Seventeen:

> Its meetings seemed to inaugurate a new form of presidential-congressional government. The meetings were secret. There were no minutes or transcripts. All conversations were strictly off the record. The gang was free to discuss all the options without fear of political retaliation. . . . This was not just separate institutions sharing power; this was a new kind of government body involving a single chamber of national leadership.[27]

When the Gang of Seventeen ultimately failed, it was replaced by an even smaller Gang of Nine, which ultimately succeeded. This secret gang "built a compromise, wrapped it in a bipartisan flag, and rammed it through Congress."[28] If Gramm-Rudman-Hollings eventually fails, if the federal budget deficit at the same time fails to correct itself, and if leaders of both the administration and Congress finally decide that some action must be taken lest permanent damage be done to the American economy, then a collusion of elites of the kind described by Light and others would appear on the face of it to be the best, perhaps the only, institutional mechanism available.[29] There is a nice irony in the idea of the representatives of the people standing together against the people but in the people's interests. It is not normally what is thought of as democracy, let alone participationist democracy, but it may be none the worse for that.

Envoi

The next few decades will probably not be altogether easy for the United States. Even if, as seems possible, a combination of Gramm-Rudman-Hollings, changes in the social security system, and some assortment of "revenue enhancements" does succeed in reducing the federal budget deficit to a more manageable size, American citizens will have to get used to the idea of a sharp diminution in America's political and military strength, and also in its economic strength, relative to that of the rest of the world.

The change in the quality of America's political relationship with the rest of the world is already well advanced. Many more countries have substantial military strength today than in the 1940s and 1950s; American resolve was to some extent weakened by the Vietnam War; and of course nuclear weapons, although undoubtedly desirable to have, have turned out to be next to useless in influencing most real-world political situations. In almost no part of the world does America's writ still run. Compare, for instance, the involvement of the United States in Lebanon in the late 1950s, when U.S. Marines were able to intervene with impunity, with its involvement there in the mid-1980s, when 241 marines were killed in a single attack and the intervening American force had somewhat ignominiously to be "redeployed offshore."

America, like Great Britain after it lost its empire, is searching for, but has yet to find, a new world role. Such a new role will take time to define, and in the meantime many in a land of superpatriots may not find it easy to accommodate themselves to an international environment in which America is no longer the unchallenged leader of the free world but is merely the most powerful among a number of powerful nations in an increasingly complex and heterogeneous universe. The international political system, as well as the American, is becoming fragmented.

The economic cloud on the horizon is, if anything, even larger. Mention was made earlier of the three eighteenth- and nineteenth-century empires: the British, the Russian, and the American. One consequence of those countries' being empires was that their economies were for long periods largely protected from the full rigors of international competition. It may be no accident that the British, the Soviet, and the American economies are all, in different ways and to varying degrees, finding it more difficult than those of many other countries to adapt to the postimperial world economic order. Countries that never had empires or had them for only short periods are doing better. The British, Soviet, and American trade deficits, reflecting the three countries' low rates of economic growth, and especially their low rates of growth of labor productivity, are only the visible outward signs of what is almost certainly, even in the case of the United States, a deeper internal malaise. It is possible that the American economy may be about to enter, may already have entered, a prolonged period of British-style relative economic decline. If so, the decline itself will be difficult for American politicians to manage or reverse. The wounds inflicted on Americans' pride and generosity of spirit could be serious.

Almost inevitably, if substantial numbers of Americans begin to worry about America's position in the world and to lose confidence in their leaders and their political institutions, they will call for "reform." They will call for a strengthened presidency or stronger political parties. Amendments to the Constitution will be proposed. It is for Americans to decide what they want to do about such proposals, but a detached observer can sound a note of warning—and of encouragement. The political system of the United States has proved itself remarkably flexible and resilient over a period of 200 years, a far longer period than most other systems have survived. There is no reason to suppose that it cannot be adapted to meet a new set of challenges, however unfamiliar. It would be a terrible mistake to put at risk for no good reason one of America's most precious assets, but one that is at the same time too easily taken for granted: its political stability. As the old saying goes, "If it ain't broke, don't fix it." And the American political system, even the new American political system, ain't broke.

Notes

CHAPTER 1: THE SEPARATED PRESIDENCY—MAKING IT WORK IN
CONTEMPORARY POLITICS

1. Richard E. Neustadt, *Presidential Power: The Politics of Leadership*
(New York: Wiley, 1960), p. 33.

2. Ibid., p. 34.

3. Ibid., p. 187.

4. Ibid.

5. David S. Broder, "Split Tickets Hurt Process of Democracy,"
Wisconsin State Journal, April 10, 1989, p. 7A.

6. James L. Sundquist, "Needed: A Political Theory for the New
Era of Coalition Government in the United States," *Political Science
Quarterly*, vol. 103 (Winter 1988–1989), pp. 613–35.

7. Ibid., p. 632.

8. For a summary of political party success see Paul Allen Beck,
"Incomplete Realignment: The Reagan Legacy for Parties and Elec-
tions," in Charles O. Jones, ed., *The Reagan Legacy: Promise and
Performance* (Chatham, N.J.: Chatham House, 1988), chap. 5.

9. Data from CBS/*New York Times* exit polls as reported in *Public
Opinion* (January/February 1989), pp. 24–25.

10. Aaron Wildavsky, "President Reagan as a Political Strategist,"
in Jones, ed., *The Reagan Legacy*, p. 290.

11. Samuel C. Patterson, "The Semi-Sovereign Congress," in
Anthony King, ed., *The New American Political System* (Washington,
D.C.: American Enterprise Institute, 1978), p. 132.

12. Comments made in a panel discussion entitled "The Role of
Congress," sponsored by Time, Inc., in Chicago, Illinois, December
5, 1972.

13. Mark J. Rozell, *The Press and the Carter Presidency* (Boulder,
Colo.: Westview Press, 1989), p. 4.

14. Richard F. Fenno, Jr., *Home Style: House Members in Their
Districts* (Boston: Little, Brown, 1978), p. 54.

15. Terry M. Moe, "The Politicized Presidency," in John E. Chubb

and Paul E. Peterson, eds., *The New Directions in American Politics* (Washington, D.C.: Brookings Institution, 1985), p. 269.
16. Fred I. Greenstein, "Change and Continuity in the Modern Presidency," in King, ed., *The New American Political System*, p. 83; and Nelson W. Polsby, *Congress and the Presidency*, 4th ed. (Englewood Cliffs, N.J.: Prentice-Hall, 1986), p. 209.
17. Moe, "The Politicized Presidency," p. 270.
18. Theodore J. Lowi, *The Personal President: Power Invested, Promise Unfulfilled* (Ithaca, N.Y.: Cornell University Press, 1985), p. xii.
19. Wildavsky, "Reagan as Strategist," p. 304.

CHAPTER 2: POLITICAL CHANGE AND THE CHARACTER
OF THE CONTEMPORARY CONGRESS

1. For discussions of these various achievements, see E. Pendleton Herring, *Presidential Leadership* (New York: Farrar and Rhinehart, 1940); and James T. Patterson, *Congressional Conservatism and the New Deal* (Lexington: University of Kentucky Press, 1967).
2. See Herman Somers, *Presidential Agency* (Cambridge, Mass.: Harvard University Press, 1950); Stephen K. Bailey, *Congress Makes a Law: The Story behind the Employment Act of 1946* (New York: Columbia University Press, 1950); Nelson W. Polsby, *Political Innovation in America* (New Haven, Conn.: Yale University Press, 1984); and Paul Hammond, *Organizing for Defense* (Princeton, N.J.: Princeton University Press, 1961).
3. Much of this legislation passed in the 89th Congress. See *Congressional Quarterly Almanac, 89th Congress, 1st Session, 1965*, vol. 21 (Washington, D.C.: Congressional Quarterly Service, 1966), pp. 65–122; and *Congressional Quarterly Almanac, 89th Congress, 2nd Session, 1966*, vol. 22 (Washington, D.C.: Congressional Quarterly Service, 1967), pp. 69–94, 99–115.
4. James McGregor Burns, *The Deadlock of Democracy: Four Party Politics in America* (Englewood Cliffs, N.J.: Prentice-Hall, 1963).
5. On crisis and its effects on innovation, see Polsby, *Political Innovation*, pp. 167–72.
6. For authoritative commentary on the Legislative Reorganization Act of 1946, see George Galloway, *Congress at the Crossroads* (New York: Crowell, 1946).
7. On Johnson, see Ralph K. Huitt, "Democratic Party Leadership in the Senate," *American Political Science Review*, vol. 55 (June 1961), pp. 331–44. On the packing of the Rules Committee, see Neil MacNeil, *Forge of Democracy: The House of Representatives* (New York: McKay, 1963), pp. 412–47; and William MacKaye, *A New Coalition*

Takes Control: The House Rules Committee Fight of 1961 (New York: McGraw Hill, 1963). On recent reforms of the House, see Norman Ornstein, "The Democrats Reform Power in the House of Representatives, 1969–1975," in Allan Sindler, ed., *America in the Seventies: Problems, Policies, and Politics* (Boston, Mass.: Little, Brown, 1977), pp. 2–48.

8. See Polsby, *Congress and the Presidency* (Englewood Cliffs, N.J.: Prentice-Hall, 1986), pp. 85–113; and "What Hubert Humphrey Wrought," *Commentary*, vol. 78 (November 1984), pp. 47–50. Also see Alan Ehrenhalt, "In the Senate of the 80s Team Spirit Has Given Way to the Role of Individuals," *Congressional Quarterly*, September 4, 1982, pp. 2175–82.

9. William S. White, *Citadel* (New York: Harper and Row, 1956). See also Joseph S. Clark, *Congress: The Sapless Branch* (New York: Harper and Row, 1964); and Ralph K. Huitt, "The Outsider in the Senate: An Alternative Role," *American Political Science Review*, vol. 55 (June 1961), pp. 556–75.

10. See, for example, Virginia Van der Veer Hamilton's biography of a highly influential and constructive southern senator, *Lister Hill: Statesman from the South* (Chapel Hill, N.C.: University of North Carolina Press, 1987).

11. Clayton Fritchey, "Who Belongs to the Senate's Inner Club?" *Harper's* (May 1967), pp. 104–10.

12. Joseph B. Gorman, *Kefauver: A Political Biography* (New York: Oxford University Press, 1971).

13. See Huitt, "Democratic Leadership in the Senate"; Clark, *Congress: The Sapless Branch*; Doris Kearns, *Lyndon Johnson and the American Dream* (New York: Harper and Row, 1976), pp. 72–159; and Rowland Evans and Robert Novak, *Lyndon B. Johnson: The Exercise of Power* (New York: New American Library, 1966), pp. 50–224.

14. See John G. Stewart, "Two Strategies of Leadership: Johnson and Mansfield," in Nelson W. Polsby, ed., *Congressional Behavior* (New York: Random House, 1971), pp. 61–92.

15. See, for example, Jeffrey H. Birnbaum, "Nevada Senator Hecht, a Barrel of Gaffes, Staves Off Spotlight," *Wall Street Journal*, August 11, 1988.

16. See Nelson W. Polsby, Miriam Gallaher, and Barry Spencer Rundquist, "The Growth of the Seniority System in the U.S. House of Representatives," *American Political Science Review*, vol. 63 (September 1969), pp. 787–807.

17. Nicholas Masters, "Committee Assignments in the House of Representatives," *American Political Science Review*, vol. 55 (June 1961), pp. 345–57.

18. See Barbara Deckard Sinclair, "Determinants of Aggregate Party Cohesion in the U.S. House of Representatives, 1901–1956," *Legislative Studies Quarterly*, vol. 2 (May 1977), pp. 155–75, esp. p. 160; and Barbara Deckard and John Stanley, "Party Decomposition and Region: The House of Representatives, 1945–1970," *Western Political Quarterly*, vol. 27 (June 1974), pp. 249–64, esp. pp. 250, 257. Also see Julius Turner and Edward V. Schneier, Jr., *Party and Constituency: Pressures on Congress* (Baltimore, Md.: Johns Hopkins Press, 1970), pp. 41–106 and 165–89.

19. See Thomas Mann and Norman Ornstein, eds., *The New Congress* (Washington, D.C.: American Enterprise Institute, 1981), especially chapters by Roger Davidson and Michael Malbin, pp. 99–177; Leroy Rieselbach, *Congressional Reform in the Seventies* (Morristown, N.J.: General Learning Press, 1977); and Ornstein, "The Democrats Reform Power."

20. See Clem Miller, in John Baker, ed., *Member of the House* (New York: Scribner's, 1962), pp. 116–31.

21. See Mark Ferber, *The Democratic Study Group: A Study of Intra-Party Organization in the House of Representatives* (Ph.D. diss., University of California at Los Angeles, 1964).

22. See three works by Eric L. Davis: "Congressional Liaison: The People and the Institutions," in Anthony King, ed., *Both Ends of the Avenue* (Washington, D.C.: American Enterprise Institute, 1983), pp. 59–96; "Legislative Liaison in the Carter Administration," *Political Science Quarterly*, vol. 94 (Summer 1979), pp. 287–301; and *Building Presidential Coalitions in Congress: Legislative Liaison in the Johnson White House* (Ph.D. diss., Stanford University, 1978). See also John Manley, "Presidential Power and White House Lobbying," *Political Science Quarterly*, vol. 93 (Summer 1978), pp. 255–75; and John Hart, *The Presidential Branch* (New York: Pergamon Press, 1987), pp. 171–175.

23. Norman Ornstein, Thomas Mann, and Michael Malbin, *Vital Statistics on Congress, 1987–1988* (Washington, D.C.: Congressional Quarterly, 1987), pp. 135–59. For a commentary, see Michael Malbin, *Unelected Representatives: Congressional Staff and the Future of Representative Government* (New York: Basic Books, 1980).

24. Charles O. Jones agrees. See his text, *The United States Congress: People, Places and Policy* (Homewood, Ill.: Dorsey, 1982), pp. 133–48, 379–408. On page 405, he says,

> Recent reforms (growth in staff, expanded use of the legislative veto, a more comprehensive and coordinated budgetary procedure) encourage even more direct and system-

atic congressional participation in program execution. Interestingly these changes appear to have been made to a substantial degree as a consequence of perceived excesses by the president—particularly during the Johnson and Nixon administrations. That is, Congress was moved to expand its capabilities to deal with all aspects of foreign and domestic issues because many members came to believe that Presidents Johnson and Nixon had exceeded their authority.

Also see his "Congress and the Presidency," in Mann and Ornstein, eds., *The New Congress*, pp. 223–49.

25. For a recent profile of congressional staff, see Harrison W. Fox, Jr., and Susan Webb Hammond, *Congressional Staffs: The Invisible Force in American Lawmaking* (New York: Free Press, 1977). Also see Richard E. Cohen, "The Hill People," *National Journal*, vol. 19, May 16, 1987, pp. 1170–71.

26. See David Price, *Who Makes the Laws? Creativity and Power in Senate Committees* (Cambridge, Mass.: Schenkman Publishing Co., 1972), pp. 329–31. Also see Michael Pertschuck, *Revolt against Regulation: The Rise and Pause of the Consumer Movement* (Berkeley: University of California Press, 1982), pp. 26–28. Also see Malbin, *Unelected Representatives*.

27. Nelson W. Polsby, "Strengthening Congress in National Policy-Making," *The Yale Review*, vol. 59 (June 1970), pp. 481–97.

28. See, for example, David B. Truman, ed., *The Congress and America's Future* (Englewood Cliffs, N.J.: Prentice-Hall, 1965), pp. 1–31.

29. Polsby, "Institutionalization of the U.S. House of Representatives," *American Political Science Review*, vol. 62 (March 1968), pp. 144–68.

30. David Brady, *Critical Elections and Congressional Policy-Making* (Stanford, Calif.: Stanford University Press, 1988).

31. Raymond E. Wolfinger and Joan Heifetz, "Safe Seats, Seniority, and Power in Congress," *American Political Science Review*, vol. 59 (June 1965), pp. 337–49.

32. Ornstein, Mann, and Malbin, *Vital Statistics on Congress*, pp. 135–39.

CHAPTER 3: THE SUPREME COURT FROM EARLY BURGER
TO EARLY REHNQUIST

1. The course of these policy initiatives and others noted later in the chapter can be traced easily in any standard constitutional law

case book. See, for example, Martin Shapiro and Rocco J. Tresolini, *American Constitutional Law*, 6th ed. (New York: Macmillan, 1983).

2. *New York Times* Co. v. United States, 403 U.S. 713 (1971); United States v. Nixon, 418 U.S. 683 (1974).

3. See Louis Fisher, *Constitutional Conflicts between Congress and the President* (Princeton, N.J.: Princeton University Press, 1985).

4. The literature on compliance and impact more generally is surveyed in Stephen Wasby, *The Impact of the United States Supreme Court: Some Perspectives* (Homewood, Ill.: Dorsey, 1970).

5. Charles Bullock and Harrell Rodgers, *Law and Social Change: Civil Rights Laws and Their Consequences* (New York: McGraw-Hill, 1972).

6. For a more complete version of this argument, see Martin Shapiro, "The Constitution and Economic Rights," in M. Judd Harmon, ed., *Essays on the Constitution of the United States* (Port Washington, N.Y.: Kennikat Press, 1978).

7. David Adamany and Joel Grossman, "Support for the Supreme Court as a National Policymaker," *Law and Policy Quarterly*, vol. 5 (1983), pp. 405–37.

8. This work is summarized in Glendon Schubert, *The Judicial Mind* (Evanston, Ill.: Northwestern University Press, 1965).

9. Much of this work is summarized in Joel B. Grossman and Richard S. Wells, *Constitutional Law and Judicial Policy Making* (New York: Wiley, 1972), pp. 168–79.

10. See Bob Woodward and Scott Armstrong, *The Brethren* (New York: Simon and Schuster, 1979); Bernard Schwartz, *Super Chief: Earl Warren and His Supreme Court* (New York: New York University Press, 1983); and Mark Cannon and David O'Brien, *View from the Bench* (New York: Chatham House, 1985).

11. See Joseph Tanenhaus et al., "The Supreme Court's Certiorari Jurisdiction: Cue Theory," in Glendon Schubert, ed., *Judicial Decision-Making* (New York: Free Press, 1963), pp. 111–27. See also Sidney Ulmer et al., "The Decision to Grant or Deny Certiorari: Further Consideration of Cue Theory," *Law and Society Review*, vol. 6 (1972), pp. 640–55.

12. See Robert G. McCloskey, *The Modern Supreme Court* (Cambridge, Mass.: Harvard University Press, 1972), chap. 4.

13. San Antonio School District v. Rodriguez, 411 U.S. 1 (1973).

14. Frontier v. Richardson, 411 U.S. 677 (1973). This case involved less favorable treatment of the dependents of female military personnel than male military personnel. Subsequently, the Burger Court struck down a number of state and federal statutes on sex discrimination grounds but refused to hold that sex was a suspect classifi-

cation. Instead, the Court held that, in order to satisfy its equal protection standard, sex classification "must serve important governmental objectives and must be substantially related to achievement of those objectives." Craig v. Boren, 429 U.S. 190 (1976).

15. On the transition from the Warren Court to the Burger Court, see Richard Y. Funston, *Constitutional Counter-Revolution* (New York: Wiley, 1977); Stephen L. Wasby, *Continuity and Change: From the Warren Court to the Burger Court* (Pacific Palisades, Calif.: Goodyear Publishing, 1976); and Wallace Mendelson, "From Warren to Burger: The Rise and Decline of Substantive Equal Protection," *American Political Science Review*, vol. 66 (1972), pp. 1226–33.

16. Roe v. Wade, 410 U.S. 113 (1973); and Doe v. Bolton, 410 U.S. 179 (1973).

17. Furman v. Georgia, 408 U.S. 238 (1972).

18. Most of the cases relevant to the developments that will be traced in the rest of this chapter can be found in William B. Lockhart et al., *Constitutional Law* (St. Paul, Minn.: West Publishing Co., 1980), which has annual supplements keeping it constantly up to date and a new edition every four or five years.

19. This approach can be traced in New Jersey v. TLO, 105 S. Ct. 733, see especially Justice Brennan dissenting at 758 (1985); United States v. Leon, 104 S. Ct. 3405 (1984); Florida v. Rodriguez, 105 S. Ct. 308 (1984); Thompson v. Louisiana, 105 S. Ct. 409 (1984); United States v. Hensley, 105 S. Ct. 675 (1985); Hayes v. Florida, 105 S. Ct. 1643 (1985); Oregon v. Elstad, 105 S. Ct. 1284 (1985).

20. See Karcher v. Daggett, 462 U.S. 725 (1983); and Brown v. Thomson, 462 U.S. 835 (1983).

21. See City of Mobile v. Bolden, 446 U.S. 55 (1980). At-large systems that in fact result in the absence of minority legislators have been rendered illegal, no matter what the intent, by recent amendments to the Voting Rights Act.

22. Davis v. Bandemer, 478 U.S. 109 (1986). See "Symposium: Gerrymandering and the Courts," *U.C.L.A. Law Review*, vol. 33, no. 1 (1989).

23. Regents of University of California v. Bakker, 438 U.S. 265 (1978); and Fullilove v. Klutznick, 448 U.S. 448 (1980).

24. See W. Van Alstyne, "Graphic Review of the Free Speech Clause," *California Law Review*, vol. 70 (1982), pp. 107–50.

25. National League of Cities v. Usery, 426 U.S. 833 (1976).

26. Garcia v. San Antonio Metropolitan Transit Authority, 105 S. Ct. 1005 (1985).

27. United States v. Carolene Products Co., 304 U.S. 144, 152n.4 (1938).

28. See Shapiro, "The Constitution and Economic Rights."

29. This and the two previous paragraphs are a summary of chap. 6 in Martin Shapiro, *Law and Politics in the Supreme Court* (New York: Free Press, 1964).

30. See Continental T.V. Inc. v. GTE Sylvania Inc., 433 U.S. 36 (1977); Northwest Wholesale Stationers Inc. v. Pacific Stationery and Printing Co., 105 S. Ct. 2613 (1985); N.C.A.A. v. Board of Regents, 104 S. Ct. 2948 (1985); and Jefferson Parish Hospital District v. Hyde, 104 S. Ct. 1551 (1984).

31. Coker v. Georgia, 433 U.S. 584 (1977).

32. Solem v. Helm, 463 U.S. 277 (1983). See also Tennessee v. Garner, 105 S. Ct. 1694 (1985).

33. Walz v. Tax Commissioner, 397 U.S. 664 (1970); and Wisconsin v. Yoder, 406 U.S. 205 (1972).

34. Committee for Public Education and Religious Liberty v. Nyquist, 413 U.S. 756 (1973).

35. Mueller v. Allen, 463 U.S. 388 (1983).

36. Lynch v. Donnelly, 104 S. Ct. 1335 (1984).

37. Cleveland Board of Education v. Loudermill, 105 S. Ct. 1487 (1985).

38. See particularly City of Cleburne v. Cleburne Living Center, 105 S. Ct. 3249 (1985).

39. For more extended discussion of the discretion left to administrators and judges by ambiguous statutes, see Peter Aranson, Ernest Gelhorn, and Glen Robinson, "A Theory of Legislative Delegation," *Cornell Law Quarterly*, vol. 68 (1983), pp. 1–97; and Martin Shapiro, "Administrative Discretion: The Next Stage," *Yale Law Journal*, vol. 92 (1983), pp. 1487–1522.

40. The developments in administrative law sketched in the next ten paragraphs can be traced in detail in Richard Stewart, "The Reformation of American Administrative Law," *Harvard Law Review*, vol. 88 (1975), pp. 1667–1784; and Martin Shapiro, *Who Guards the Guardians?* (Athens, Ga.: University of Georgia Press, 1988).

41. Shep Melnick, *Regulation and the Courts* (Cambridge: Harvard University Press, 1983).

42. Vermont Yankee Nuclear Power Corp. v. Natural Resources Defense Council, Inc., 435 U.S. 519 (1978).

43. See particularly Motor Vehicle Manufacturers Assoc. v. State Farm Mutual Automobile Insurance Co., 103 S. Ct. 2856 (1983); Industrial Union Dept. AFL-CIO v. American Petroleum Institute, 448 U.S. 607 (1980); American Textile Manufacturers Institute v. Donovan, 452 U.S. 490 (1981); Board of Education v. Rowley, 458

U.S. 176 (1982); and Chemical Manufacturers Association v. Natural Resources Defense Council, 105 S. Ct. 1102 (1985).

44. City of Cleburne v. Cleburne Living Center, 105 S. Ct. 3249 (1985).

45. See Frank H. Easterbrook, "The Court and the Economic System," *Harvard Law Review*, vol. 98 (1984), pp. 4–60.

CHAPTER 4: POLITICAL PARTIES—DECLINING, STABILIZING, OR RESURGING?

1. The decline of party literature is summarized in William Crotty and Gary Jacobson, *American Parties in Decline* (Boston: Little, Brown, 1980).

2. Gerald Pomper, "An American Epilogue," in Vernon Bogdanor, ed., *Parties and Democracy in Britain and America* (New York: Praeger, 1984), p. 271.

3. See M. P. Wattenberg, *The Decline of American Political Parties 1952–1984* (Cambridge, Mass.: Harvard University Press, 1986).

4. Joseph A. Schlesinger, "On the Theory of Party Organization," *Journal of Politics*, vol. 46, no. 2 (May 1984).

5. David E. Price, *Bringing Back the Parties* (Washington, D.C.: Congressional Quarterly Press, 1984), p. 78.

6. *New York Times*, January 2, 1989.

7. T. M. Konda and L. Sigelman, "Public Evaluations of the American Parties 1952–1984" *Journal of Politics*, vol. 49 (1987), pp. 814–29.

8. Arthur Schlesinger, Jr., "The Crisis of the Party System II," *Wall Street Journal*, May 10, 1978; Walter Dean Burnham, *The Current Crisis in American Politics* (New York: Oxford University Press, 1982), p. 115.

9. For an account of recent Republican party development that emphasizes this theme see Martin Shefter and Benjamin Ginsberg, "Reaganism Well into the 21st Century," *Washington Post*, September 15, 1985.

10. See Samuel Beer, "In Search of a New Public Philosophy," in Anthony King, ed., *The New American Political System* (Washington, D.C.: American Enterprise Institute, 1978).

11. For an in-depth account of the reforms in the Democratic party during this period, see Byron Shafer, *Quiet Revolution* (New York: Russell Sage Foundation, 1983).

12. From a speech given at the Democratic Leadership Council meeting on March 10, 1989. "Jackson, Robb Tussle over Democratic Strategy," *Washington Post*, March 11, 1989.

NOTES

13. James Sundquist, "Congress and the President: Enemies or Partners?" *Congress Reconsidered* (New York: Praeger, 1977), p. 242.

14. Jones "Nominating 'Carter's Favorite Opponent,' " in Austin Ranney, ed., *The American Elections of 1980* (Washington, D.C.: American Enterprise Institute, 1981), p. 98.

15. Sidney Milkis, "The Modern Presidency and the Transformation of the American Party System" (Paper presented at the 1987 American Political Science Association Meeting), p. 68.

16. Speech to the 12th Annual Conservative Political Action Conference, March 1, 1985.

17. See Samuel Lubell, *The Future of American Politics* (New York: Doubleday, 1951), p. 212.

18. Gallup surveys showed that after 1984 for the first time Republicans started consistently to rank ahead of the Democrats as the party better for prosperity. See *Gallup Report,* October 1988, p. 5.

19. This is the view of Alan Baron and Howard Rosenthal. See *Wall Street Journal,* November 14, 1988.

20. For further elaboration of this view, see John Chubb and Paul Peterson, "Realignment and Institutionalization," in Chubb and Peterson, eds., *The New Direction in American Politics* (Washington, D.C.: Brookings Institution, 1985).

21. The notion of competition here is being used in an analytic sense. In the real world, there are elements of cooperation as well as competition, and parties sometimes work with or exert control over PACs and interest groups. Overall, however, there is enough truth in the idea of competition to justify its use as a helpful simplification.

22. The classic statements of this argument have been made by Martin Van Buren, V. O. Key, and Leon Epstein. This case for parties is a quite different one from that made by Woodrow Wilson and other modern proponents of the "responsible" party model. The former seeks "strong" parties to improve the functioning of the government *under* the Constitution; the latter seeks strong parties to change or alter the character of the Constitution itself, which is regarded as radically deficient. It is highly unfortunate that the term "strong parties" is applied to both cases, for they have nothing to do with each other.

23. By the national party here, I am referring for each party to the national committees plus the two congressional campaign committees.

24. For an account of the increased organizational capacity of the state parties, as measured by budgets and full-time employees, see James Gibson, Cornelius Cotter, John Bibby, and Robert Huckshorn,

"Assessing Party Organizational Strength," *American Journal of Political Science*, vol. 27 (May 1983), pp. 194–205; and the ACIR's *The Transformation in American Politics: Implications for Federalism* (Washington, D.C.: 1986), chap. 4.

25. According to David R. Mayhew, only thirteen states can be classified as having had strong party organizations during most of this century. See *Placing Parties in American Politics* (Princeton, N.J.: Princeton University Press, 1986).

26. William Crotty and Gary Jacobson, *American Parties in Decline* (Boston: Little, Brown, 1980).

27. Cited in Gary Orren, "The Nomination Process," in Michael Nelson, ed., *The Elections of 1984* (Washington, D.C.: Congressional Quarterly, 1985), p. 32.

28. Garry Orren and Nelson Polsby, "New Hampshire: Springboard of Nomination Politics," in Garry Orren and Nelson Polsby, eds., *Media and Momentum* (Chatham, N.J.: Chatham House, 1987), p. 4. For the first systematic attempts to deal with voting behavior in presidential primaries, see Scott Keeter and Cliff Zukin, *Uninformed Choice* (New York: Praeger, 1983); and Larry Bartels, *Presidential Primaries and the Dynamics of Public Choice* (Princeton, N.J.: Princeton University Press, 1988).

29. David Truman described the role of interests under the old system as follows: "The national parties, as they assemble quadrennially to nominate candidates for the Presidency, are not leagues of organized interest groups but coalitions of state parties and factions with group ties of varying intimacy." In Norman Zucker, ed., *The American Party Process* (New York: Dodd, Mead, & Co., 1968), p. 363.

30. Michael Malbin "The Conventions, Platforms, and Issue Activists," in Ranney, ed., *American Elections of 1980*, p. 136.

31. *Hunt Commission Report*, 1982, p. 16. This rule shows that if elected officials are virtually guaranteed seats as delegates, they can actually be induced to attend the convention! In 1976, only 18 percent of the Democratic senators and 14 percent of the Democratic House members attended the party convention. By 1984, these figures had risen to 61 percent and 66 percent, respectively.

32. In addition to reducing the number of superdelegates, the convention agreed to ban bonus delegates that some states awarded to the candidate receiving a plurality in each congressional district. This change moves the system back to a slightly more proportional allocation of delegates. The rule changes in 1988 were significant but left the existing system essentially intact. They were made by the now usual procedure of the victorious candidate giving in to the demands of the loser in order to achieve party harmony. See *Congressional Quarterly Weekly Report*, July 2, 1988, pp. 1799–1801.

33. In 1984, the convention passed a resolution that called for a fairness commission that would eliminate superdelegates. By the time the commission reported in 1986, it had actually enlarged the number of superdelegates.

34. Harold Bass, "The Presidency and the National Party Organization," in Robert Harmel, ed., *Presidents and Their Parties* (New York: Praeger, 1984), p. 61.

35. William Crotty, "The National Committees as Grass-roots Vehicles of Representation," in William Crotty, ed., *The Party Symbol* (San Francisco: W. H. Freeman, 1980), pp. 40–41.

36. Cited in Sydney Milkis, "The Modern Presidency," p. 67.

37. Charles Clapp, *The Congressman* (Washington, D.C.: Brookings Institution, 1963), p. 34.

38. Ibid. See also Steven and Barbara Salmore, *Candidates, Parties and Campaigns* (Washington, D.C.: Congressional Quarterly Press, 1985).

39. Richard Fenno, *Homestyle* (Boston: Little, Brown, 1978), p. 113.

40. Alan Abramowitz, "In Congressional Elections, Lack of Money Is the Root of All Evil," *New York Times*, June 27, 1989. The remaining 13 percent went to candidates for open seats.

41. David Adamany, "Political Parties in the 1980s," in Michael Malbin, ed., *Money and Politics in the United States* (Chatham, N.J.: Chatham House, 1984), p. 71. This claim may be a bit misleading. Parties are mentioned in passing in the 1940 Hatch Act, and the spending limits of political committees clearly applied to the national committees.

42. Ibid., p. 74. See also Xandra Kayden and Eddie Mahe, *The Party Goes On* (New York: Basic Books, 1985), pp. 187–89.

43. Cited in Salmore and Salmore, *Candidates, Parties and Campaigns*, p. 238.

44. Paul Herrnson, *Party Campaigning in the 1980s* (Cambridge, Mass.: Harvard University Press, 1988), p. 130.

45. Abramowitz, "In Congressional Elections, Lack of Money Is the Root of All Evil."

46. Philip Williams, "Power and the Parties: The United States," in Bogdanor, ed., *Parties and Democracy in Britain and America*, p. 10. The importance of American parties, however, was much greater in the nineteenth century. Lord Bryce wrote in 1889: "In America, the great moving forces are the parties. The government counts for less than in Europe, the parties count for more." *The American Commonwealth*, vol. 2 (New York: Macmillan, 1889), p. 5.

47. Henry Jones Ford, *The Growth and Development of American*

Politics (New York: Da Capo Press, 1967), pp. 326–27 (originally published in 1898).

48. Anthony King, "The American Polity in the Late 1970s: Building Coalitions in the Sand," in King, ed., *The New American Political System*, p. 393. For the best concrete exploration of politics under this "new" system, see Martha Derthick and Paul Quirk, *The Politics of Deregulation* (Washington, D.C.: Brookings Institution, 1985).

49. In the words of Melissa Collie and David Brady, "the renewed institutional strength of party in the House has been more than counterbalanced by the trend toward fragmentation and dispersal of power." "The Decline of Partisan Voting Coalitions in the House of Representatives," *Congress Reconsidered* (Washington, D.C.: Congressional Quarterly Press, 1985), p. 275.

50. Gary C. Jacobson, "Republican Advantage in Campaign Finance," in John Chubb and Paul Peterson, eds., *The New Direction in American Politics* (Washington, D.C.: Brookings Institution, 1985), p. 169.

51. James Sundquist, "Needed: A New Political Theory for the New Era of Coalition Government in the United States." Paper presented at the American Political Science Association meeting, Sept 1–4, 1988, pp. 1–2 and 31.

52. Elrod v. Burns, 427 U.S. 347 (1976), p. 369.

53. State laws governing financing of campaigns today present a bewildering spectacle that I cannot even begin to summarize here. Ten states in some way assist the financing of parties—Alabama, California, Idaho, Iowa, Kentucky, Maine, North Carolina, Rhode Island, Utah, and Virginia—but it is a matter of dispute whether this assistance actually helps the parties or makes them more dependent on the state and subject to greater regulation. *The Transformation in American Politics: Implications for Federalism* (Washington, D.C.: Advisory Council on Intergovernmental Relations, August 1986), pp. 306–7.

54. Republican Party of the State of Connecticut v. Tashjian, (1986), March Fong Eu v. San Francisco County Democratic Central Committee (1989).

55. E. E. Schattschneider, *Party Government* (New York: Rinehart, 1942), p. 129.

56. James Reichley, "The Rise of National Parties," in Chubb and Peterson, eds., *The New Direction in American Politics*, p. 176.

57. Gerald Pomper, "An American Epilogue," in Bogdanor, ed., *Parties and Democracy in Britain and America*, p. 274.

58. Indeed, many state contributions are actually made by the national parties, a pass-through now deemed legal.

59. Reichley, "The Rise of National Parties," p. 190.

60. Cited in John Bibby, "Political Parties and Federalism," in *Publius*, vol. 9 (Winter 1979), p. 234.

61. Remarks by Congressman Donald Fraser before the Democratic Party Commission on Rules, January 15, 1970. Cited in William Crotty, *Party Reform* (New York: Longman, 1983), p. 138.

62. William Riker, *Federalism: Origin, Operation, Significance* (Boston: Little, Brown, 1964), p. 91.

63. Lord Macaulay, *Critical and Historical Essays*, vol. 3 (New York: Putnam's Sons, 1903), p. 399.

64. For the end-of-ideology thesis, see, for example, Robert Lane, "The Politics of Consensus in an Age of Affluence," *American Political Science Review*, vol. 59 (1965), pp. 874–95. For a statement of the "post-materialist" new class argument, see Robert Inglehart, "Post-Materialism in an Environment of Insecurity," *American Political Science Review*, vol. 75 (1981), pp. 880–900.

65. For an account of the possibilities for legal changes, see Larry J. Sabato, *The Party's Just Begun* (Glenview, Ill.: Scott, Foresman, and Company, 1988).

CHAPTER 5: FROM A PARTISAN TO A CANDIDATE-CENTERED ELECTORATE

1. V. O. Key, *The Responsible Electorate* (Cambridge, Mass.: Harvard University Press, 1966), p. 2.

2. "1988, You're No 1960," *Time*, October 24, 1988, p. 21.

3. Theodore H. White, *The Making of the President, 1960* (New York: Atheneum, 1961), p. 94.

4. Charles Brereton, *First in the Nation: New Hampshire and the Premier Presidential Primary* (Portsmouth, N.H.: Peter E. Randall, 1987).

5. Jack Dennis, "Trends in Public Support for the American Party System," *British Journal of Political Science*, vol. 5 (1975), pp. 187–230.

6. Larry J. Sabato, *The Party's Just Begun: Shaping Political Parties for America's Future* (Glenview, Ill.: Scott, Foresman and Company, 1988), p. 133.

7. Walter Dean Burnham, "The 1984 Elections and the Future of American Politics," in Ellis Sandoz and Cecil V. Crabb, Jr., eds., *Election 84: Landslide without a Mandate?* (New York: Mentor, 1985), p. 235.

8. In 1988, for the first time, the R^2 for all three of Burnham's measures fell below 0.10.

9. Martin P. Wattenberg, *The Decline of American Political Parties,*

1952–1984 (Cambridge, Mass.: Harvard University Press, 1986), p. 156.

10. Philip E. Converse, "The Nature of Belief Systems in Mass Publics," in David Apter, ed., *Ideology and Discontent* (Glencoe, Ill.: Free Press, 1964).

11. Burnham, "The 1984 Elections," p. 248.

12. Emmett H. Buell, Jr., "Divisive Primaries and Participation in Fall Presidential Campaigns: A Study of 1984 New Hampshire Primary Activists," *American Politics Quarterly*, vol. 14 (1986), pp. 376–90.

13. Walter J. Stone, "Prenomination Candidate Choice and General Election Behavior: Iowa Presidential Activists in 1980," *American Journal of Political Science*, vol. 28 (1984), pp. 361–78.

14. James I. Lengle, "Divisive Presidential Primaries and Party Electoral Prospects, 1932–1976," *American Politics Quarterly*, vol. 8 (1980), pp. 261–77.

15. Patrick J. Kenney and Tom W. Rice, "The Relationship between Divisive Primaries and General Election Outcomes," *American Journal of Political Science*, vol. 31 (1987), pp. 31–44.

16. G. Bingham Powell, Jr., "American Voter Turnout in Comparative Perspective," *American Political Science Review*, vol. 80 (1986), pp. 17–44.

17. Angus Campbell, Philip E. Converse, Warren E. Miller, and Donald E. Stokes, *The American Voter* (New York: Wiley, 1960), p. 328.

18. Ibid., p. 313.

19. Philip E. Converse, "Religion and Politics: The 1960 Election," in Angus Campbell et al., eds., *Elections and the Political Order* (New York: Wiley, 1966).

20. Martin P. Wattenberg and Arthur H. Miller, "Decay in Regional Party Coalitions: 1952–1980," in Seymour Martin Lipset, ed., *Party Coalitions in the 1980s* (San Francisco: Institute for Contemporary Studies, 1981).

21. Blacks are even more likely than whites to possess fundamentalist religious attitudes, but their racial identification has overriding importance when it comes to voting behavior. Regardless of religious attitudes or economic status, a black voter was almost sure to be a Democratic voter in the 1980s. Therefore, combining blacks and whites in the same analysis would obscure the relationship between fundamentalism and voting.

22. David Easton, *The Political System: An Inquiry into the State of Political Science* (New York: Knopf, 1953).

23. Thomas B. Edsall, *The New Politics of Inequality* (New York: Norton, 1984), p. 209.

24. Philip E. Converse, "On the Possibility of Major Political Realignment in the South," in Angus Campbell et al., eds., *Elections and the Political Order*, p. 213.

25. The South is broadly defined in this section to include the states of the Confederacy as well as the border states of Kentucky, Maryland, Oklahoma, Tennessee, and West Virginia and the District of Columbia. This choice stems partly from my own roots in this part of the country and observation that many people in these states identify with the South. Indeed, an analysis of the group identification question regarding the South reveals that in 1984, 51 percent of those interviewed in the border South, 46 percent in the Deep South, and just 17 percent in the non-South said they felt close to southerners.

26. The only southern units not included in the NES 1988 Super Tuesday survey were South Carolina, West Virginia, and the District of Columbia, which cast just 6 percent of the vote in the South in 1988. An analysis of the data from 1980 to 1986 combined shows that when South Carolina, West Virginia, and the District of Columbia are excluded from the analysis, the percentage of Republicans decreases by a mere 0.5 percentage point. Thus it can safely be said that the 1988 NES Super Tuesday survey is representative of the South as a whole.

27. Joseph A. Califano, Jr., "Tough Talk for the Democrats," *New York Times Magazine*, January 8, 1989, p. 28.

28. Earl Black and Merle Black, *Politics and Society in the South* (Cambridge, Mass.: Harvard University Press, 1987), chap. 9.

29. A Gallup/Times-Mirror study, for example, showed that the pledge of allegiance issue was more salient in the South than in any other region in 1988. In the South 51 percent of voters said the pledge issue had been very important to them, compared with 29 percent in the Northeast and 37 percent in the West and Midwest. See E. J. Dionne, Jr., "Solid South Again, but Republican," *New York Times*, November 13, 1988.

30. Thomas Ferguson and Joel Rogers, *Right Turn: The Decline of the Democrats and the Future of American Politics* (New York: Hill and Wang, 1986), chap. 1.

31. See Wattenberg, *Decline of Political Parties*, p. 153.

32. Anthony Downs, *An Economic Theory of Democracy* (New York: Harper and Row, 1957), p. 137.

33. Byron E. Shafer, *Bifurcated Politics: Evolution and Reform in the*

National Party Convention (Cambridge, Mass.: Harvard University Press, 1988), p. 111.

CHAPTER 6: BROADCASTING, NARROWCASTING, AND POLITICS

1. For an insightful review of this process, see Nelson W. Polsby, *Consequences of Party Reform* (New York: Oxford University Press, 1983), chap. 4.

2. In the considerable body of scholarly literature describing the content and consequences of the post-1968 reforms, I have found especially useful Polsby, *Consequences of Party Reform;* Byron Shafer, *Quiet Revolution: Reform Politics in the Democratic Party* (New York: Russell Sage Foundation, 1984); Jeane J. Kirkpatrick, *The New Presidential Elite* (New York: Russell Sage Foundation, 1976); James W. Ceaser, *Reforming the Reforms* (Cambridge, Mass.: Ballinger, 1982); Martin P. Wattenberg, *The Decline of American Political Parties, 1952–1980* (Cambridge: Harvard University Press, 1986); William J. Crotty, *Political Reform and the American Experiment* (New York: Harper & Row, 1977); and Crotty, *Decision for the Democrats* (Baltimore: Johns Hopkins University Press, 1978). I have tried to put the post-1968 reforms in historical perspective in my *Curing the Mischiefs of Faction: Party Reform in America* (Berkeley: University of California Press, 1975); Leon D. Epstein has presented a somewhat different perspective in *Political Parties in the American Mold* (Madison: University of Wisconsin Press, 1986).

3. An excellent study of the role of the media in accelerating and retarding momentum for the aspirants in presidential nomination contests is Larry M. Bartels, *Presidential Primaries and the Dynamics of Public Choice* (Princeton: Princeton University Press, 1988).

4. The two-step flow theory was set forth mainly in Paul F. Lazarsfeld, Bernard Berelson, and Hazel Gaudet, *The People's Choice,* 2d ed. (New York: Columbia University Press, 1948); and Elihu Katz and Paul F. Lazarsfeld, *Personal Influence* (New York: Free Press, 1955).

5. The most influential study of American voting behavior published before the 1970s, for example, paid little attention to the mass media: the index to Angus Campbell, Philip E. Converse, Warren E. Miller, and Donald E. Stokes, *The American Voter* (New York: Wiley, 1960), had only one reference to communications, one to mass media, and none to newspapers, radio, or television.

6. See, for example, the studies summarized in Sidney Kraus and Dennis Davis, *The Effects of Mass Communication on Political Behavior* (University Park: Pennsylvania State University Press, 1976), especially chap. 3.

7. Austin Ranney, *Channels of Power: The Impact of Television on American Politics* (New York: Basic Books, 1983).

8. U. S. Bureau of the Census, *Statistical Abstract of the United States 1988* (Washington, D.C.: Government Printing Office, 1988), pp. 526–27.

9. For more detailed accounts of the networks' heyday, see Adolf F. Reel, *The Networks: How They Stole the Show* (New York: Scribner's, 1979); and Harry Castleman and Walter J. Podrazik, *Watching TV: Four Decades of American Television* (New York: Scribner's, 1982).

10. Federal Communications Commission, "Fairness Doctrine and Public Interest Standards, Fairness Report regarding Handling of Public Issues," *Federal Register*, vol. 39 (1974), pp. 26372, 26374, par. 15. See also Steven J. Simmons, *The Fairness Doctrine and the Media* (Berkeley: University of California Press, 1978); and Harvey L. Zuckman and Martin J. Gaynes, *Mass Communications Law in a Nutshell*, 2d ed. (St. Paul, Minn.: West Publishing, 1983), pp. 406–7.

11. Simmons, *The Fairness Doctrine and the Media*, p. 246, nn. 202, 203.

12. From 1952 to 1976, for example, all three networks broadcast gavel-to-gavel coverage of the Democratic and Republican national conventions; that is, they were on the air live not only during all of the conventions' formal proceedings but also at other times and broadcast as much as eight or nine hours per day for four or five days. All three received increasing complaints from viewers about the preemption of entertainment programs. In 1980 ABC abandoned gavel-to-gavel coverage in favor of nightly two-hour summaries of each day's highlights. CBS and NBC said that this proved only that ABC was not providing serious news coverage, but in 1984 and 1988 both networks followed ABC's lead by providing only two hours of prime-time coverage each night, consisting mainly of remarks by their own commentators and interviews of politicians by their correspondents rather than of speeches from the podium.

13. Compare Epstein, *News from Nowhere*, pp. 59–63.

14. Michael J. Robinson, "Television and American Politics, 1956–1976," *Public Interest* (Summer 1977), pp. 3–39; and "American Political Legitimacy in an Era of Electronic Journalism: Reflections on the Evening News," in Douglass Cater and Richard Adler, eds., *Television as a Social Force: New Approaches to TV Criticism* (New York: Praeger, 1975), pp. 97–139.

15. See, for example, the ABC News poll, June 15–19, 1984.

16. For samples of each kind of attack, see Edith Efron, *The News Twisters* (Los Angeles: Nash Publishing, 1971); Joseph Keeley, *The Left-Leaning Antenna: Political Bias in Television News* (New Rochelle,

N.Y.: Arlington House, 1971); Robert Cirino, *Don't Blame the People* (New York: Random House, 1972); David L. Altheide, *Creating Reality: How TV News Distorts Events* (Beverly Hills, Calif.: Sage Publications, 1977); and Lance Bennett, *News: The Politics of Illusion*, 2d ed. (New York: Longman, 1988).

17. Ranney, *Channels of Power*, p. 43. For expositions of the structural bias view, see ibid., pp. 42–62; Epstein, *News from Nowhere*; C. Richard Hofstetter, *Bias in the News* (Columbus: Ohio State University Press, 1976); and Michael J. Robinson and Margaret A. Sheehan, *Over the Wire and On TV: CBS and UPI in Campaign '80* (New York: Russell Sage Foundation, 1983).

18. Paul H. Weaver, "Is Television News Biased?" *Public Interest* (Winter 1972), pp. 57–74, at p. 69.

19. The Supreme Court most fully enunciated the scarcity doctrine in National Broadcasting Co. v. United States, 319 U.S. 190 (1943). For a succinct discussion of the doctrine's content and impact, see Zuckman and Gaynes, *Mass Communications Law in a Nutshell*, pp. 328–31.

20. The other leading case upholding the FCC's power to regulate the political content of radio and television programs is Red Lion Broadcasting Company v. Federal Communications Commission 395 U.S. 367 (1969).

21. Simmons, *The Fairness Doctrine and the Media*, p. 191.

22. See Zuckman and Gaynes, *Mass Communications Law in a Nutshell*, pp. 395–98.

23. Anthony King, "The American Polity in the Late 1970s: Building Coalitions in the Sand," in Anthony King, ed., *The New American Political System* (Washington, D.C.: American Enterprise Institute, 1978), pp. 388–91.

24. For the impact of doubling the time of the nightly newscasts, see Robinson, "American Political Legitimacy in an Era of Electronic Journalism."

25. Ranney, *Channels of Power*, chaps. 3–6.

26. For demonstrations of the networks' role in selecting presidential candidates, see Bartels, *Presidential Primaries and the Dynamics of Public Choice*; and Garry R. Orren and Nelson W. Polsby, eds., *Media and Momentum: The New Hampshire Primary and Nomination Politics* (Chatham, N.J.: Chatham House, 1987).

27. Norman H. Nie, Sidney Verba, and John R. Petrocik, *The Changing American Voter* (Cambridge: Harvard University Press, 1976), figure 4.3, p. 53. See also Samuel J. Eldersveld, *Political Parties in American Society* (New York: Basic Books, 1982), pp. 78–79. A 1986 voter survey by Yankelovich, Clancy, and Shulman found that 48

percent of self-identified Democrats, 53 percent of Republicans, and 87 percent of Independents reported splitting their tickets. *Public Opinion* (January/February 1987), p. 34.

28. Norman J. Ornstein, "The Open Congress Meets the President," in Anthony King, ed., *Both Ends of the Avenue* (Washington, D.C.: American Enterprise Institute, 1983), p. 202.

29. Ranney, *Channels of Power*, p. 154.

30. For similar views on the advent of narrowcasting, see Susan Tyler Eastman, Sidney W. Head, and Lewis R. Klein, *Broadcast Programming: Strategies and Policies*, 2d ed. (Belmont, Calif.: Wadsworth, 1985); Robert W. Haigh, George Gerbner, and Richard B. Byrne, eds., *Communications in the Twenty-First Century* (New York: Wiley-Interscience, 1981); and Joseph Martin, *Future Developments in Telecommunications*, 2d ed. (Englewood Cliffs, N.J.: Prentice-Hall, 1977).

31. For details, see Daniel L. Brenner and Monroe F. Price, *Cable Television and Other Nonbroadcast Video: Law and Politics* (New York: Clark Boardman, 1986); James W. Roman, *Cable Mania* (Englewood Cliffs, N.J.: Prentice-Hall, 1983); Joseph Martin, *The Wired Society* (Englewood Cliffs, N.J.: Prentice-Hall, 1978); and Ralph M. Negrine, ed., *Cable Television and the Future of Broadcasting* (New York: St. Martin's Press, 1985).

32. Bureau of the Census, *Statistical Abstract of the United States 1988*, table 878, p. 523.

33. Geoffrey Colvin, "The Crowded New World of TV," *Fortune*, September 17, 1984, pp. 156–66. See also ibid., pp. 527, 531.

34. Compare Corporation for Public Broadcasting, *The Low Power Television Guidebook: A Primer on the Low Power Service* (Washington, D.C.: CPB, 1980); and Jacquelyn Biel, *Low Power Television: Development and Current Status of the LPTV Industry* (Washington, D.C.: National Association of Broadcasters, 1985).

35. Colvin, "The Crowded New World of TV," p. 166.

36. Epstein, *News from Nowhere*, pp. 93–96.

37. Compare James G. Webster, "Audience Behavior and the New Media Environment," *Journal of Communication*, vol. 36 (Summer 1986), pp. 77–91, at p. 81.

38. See Marvin Smith, *Radio, TV & Cable* (New York: Holt, Rinehart and Winston, 1985), pp. 174–75; Joseph S. Johnson and Kenneth K. Jones, *Modern Radio Station Practices*, 2d ed. (Belmont, Calif.: Wadsworth, 1978); and Edd Routt, James B. McGrath, and Fredric A. Weiss, *The Radio Format Conundrum* (New York: Hastings House, 1978).

39. U.S. Bureau of the Census, *Statistical Abstract of the United*

States in 1986, (Washington, D.C.: Government Printing Office, 1986), table 935, p. 547.

40. "Why TV News Has Been Losing Its Audience," *Business Week*, April 16, 1984, pp. 137–41.

41. Epstein, *News from Nowhere*, pp. 67–68.

42. *New York Times*, June 21, 1987.

43. *New York Times*, August 5, 1987.

44. Compare Zuckman and Gaynes, *Mass Communications Law in a Nutshell*, p. 434.

45. Almost every commentator on the coverage of politics by American television in the network era has emphasized (most of them disapprovingly) the dominance of horse race journalism. For some representative examples, see Thomas E. Patterson, *The Mass Media Election* (New York: Praeger, 1980); Robinson and Sheehan, *Over the Wire and On TV*; and David L. Paletz and Robert M. Entman, *Media Power Politics* (New York: Free Press, 1981).

CHAPTER 7: THE PARADOX OF INTEREST GROUPS IN WASHINGTON— MORE GROUPS, LESS CLOUT

1. Jeffrey H. Birnbaum and Alan S. Murray, *Showdown at Gucci Gulch* (New York: Random House, 1987).

2. Arthur Close et al., eds., *Washington Representatives, 1988* (Washington, D.C.: Columbia Books, 1988).

3. Craig Colgate, ed., *National Trade and Professional Associations of the United States, 1982* (Washington, D.C.: Columbia Books, 1982).

4. David Yoffie, "Interest Groups v. Individual Action: An Analysis of Corporate Political Strategies," Working paper, Harvard Business School, 1985.

5. Kay Lehman Schlozman and John T. Tierney, *Organized Interests and American Democracy* (New York: Harper and Row, 1986), p. 76; see also Jack L. Walker, "The Origins and Maintenance of Interest Groups in America," *American Political Science Review*, vol. 77 (1983), pp. 390–406.

6. Mancur Olson, *The Logic of Collective Action* (Cambridge, Mass.: Harvard University Press, 1965).

7. Robert H. Salisbury, "Interest Representation: The Dominance of Institutions," *American Political Science Review*, vol. 78, pp. 64–76.

8. See Lawrence Mone, "Thinkers and Their Tanks Move on Washington," *Wall Street Journal*, March 15, 1988. Think tank lobbying is described in David Shribman, "Lobbying of Bush Transition Office Is Turning to Matters of Policy from Personnel Choices," *Wall Street Journal*, January 3, 1989. See also Martha Derthick and Paul

Quirk, *The Politics of Deregulation* (Washington, D.C.: Brookings Institution, 1985).

9. See Robert L. Nelson, John P. Heinz, Edward O. Laumann, and Robert H. Salisbury, "Private Representation in Washington: Surveying the Structure of Influence," *American Bar Foundation Research Journal* (1987), pp. 141–200.

10. William P. Browne, *Private Interests, Public Policy, and American Agriculture* (Lawrence: University of Kansas Press, 1988).

11. See Edward O. Laumann and David Knoke, *The Organizational State: Social Choice in National Policy Domains* (Madison: University of Wisconsin Press, 1987).

12. See my essay, "Washington Lobbyists: A Collective Portrait," in Allan J. Cigler and Burdett A. Loomis, eds., *Interest Group Politics*, 2d ed. (Washington, D.C.: Congressional Quarterly Press, 1986), pp. 146–61.

13. Byron Shafer, *Bifurcated Politics* (Cambridge, Mass.: Harvard University Press, 1988), chap. 4.

14. See Robert H. Salisbury, John P. Heinz, Edward O. Laumann and Robert L. Nelson, "Who Works with Whom? Interest Group Alliances and Opposition," *American Political Science Review*, vol. 81, pp. 1217–34. The excellent essay by Jeffrey M. Berry, "Subgovernments, Issue Networks, and Political Conflict," stresses the importance of increased conflict as a destabilizing force. Berry's essay came to my attention after I had completed my own, but it is clear that our thinking has moved along closely related lines. His work appears in Richard Harris and Sidney Milkis, eds., *Remaking American Politics* (Boulder, Colo.: Westview Press, 1989), pp. 239–60.

15. Terry Moe, "Interests, Institutions, and Positive Theory: The Politics of the NLRB," *Studies in American Political Development*, vol. 2 (1987), pp. 236–99.

16. Charles O. Jones, "American Politics and the Organization of Energy Decision Making," *Annual Review of Energy*, vol. 4 (1979), pp. 99–121.

17. Hugh Heclo, "Issue Networks and the Executive Establishment," in Anthony King, ed., *The New American Political System* (Washington, D.C.: American Enterprise Institute, 1978), pp. 87–124.

18. Theodore Lowi, *The End of Liberalism* (New York: W. W. Norton, 1969).

19. John Mark Hansen, "Choosing Sides: The Creation of an Agricultural Policy Network in Congress, 1919–1932," *Studies in American Political Development*, vol. 2 (1987), pp. 183–229.

20. Robert H. Salisbury, John P. Heinz, Edward O. Laumann, and

Robert L. Nelson, "Iron Triangles: Similarities and Differences among the Legs" (Paper presented to the annual meeting of the American Political Science Association, Washington, D.C., September 1988).

21. R. Kenneth Godwin, *One Billion Dollars of Influence: The Direct Marketing of Politics* (Chatham, N.J.: Chatham House, 1988).

22. See my essay "Political Movements in American Politics: An Essay on Concept and Analysis," *National Journal of Political Science*, vol. 1 (1989), pp. 15–30.

23. See, for example, Andrew McFarland, *Common Cause: Lobbying in the Public Interest* (Chatham, N.J.: Chatham House, 1984); and Jeffrey M. Berry, *Lobbying for the People* (Princeton, N.J.: Princeton University Press, 1977).

24. Much of this section is based on the research of Craig Humphries, whose doctoral dissertation, *The Political Behavior of American Corporations*, analyzes corporate strategies of political action in careful detail. I am grateful to Dr. Humphries for permission to use some of his data and for his helpful comments on this paper.

25. See Kirk Victor, "Being Here," *National Journal*, August 6, 1988, pp. 2021–25.

26. Burdett A. Loomis, "Coalitions of Interests: Building Bridges in a Balkanized State," in Cigler and Loomis, eds., *Interest Group Politics*, pp. 258–74.

27. For a discussion of this development among manufacturing trade associations concerned about trade issues, see Leonard H. Lynn and Timothy J. McKeown, *Organizing Business: Trade Associations in America and Japan* (Washington, D.C.: American Enterprise Institute, 1988), pp. 110–12. See also Jeffrey M. Berry, *The Interest Group Society* (Boston: Little, Brown, 1984), pp. 202–5.

28. George Melloan, "What to Do When Your Own Lobby Is against You," *Wall Street Journal*, February 16, 1988.

29. Actually, the N is 990; ten firms on the *Fortune Magazine* list were either subsidiaries of other firms or agricultural cooperatives. *Fortune Magazine*, May 3, 1982.

30. See n. 24.

31. Schlozman and Tierney, *Organized Interests and American Democracy*, chap. 7.

32. Shafer, *Bifurcated Politics*.

33. For a careful, measured analysis of PACs in American politics placed in their larger historical and political context, see Frank J. Sorauf, *Money in American Elections* (Glenview, Ill.: Scott, Foresman, 1988). A richly detailed analysis of corporate PACs is Theodore J. Eismeier and Philip H. Pollock III, *Business, Money, and the Rise of*

Corporate PACs in American Elections (New York: Quorum Books, 1988).

34. Lester Milbrath, *The Washington Lobbyists* (Chicago: Rand McNally, 1963).

35. Laumann and Knoke, *The Organizational State*, p. 3.

36. Ibid., p. 15.

CHAPTER 8: FEDERALISM—THE GREAT "COMPOSITION"

1. *The Federalist Papers* (New York: Mentor Books, 1961), p. 246.

2. K. C. Wheare, *Federal Government*, 4th ed. (New York: Oxford University Press, 1964), p. 62. See also Richard H. Leach, *American Federalism* (New York: W. W. Norton and Co., 1970), p. 1.

3. *Federalist Papers*, p. 108.

4. Daniel J. Elazar, *Exploring Federalism* (Tuskaloosa: University of Alabama Press, 1987), p. 6.

5. Maurice J. C. Vile, "Federal Theory and the 'New Federalism,' " in D. Jaensch, ed., *The Politics of New Federalism* (Adelaide: Australian Political Studies Association, 1977), p. 1.

6. Michael D. Reagan and John G. Sanzone, *The New Federalism* (New York: Oxford University Press, 1981), p. 19.

7. Richard P. Nathan and Margarita M. Balmaceda, "Comparing Federal Systems of Government," chapter in book to be published by Oxford University Press.

8. Ibid.

9. Kenneth N. Vines, "The Federal Setting of State Policies," in Herbert Jacob and Kenneth N. Vines, eds., *Politics and the American States: A Comparative Analysis*, 3d ed. (Boston: Little, Brown, 1976), p. 20.

10. Richard P. Nathan and Fred C. Doolittle, eds., *Reagan and the States* (Princeton, N.J.: Princeton University Press, 1987).

11. Jerry Hagstrom, "Liberal and Minority Coalitions Pleading Their Cases in State Capitals," *National Journal*, vol. 17, no. 8 (February 23, 1985), p. 426.

12. Steven D. Gold, "Developments in State Finances, 1983 to 1986," *Public Budgeting and Finance*, vol. 7, no. 1 (Spring 1987), p. 15.

13. Steven D. Gold and Corina L. Eckl, "State Budget Actions in 1984," Fiscal Affairs Program, National Conference of State Legislatures, Legislative Paper 45, September 1984, p. 1.

14. James T. Patterson, *The New Deal and the States: Federalism in Transition* (Princeton, N.J.: Princeton University Press, 1969), p. 4.

15. Ibid., p. 7.

16. Allan Nevins and Henry Steele Commager, *A Pocket History of*

the United States (New York: Washington Square Press, 1981), pp. 346ff.

17. U.S. Advisory Commission on Intergovernmental Relations, *The Question of State Government Capability*, report A-98 (Washington, D.C., 1985), p. 2.

18. In Baker v. Carr, voters in Tennessee successfully challenged the failure of the state legislature to reapportion its membership. The key issue was what was felt to be the overrepresentation of rural areas and interests in the state legislature. Before the Supreme Court ruling in 1962, the last time the legislature had been reapportioned was in 1901. See Walter F. Murphey and C. Herman Pritchett, *Courts, Judges, and Politics: An Introduction to the Judicial Process* (New York: Random House, 1974), pp. 46–52; and Deil S. Wright, *Understanding Intergovernmental Relations* (North Scituate, Mass.: Duxbury Press, 1978), pp. 204–5.

19. Martha Derthick, "American Federalism: Madison's Middle Ground," *Public Administration Review*, vol. 47, no. 1 (January–February 1987), p. 72.

20. Denis P. Doyle and Terry W. Hartle, *Excellence in Education: The States Take Charge* (Washington, D.C.: American Enterprise Institute, 1985), p. 1. Some credit for this spurt of educational reforms in the states should be assigned to action by the federal government, namely, the publication of the report *A Nation at Risk* in April 1983. See National Commission on Excellence in Education, *A Nation at Risk: The Imperative for Educational Reform*, a report to the nation and the secretary of education (Washington, D.C., 1983).

21. New State Ice Company v. Ernest A. Liebmann, 285 U.S. 262–311, *United States Supreme Court Reports* 76 L. Ed. (1931), p. 771.

22. Jack L. Walker, "The Diffusion of Innovation among the American States," *American Political Science Review*, vol. 63 (1969), pp. 880–99. (Walker's analysis is for the period 1870–1969.) See also Virginia Gray, "Innovation in the States: A Diffusion Study," *American Political Science Review*, vol. 67 (1973), pp. 1174–85.

23. Woodrow Wilson, *Constitutional Government in the United States* (New York: Columbia University Press, 1880; reprinted 1961), p. 173.

24. Martin Diamond, "What the Framers Meant by Federalism," in Robert A. Goldwin, ed., *A Nation of States: Essays on the American Federal System* (Chicago: Rand McNally and Co., 1961), p. 32.

25. As cited ibid., p. 27.

26. Ibid., p. 37.

27. Ibid.

28. Tocqueville, as quoted by Martin Diamond, "The Ends of Federalism," *Publius*, vol. 3, no. 2 (Fall 1973).

29. Wheare, *Federal Government*, p. 33.

30. Arthur W. MacMahon, "The Problem of Federalism: Survey," in Arthur W. MacMahon, ed., *Federalism Mature and Emergent* (Garden City, N.Y.: Doubleday, 1955), p. 4.

31. Ibid.

32. City of Clinton v. Cedar Rapids and Missouri RR Co., 24 Iowa 475 (1868), as quoted in James A. Maxwell and J. Richard Aronson, *Financing State and Local Governments* (Washington, D.C.: Brookings Institution, 1977), p. 11. See also Edward S. Corwin, "The Passing of Dual Federalism," *Virginia Law Review*, vol. 36, no. 1 (February 1950), pp. 1–24.

33. Morton Grodzins, "The Federal System," in *Goals for Americans: The Report of the President's Commission on National Goals* (New York: Columbia University Press, 1960), p. 265.

34. Reagan and Sanzone, *The New Federalism*, p. 75.

35. Roscoe C. Martin, *The Cities and the Federal System* (New York: Atherton Press, 1955), p. 171.

36. Martha Derthick, "Preserving Federalism: Congress, the States, and the Supreme Court," *Brookings Review* (Winter/Spring 1986).

37. *United States Supreme Court Reports*, 89 L. Ed. 2d., no. 9, March 22, 1985, p. 1032. See also Thomas Anton, *American Federalism and Public Policy: How the System Works* (Philadelphia: Temple University Press, 1989), pp. 14–16.

38. *United States Supreme Court Reports*, 89 L. Ed. 2d., no. 9, March 22, 1985, p. 1040.

39. Ibid., p. 1052.

40. Daniel J. Elazar, *The American Partnership: Intergovernmental Cooperation in the Nineteenth Century in the United States* (Chicago: University of Chicago Press, 1962).

41. Ibid., p. 336.

42. Carl J. Friedrich, *Trends of Federalism in Theory and Practice* (New York: Praeger, 1968), p. 173.

43. Ibid., p. 7.

44. Geoffrey Brennan and James M. Buchanan, *The Power to Tax: Analytical Foundations of a Fiscal Constitution* (Cambridge: Cambridge University Press, 1980), pp. 16, 174. See also Anton, *American Federalism and Public Policy*, esp. pp. 27–28.

45. Richard M. Nixon, White House Memorandum, June 1970.

46. Richard M. Nixon, Remarks, Winter Session of the National Governors' Association, Washington, D.C., February 27, 1970.

47. Lillian Rymarowicz and Dennis Zimmerman, "Federal Aid to Local Governments: 1980 Retrenchment," *Congressional Research Ser-*

vice Review, vol. 9, no. 10 (November/December 1980), p. 18. Figures are adjusted to omit revenue sharing.

48. President Carter in 1979 established a Commission for the National Agenda for the Eighties, chaired by William J. McGill, former president of Columbia University. The McGill commission's most controversial and surprising conclusion was that the national government's strategy in dealing with urban problems should move away from "a narrowly circumscribed concept of local economic development" with "emphasis placed on revitalizing specific places." The commission said, "The results for most distressed places have not been encouraging." The commission instead favored policies "to direct greater concentrations of federal resources directly to people, wherever they may live, rather than indirectly to people through places and political jurisdictions." See President's Commission for a National Agenda for the Eighties, Report of the Panel on Policies and Prospects for Metropolitan and Nonmetropolitan America, *Urban America in the Eighties: Perspectives and Prospectives* (Washington, D.C., 1980), chap. 7.

49. For studies that find states more responsive to distressed communities than the national government, see, for example, Thomas K. Dye and Thomas Hurley, "The Responsiveness of Federal and State Governments to Urban Problems," *Journal of Politics*, vol. 40 (1978), pp. 196–201; and *By-passing the States: Wrong Turn for Urban Aids* (Washington, D.C.: National Governors' Association, 1980). Other studies report contrary findings. A study by the U.S. Advisory Commission on Intergovernmental Relations, for example, concluded that state aid is basically nonequalizing. See U.S. Advisory Commission on Intergovernmental Relations, *The States and Intergovernmental Aid*, report A-59 (Washington, D.C.: ACIR, 1977), p. 25.

CHAPTER 9: A WORLD OF DIFFERENCE—THE PUBLIC PHILOSOPHIES AND POLITICAL BEHAVIORS OF RIVAL AMERICAN CULTURES

1. Anthony King, ed., *The New American Political System* (Washington, D.C.: American Enterprise Institute, 1978).
2. Ibid., pp. 25–26.
3. Ibid., p. 28.
4. Ibid., p. 31.
5. Ibid., p. 40.
6. For further discussion of why left-right differences are inadequate and why these cultural categories are superior, see Aaron Wildavsky, "Choosing Preferences by Constructing Institutions: A

NOTES

Cultural Theory of Preference Formation," *American Political Science Review*, vol. 81, no. 1 (March 1987), pp. 3–21; and Richard Ellis and Aaron Wildavsky, *Dilemmas of Early American Presidents from Washington through Lincoln* (New Brunswick, N.J.: Transaction Press, 1989).

7. Samuel Huntington, *American Politics: The Promise of Disharmony* (Cambridge, Mass: Belknap Press, Harvard University Press, 1981), pp. 3–4.

8. See Richard Ellis and Aaron Wildavsky, "A Cultural Analysis of the Role of Abolitionists in the Coming of the Civil War," *Comparative Studies in Society and History*, vol. 31. no. 1 (Winter 1990), pp. 89–116.

9. Huntington, *American Politics*, pp. 39, 41.

10. Ibid., p. 237.

11. Material for this section is drawn from a series of earlier papers on similar themes: "The Three Cultures: Explaining Anomalies in the American Welfare State," *The Public Interest*, no. 69 (Fall 1982), pp. 45–58; "Industrial Policies in American Political Cultures," in Claude E. Barfield and William A. Schambra, eds., *The Politics of Industrial Policy* (Washington, D.C.: American Enterprise Institute, 1986), pp. 15–32; "Federalism Means Inequality," *Society*, vol. 22, no. 2 (January/February 1985), pp. 42–49; "President Reagan as a Political Strategist," in Kay Lehman Schlozman, ed., *Elections in America* (Boston: Allen & Unwin, 1987), pp. 221–38; "No War without Dictatorship, No Peace without Democracy," *Social Philosophy & Policy*, vol. 3, no. 1 (Autumn 1985), pp. 176–91; and Richard Ellis and Aaron Wildavsky, "A Cultural Analysis of the Role of Abolitionists in the Coming of the Civil War."

12. See Aaron Wildavsky, "The Media's 'American Egalitarians,' " *The Public Interest*, no. 88 (Summer 1987), pp. 94–104.

13. See R. Brickman, S. Jasanoff, and T. Ilgen, *Chemical Regulation and Cancer: A Crossnational Study of Policy and Politics* (Ithaca, N.Y.: Cornell University Press, 1982); Steven Kelman, *Regulating America, Regulating Sweden: A Comparative Study of Occupational Safety and Health Policy* (Cambridge, Mass.: MIT Press, 1981); L. J. Lundquist, *The Hare and the Tortoise: Clean Air Policies in the United States and Sweden* (Ann Arbor, Mich.: University of Michigan Press, 1980).

14. See Mary Douglas and Aaron Wildavsky, *Risk and Culture* (Berkeley: University of California Press, 1982).

15. See Daniel Polisar and Aaron Wildavsky, "From Individual to System Blame: A Cultural Analysis of the Law of Torts," *Journal of Policy History*, vol. 1, no. 2 (April 1989).

16. See Joe White and Aaron Wildavsky, "Public Authority and the Public Interest: What the 1980s Budget Battles Have to Tell Us

334

about the American State," *Journal of Theoretical Politics*, vol. 1, no. 1 (January 1989), pp. 7–31.

17. Owen Harries, "Best-Case Thinking," *Commentary*, vol. 77, no. 5 (May 1984), pp. 23–28; quotation on p. 27.

18. George Shultz, "Power and Diplomacy," Address to the Veterans of Foreign Wars, Chicago, August 20, 1984 (U.S. Dept. of State, Bureau of Public Affairs, Current Policy no. 606).

19. Samuel H. Beer, "In Search of a New Public Philosophy," in Anthony King, ed., *The New American Political System* (Washington, D.C.: American Enterprise Institute, 1978), p. 44.

20. A combination of Charles Murray's *Losing Ground* (New York: Basic Books, 1984), and Lawrence Mead's *Beyond Entitlement: The Social Obligations of Citizenship* (New York: Free Press, 1986) would do the trick.

21. See Aaron Wildavsky, "Resolved, That Individualism and Egalitarianism Be Made Compatible in America: Political Cultural Roots of Exceptionalism" (Paper prepared for the Conference on American Exceptionalism at Nuffield College, Oxford, April 14–16, 1988).

CHAPTER 10: THE AMERICAN POLITY IN THE 1990s

1. See Samuel H. Beer, "In Search of a New Public Philosophy," in Anthony King, ed., *New American Political System*, (Washington, D.C.: American Enterprise Institute, 1978).

2. Austin Ranney, "The Political Parties: Reform and Decline," in ibid., pp. 230–36.

3. Hugh Heclo, "Issue Networks and the Executive Establishment," in ibid., chap. 3.

4. Tip O'Neill, with William Novak, *Man of the House* (New York: St. Martin's Press, 1988), pp. 339–42.

5. Of course, the phrase "direct link between the individual politician and the individual citizen" is, as Ranney recognizes, misleading. In the first place, the link is one way. In the second, what the citizen sees and hears is usually what the politicians and the broadcasters want him to see and hear. Spontaneity is rare—and becoming more so. Speaker O'Neill in *Man of the House* provides additional support for Ranney's case by noting the extent to which the Watergate Babies and their peers were media oriented: "Some of them became very popular with the news media, which like nothing better than to feature politicians blasting each other" (p. 341).

6. See above, p. 96.

7. See Fred I. Greenstein, "Change and Continuity in the

Modern Presidency," in King, ed., *New American Political System*, chap. 2.

8. See the comments of Hedrick Smith in *The Power Game: How Washington Works* (New York: Random House, 1988), p. 464.

9. A broadly similar view is expressed, though with more asperity, in Bob Schieffer and Gary Paul Gates, *The Acting President* (New York: E. P. Dutton, 1989). A view more favorable to Reagan can be found in Aaron Wildavsky, "President Reagan as a Political Strategist," in Charles O. Jones, ed., *The Reagan Legacy: Promise and Performance* (Chatham, N.J.: Chatham House, 1988), pp. 289–305.

10. See above, p. 3.

11. King, "The American Polity in the 1970s: Building Coalitions in the Sand," in King, ed., *New American Political System*, pp. 388–91.

12. Ibid., p. 391.

13. Smith, *The Power Game*, chap. 13.

14. Ibid., p. 453.

15. As Smith points out in ibid., pp. 451–81, the circumstances of 1981 were highly unusual. The Republicans had just captured not only the presidency but the Senate. They were effectively led in both the Senate and the House of Representatives. They believed that they had a chance of bringing about a major party realignment in their favor. They believed that the circumstances of Reagan's 1980 victory constituted a kind of electoral "mandate" for budget and tax cutting. There was a widespread desire, not only among Republicans, to see someone, anyone, succeed in the Oval Office. Reagan was powerfully assisted, in addition, by the assassination attempt on him and his responses to it. Such factors—and there were others—were not likely to be repeated in unison.

16. Ibid., pp. 482, 484, 487.

17. Ibid., p. 451.

18. King, "The American Polity in the 1970s," p. 393.

19. See above, p. 31.

20. Smith, *The Power Game*, pp. 455–56, 464. Almost everyone who has written about the events of 1981 has written in similar terms. See, for example, Paul E. Peterson and Mark Rom, "Macroeconomic Policymaking: Who Is in Control?" in John E. Chubb and Paul E. Peterson, eds., *Can the Government Govern?* (Washington, D.C.: Brookings Institution, 1989), pp. 139–82. Peterson and Rom refer to "a rush of popular support that overwhelmed remaining congressional opposition to [Reagan's] policies" (p. 214).

21. James D. Savage, *Balanced Budgets and American Politics* (Ithaca, N.Y.: Cornell University Press), pp. 1, 207–09.

22. Quoted in Anthony King, "A Mile and a Half Is a Long Way," in Anthony King, ed., *Both Ends of the Avenue: The Presidency, the Executive Branch, and Congress in the 1980s* (Washington, D.C.: American Enterprise Institute, 1983), p. 262. King argues at some length (pp. 256–62) for the importance of "mood" or "atmosphere" or "climate," including, not least, the prevailing climate of ideas. For remarks in a similar vein, see James Q. Wilson, "American Politics, Then and Now," *Commentary*, vol. 67 (February 1979), pp. 44–45.

23. Martha Derthick and Paul J. Quirk, *The Politics of Deregulation* (Washington, D.C.: Brookings Institution, 1985), p. 57. The Derthick and Quirk volume is about the politics of deregulation, but it is not only about that. It is one of the most original and sensitive analyses of Washington policy making to be produced in recent years.

24. Ibid., p. 247.

25. The classic work on the tax reform is Jeffrey H. Birnbaum and Alan S. Murray, *Showdown at Gucci Gulch: Lawmakers, Lobbyists, and the Unlikely Triumph of Tax Reform* (New York: Random House, 1987). See esp. chaps. 9–11.

26. Paul Light, *Artful Work: The Politics of Social Security Reform* (New York: Random House, 1985).

27. Ibid., p. 143, italics removed.

28. Ibid., p. 232.

29. It is odd that so little has so far been written by political scientists on the politics of the Reagan budget deficit, though see, among other things, the chapter by Peterson and Rom referred to in n. 20, the same authors' "Lower Taxes, More Spending, and Budget Deficits," in Jones, ed., *The Reagan Legacy*, pp. 213–40; B. B. Kymlicka and Jean V. Matthews, eds., *The Reagan Revolution?* (Chicago: Dorsey Press, 1988), part 4; and, not least, William A. Niskanen, *Reaganomics: An Insider's Account of the Policies and the People* (New York: Oxford University Press, 1988).

Index

A. C. Nielsen, 178, 195
Accuracy in Media, 180
Adamany, David, 120
Administrative Procedures Act
  (1946), 79, 80
Advisory Commission on Inter-
  governmental Relations, 242,
  251
Africa, 288
Agincourt, 301
Agnew, Spiro T., 180
AIDS (Acquired Immunodefi-
  ciency Syndrome), 275
Aid to Families with Dependent
  Children (AFDC), 254–55, 258
Altheide, David, 180
American Bankers Association,
  219
American Broadcasting Compa-
  nies (ABC), 178
American Council of Education
  (ACE), 219
American Council of Life Insur-
  ance, 219
American Creed, 266–68
American empire, 288–89, 304
American Enterprise Institute,
  iii, 206
American Farm Bureau Federa-
  tion (AFBF), 208
American Federation of Labor–
  Congress of Industrial Organ-
  izations (AFL-CIO), 211, 223
American Medical Association
  (AMA), 208, 209
American Petroleum Institute,
  208

American Political Science Asso-
  ciation Committee on Political
  Parties, 174
*American Politics: The Promise of
  Disharmony* (Huntington), 266
American Voter, The (Campbell et
  al.), 156–57
Anderson, John B., 6, 89
"Approval elections," 12, 13
Archer-Daniels-Midland, 208
Arizona, 235
Arkansas, 51
Artful Work (Light), 302
Articles of Confederation, 231
Association of American Uni-
  versities (AAU), 219
Atomic Energy Commission, 30
"Attack videos," 143
Atwater, Lee, 117
Austria, 233

Baker, Howard, 96, 172
Baker v. *Carr*, 242
Beer, Samuel H., 263–64, 282
Beethoven, Ludwig van, 288
Bennett, Lance, 180
Bentsen, Lloyd, 97
Berkeley, Bishop George, 288
Bible, 161
Biden, Joseph, 140
Black Entertainment Television,
  195
Blackmun, Harry A., 60, 67, 248
Blacks, 45, 49, 51, 99, 158, 160,
  194, 195
Boggs, Thomas, 207
"Boll Weevils," 297

presidential candidates
  from, 10, 35–36, 45, 172–73
Shafer, Byron, 172, 210, 222
Shapiro, Martin, iii
Shriver, Sargent, 8
Shultz, George, 280
Siberia, 288
Simmons, Steven J., 184
Simon, Paul, 98
"Sloppy hexagon," 212
Smith, Alfred E., 144
Smith, Hedrick, 297, 300
Social Security Act, 76
Social Security Administration, 76
South (United States), 2, 7, 38–39, 44–45, 94, 99, 100, 122, 160, 165–66, 168–69, 242, 293
South Carolina, 112, 166
South Dakota, 18, 235
Southwest (United States), 13
Soviet Union, 171, 231, 276, 277, 278, 279
Soy Bean Association, 208
Spain, 231
Spanish International Network, 195
Split-ticket voting, 2, 146–48, 291
State legislatures, 5
States' Rights ticket, 165
Stevens, John Paul, 60, 67
Stevenson, Adlai, 144
Stewart, Potter, 59
Stone, Walter J., 152
Student Non-violent Coordinating Committee, 267
Students for a Democratic Society, 263
Sundquist, James L., 4–5, 9, 15, 27, 125–26
Super Tuesday, 113, 153, 167
Supreme Court, iii, 31, 47–85, 127, 128, 132, 183, 184, 242, 246, 248–49, 293

Switzerland, 233
Symington, Stuart, 36

Taft, Robert A., 35, 36, 293
Taft-Hartley Act, 143
Taney, Roger B., 246
Tax cuts (1981), 11, 22–23, 169, 294, 297, 298, 300
Tax Reform Act (1986), 203, 228, 298, 301–2
Teamsters Union, 212
Television, 33–35, 45, 106, 140, 143, 175–201, 292–93
Tenth Amendment, 249, 253
Texas, 7, 139, 234–35
This Constitution, 289
Thompson, Frank, 38
Thurmond, Strom, 165, 166
Tierney, John, 221–22, 224
Time magazine, 140
Tocqueville, Alexis de, 205, 244–45, 282
Tower of Babel, 31
Truman, David B., 205
Truman, Harry S, 17, 31, 247, 258
Turnout, election, 7, 14, 154–55
Twenty-fifth Amendment, 25

United Auto Workers, 212
United States v. *Nixon*, 50
Urban Institute for Policy Analysis, 206
USA network, 195
U.S. Chamber of Commerce, 211
U.S. Marines, 303

Van Buren, Martin, 14, 102
Vandenberg, Arthur, 35, 36
Verba, Sidney, 188
Vermont Yankee case, 79, 81
Veterans Administration, 225
Vietnam War, 2, 40, 92, 148, 273, 303
Vile, Maurice, 232, 250
Vines, Kenneth N., 234
Voting Rights Act, 155